REBUILDING WESTERN CIVILIZATION

BOOKS BY SEYMOUR W. ITZKOFF

Cultural Pluralism and American Education	1969
Ernst Cassirer: Scientific Knowledge and the Concept of Man	1971, 1997 (2nd edition)
A New Public Education	1976
Ernst Cassirer, Philosopher of Culture	1977
Emanuel Feuermann, Virtuoso	1979, 1995 (2nd edition)
The Evolution of Human Intelligence	
1 *The Form of Man, The Evolutionary Origins of Human Intelligence*	1983
2 *Triumph of the Intelligent, The Creation of Homo sapiens sapiens*	1985
3 *Why Humans Vary in Intelligence*	1987
4 *The Making of the Civilized Mind*	1990
How We Learn to Read	1986
Human Intelligence and National Power	1991
The Road to Equality, Evolution and Social Reality	1992
The Decline of Intelligence in America, A Strategy for National Renewal	1994
Children Learning to Read, A Guide for Parents and Teachers	1996
Who Are the Jews?	
1 Soul of the *Israelites*	2004
2 A Nation of Philosophers	2004
The Human Prospect	
1 *The Inevitable Domination by Man, An Evolutionary Detective Story*	2000
2 *2050: The Collapse of the Global Techno-Economy*	2003
3 *Intellectual Capital in Twenty-First-Century Politics*	2003
4 *Rebuilding Western Civilization, Beyond the Twenty-First-Century Collapse*	2005

The Human Prospect--IV

Rebuilding Western Civilization

Beyond the Twenty-First-Century Collapse

Seymour W. Itzkoff
Smith College

PAIDEIA PUBLISHERS

Ashfield, Massachusetts

Library of Congress, Cataloging-in-Publication Data

Itzkoff, Seymour W.
   Rebuilding western civilization : beyond the twenty-first-century collapse / Seymour W. Itzkoff.
     p. cm -- (The human prospect ; 4)
   Includes bibliographical references and index.
   ISBN 0-913993-21-2 (cloth : alk. paper)
     1. Civilization, Western--History--21st century. 2. Intellect. 3. Population--Economic aspects. 4. Human evolution. 5. Social evolution. I. Title.

CB245.I88 2005
303.49182'1--dc22

2004057319

Paideia Publishers
P.O. Box 343
Ashfield, MA 01330

Copyright © 2005 by Seymour W. Itzkoff
ISBN 0-913993-21-2

Printed in the United States of America

Dedicated to the Class of 2050

From a member of the Class of 1950

We should have done better by you!

Table of Contents

Foreword ix

Part I—A Failing Civilization

Chapter 1 The Crisis of Our Time 11
Chapter 2 Reason's Defeat, Civilization's Fall 23
Chapter 3 Cassandra's Revenge 38
Chapter 4 Civilizational Intelligence 59

Part II—The Possible

Chapter 5   Shaping Our Human Nature 85
Chapter 6   Democratic Polity 100
Chapter 7   Twenty-Second-Century Economics: Beyond Mass Production 114
Chapter 8   Religion Digs Deep 129
Chapter 9   Art: Civilization's Center 145
Chapter 10 Universality and Nationality 161
Chapter 11 Tomorrow 181
Appendix: Western Civilization Begins at Sumer 192
             Chronology, Sumeria, Early Mesopotamia 214
             Maps: Sumeria, Early Mesopotamia; Ancient Near East ... 216
Index 220

Foreword

Rebuilding Western Civilization is the fourth book in a series that I have entitled "The Human Prospect." The basic thrust of its argument is that in order for modern humans to venture onto the timeline of unknown tomorrows, they should have some conception of the significance both of the evolutionary truths and the cultural and civilizational implications of our human heritage.

Of equal importance is the non-ideological assessment of these facts to allow us to deal with the challenges of the moment and the future with secular rationality. It is the argument of my writings that we have failed this challenge. As a result, our descendants will see the twentieth and twenty-first centuries as the dark ages of human existence, an era in which the heritage of high *Homo sapiens sapiens* intelligence was literally destroyed in a frenzy of genocides, including the *Holocaust*. Add to the mix an irrational belief and policy system that viewed all humans as having the same potential intelligence to contribute to the continuity of Western civilization's creation of modernity. Thus, the passion to redistribute the wealth of the middle classes to the permanently incapable.

Civilized humans today join in a consensus of opinion that desires political democracy, an egalitarian, classless economic structure, a life lived in congruence with science and secular human knowledge. The social and political processes and policies that have been set in ideological stone are thus destined in this century, to efface these visions in a permanent series of insoluble crises that will bring down the very foundations of our Western civilizational heritage.

Consider two factors, (1) The ongoing engorgement of vast populations of humans that are physically destroying our ecological heritage as well as our ability to manage the social system as it served once served humans in the developed democracies. We will have between nine and ten billion humans on our planet by mid-century. They will all cry out for the amenities of civilization as promised them by our "brightest and most beautiful" And, they will be denied.

(2) The bulk of this population surge will be from the lower levels of human intelligence variability. They will not on their own be able to produce the institutions, wealth, and culture that they will need to live lives becoming to this

civilizational heritage. The social stresses incurred by our promises and the inevitable failures will eventually bring down the international system.

A civilizational model can exist that would allow our dreams for our children and grandchildren to be fulfilled. The major thrust of *Rebuilding Western Civilization* is devoted to outlining an intellectual blueprint that incorporates a transition to a demography that is rationally in keeping with the ecological and technological requirements for middle-class life. Also, I try to explain the necessity of high intelligence so as to sustain the political, economic, and esthetic vision that the Western civilizational tradition has provided for us.

Civilization has its ancient literate roots. We are in touch with at least five thousand years of recorded history. These many centuries can tell us much about what is humanly possible in the building and development of highly cognitive cultures. We also have a contemporary scientific literature that tells us much about human behavior, its potential for creativity, as well as its latent dysfunctionality.

In *Rebuilding Western Civilization* is presented what I hope will be an opening dialogue about the *possible* for this human species, regardless of race or ethnic heritage. These latter differences I believe to be irrelevant to the creation of a post-twenty-first-century global civilization that encompasses the best exemplars of all ethnicities and national human groupings.

It is the responsibility of us all to think beyond failing ideologies and the censorious retributions that they engender. We will need to reincarnate the ancient vertebrate backbone, face up to scientific fact as illuminated by human experience, the only path to building a better world, a moral humanity of the thoughtful and responsible.

My deepest thanks, as always, to Patricia Stroman, both for her sustaining support for these projects, as well as her literary acumen in disciplining these writings.

Northampton, Massachusetts
March 2005

Part I—A Failing Civilization

Chapter 1

The Crisis of Our Time

Civilization: "An advanced state of human society, in which a high level of art, science, religion, and government has been reached."
The American College Dictionary

Global Unraveling

It is not so much "decline," as Spengler phrased it after World War I. Rather the West is going through a chaotic spiral into global paralysis. As I explain in this book and in my earlier writings, we do not have the worldwide intelligence levels in this oncoming mass of humans that can take our new technological civilization upward to new levels of creativity and civility. Had we not gone through a century of ideological political madness, what is happening today to a world of c.6.5 billion people, going on 9-10 billion need not to have occurred.

Ironic it is, because by any historic standard we have had a situation since the beginning of the twentieth century in which the material needs of the then-existing world population, c.1.5+ billion in 1900, could have been fulfilled. We could have advanced in levels of luxury and comfort coveted by the middle classes of Western Europe, as well as the United States and Canada. The cars were there, the airplane well on its way, electricity, gasoline-powered agricultural combines, all the machines and techniques that we have today in spruced-up venues, plus television, computers, the internet.

With no great increase in population over this 1.5 billion people on earth, then, the progress toward today's sophistication in communication, information, transportation might have come about, even if at a slower pace. Instead, terrible blood-letting in World Wars I and II, the primeval *Holocaust* and the other genocides have indelibly tainted this century.

What civilizational utility can there be in this vast population upsurge to the 9 or 10 billion mark but the utter devastation of our ecological system? In contradistinction to the environmentalist "greens," who engage in palliative politics, a lid on corporate air and water pollution, more efficient auto engines, cleaner power plants, it is the raw weight of *people* that is causing the problem. Given many fewer humans, the technologies that we have developed over the century could have led us to a much more humane century.

One could argue that this rant is really 20-20 hindsight. Today we have c.6.5 billion people, tyrannies disgorging terrorist youth in the thousands, pandemics such as AIDS, vast crime-ridden urban favelas. The situation threatens, momentarily, even as we have finally suppressed twentieth-century communist and fascist tyrannies, substituted rational free market, democratically-oriented additions to our Western civilizational constellation of peoples.

Our civilization is spiraling downward because of this explosion of humans over the past fifty years, now unanimously predicted to continue over the next fifty. A massive underclass has been created from those areas of the world that shows no evidence of being able to handle the cognitive (educational) requirements of modernity.

This underclass is exploding in numbers from the most underdeveloped semi-tribal traditions, producing a situation that weighs heavily on the shoulders of the West. The West has been complicit. It has contributed the medical and sanitary wherewithal to stave off the traditional scythe. Infant and female birth mortality has been reduced, extending life expectancy for all. It is now possible for many more humans to reach maturity and procreate.

Birth control requires foresight, personal discipline, a grasp of futurity. Unfortunately, the moment the western social workers leave a village, the people return to their old ways. As a result these dependent humans live lives far more wretched than when they were liberated from the supposed Western colonial "oppressors."

Anyone with an I.Q. over 90, a fifth grade education, and a television can confirm this decline in the general human condition. Why then are our leadership cadres completely unwilling or incapable of recognizing the scope of the problem, mobilizing a rational long-term rescue operation that could forestall this spiraling disaster?

Two reasons:

A) The leadership has not taken seriously the problem of civilization building, nor agreed to what it can achieve as a modern twenty-first-century global community. The current sense of our internationalist future does not even meet the realism embodied in one of Stalin's five-year plans. Whether it is the leadership of the United States or Britain, the international organizations, U.N., World Bank, IMF, WTO, the reality is that these institutions today constitute the ruling cliques of the world. Indeed, wonderful ideals built into the originating organizations. Unfortunately, they are now run by bureaucrats, elected or not, whose aim is to gather their spoils and retire to the spas.

There is a dim sense that some type of participatory democracy is at least an honorific value for peoples and nations. Even here, less than perfect tyrannies, autocracies, and "managed" democracies proliferate, vote in the United Nations, and receive the economic largesse of the national and international powers. So long as they do not threaten the existence of the West, as did Osama bin Laden and Saddam Hussein, we accept, begrudgingly, this steady unraveling.

B) There is as yet no perception of the danger to the very life fiber of the Western civilizational tradition by these exploding, aimless masses of humans. The leadership publicly asserts its belief that the so-called developing world can be transformed into Western secular democracies. All 10 billion of us supposedly will, by 2050, become participating contributors to this inchoate hope for stability, if not progress. All we need to do is to give these peoples a nudge.

Unfortunately, all the empirical evidence argues against this utopian dream. The reason: intelligence levels below those necessary to create and maintain the institutions of Western civilization as they have been constructed over the past six or seven thousand years. It is impossible for anyone, except perhaps the Chinese founder of Singaporean prosperity, Mr. Li Kuan Yu, to speak about human intelligence levels as the key to prosperity, equality, and, then, peace.[1] The failure of the United Nations in its sixty years of hopeful rhetoric, the proliferation of failed nations literally ruling our destiny, ought to hint at the problem.

Meaning of Civilization

The term *civilization* is clearly value-laden. We thus use this word honorifically. Today, what one person might call a way of life that is barbaric, defined by terror acts against innocent humans, suffused by religious superstition, individual obeisance, ruled by clerical pretenders to the word of Deity, incompetent in the arts and sciences, is defined by some as a contender civilization. Such a way of life is contrasted with Western civilization as it has developed in Europe and North America. This supposedly Eur-Asian civilization is now being transferred to the Northeast Asiatic nations into a transcontinental movement of ideas, values, and law.[2] In reality, no other contender civilization meets the above definition.

Our new global concept of civilization *is* worth fighting for. It is at the heart of the education that tens of millions have received over the course of centuries. In order to for us to retain what we have been taught to nurture, to treasure, we must continuously argue about the concretia that constitute the concept of *civilization*.

To argue the case for its oncoming collapse and the need to renew and rediscover this value that we call civilization, it is necessary to do more than call upon a dictionary definition. We must enhance this term through reference to the history of peoples who themselves have searched for a model of the better life.

One of the impediments to the study of civilization *per se* is the counterargument that the concept is born of an incorrect exclusivity. So-called civilization, in this thinking, is an ethnocentric concoction of Western elitists. The more inclusive concept, "cultures," as we have studied them in anthropology, more accurately reflects our human uniqueness in the biological world. Out of this concept has come the term "cultural relativism," meaning no developmental, historical, or moral superiority of one culture over another. As long as it meets basic human social needs, and creates the universal institutions of human life, religion, technology, the arts, ordered familial child-rearing institutions, all is well.[3]

We were all fascinated as undergraduates by the self-satisfying mythologies about piquant but parallel cultures to our own, as presented by Ruth Benedict and Margaret Mead.[4] They deflated our egoism about the power of Western technology and its military reach. However, time has told us another story about the relativistic status of these non-Western societies. Today, they are mired in subsistence economies, occasionally employed in Hilton tourist hotels, *et al.*, condescended to by medical support from the West, as well as never-ending economic and military "philanthropy" to survive. At international folk festivals, out come the costumes, the dance, the quaint instruments, the local culinary delicacies; they even can be found performing at Lincoln Center. These populations are now in demographic surfeit. They scream their desires for the emoluments of Western life, but they never emerge from the international handout.

At one time the entire world was at this primeval cultural level. After all, we have stone tools fabricated by humans that go back several hundred thousands of years, controversially to over a million years. These small-brained members of our genus *Homo* presumably participated in all the cultural emoluments that we embrace. However, dance, music, sociality and politics are the soft stuff of cultural activity, in contrast to the surviving stone tools. Rarely, we find pollen grains with the burials, else shells, that could indicate elaborate rites at the death of a "loved" one. Here, too, so human.

But cultures have moved on in time. The brain swells, the possibilities for objectification in thought, complex cultural institutions, and a dynamic of creative change intrude. Somewhere along this timeline of biocultural evolution a stage is reached in human thought and behavior that transcends the generic catch-all of universal cultural behavior. We then make the transition into *civilization*. This is the focus of our inquiry. What was the nature of this transition?

How did those first civilizations accomplish it? What was their own evaluation of social purpose, of innovation? We evaluate our own work. So must they have.

Why the Myopia?

At this stage in history, shouldn't our educated knowledge of the universe, life and society allow us to have a better fix on who we are as humans in the biophysical world, to allow us to do some realistic planning? From such considerations, ought we not be able to muster the policy will to persuade our yet-disparate world leadership of a better way?

Leaving aside for the moment the issue of human intelligence capacities and incapacities, our discussions, in our classrooms, halls of government, and in the responsible media of the free world ought to deal with our conjoint direction through history. Why aren't we looking beyond the next election or U.N budget evaluation? The most reasonable answer, probably similar to the French Academy's nineteenth-century refusal to accept further submissions to the puzzle of the origination of languages: question not answerable.

Are we to conclude that such inquiries are utopian, especially considering the pace of political, technological, and economic change? The most that we can do, given the existing ferment of social change, is to contain the ever lengthening number of short-term crises. We are well experienced in the shrieking Cassandra-like fears over the disappearance of natural resources or global warming and pollution. The sense is that inventive minds will find solutions to all these problems, if only we can stave off the deluge five yards, or five minutes away.

We rely on those in the intellectual community—the universities, the innumerable think tanks—to think outside the box, for even medium-length analysis, not the futurologists that dream of utopian interplanetary visits. Is there any coherency in our planning, seeking other resolutions to the avalanche of problems, that might deviate from the assumed paradigm?

Part of the problem is that the intellectual community, and thus the timid political community, still adheres to the cultural relativistic view of social life. Many, for example, argue that the condition of Muslim women in the twenty-first century constitutes one among many alternative models of family or sexual relationships. Therefore, it is not legitimate to critique seemingly deviant patterns of beliefs and behaviors from the Western standpoint.

The corruption in the United Nations revealed Europe as having its hands in Saddam Hussein's pocket. Receiving the oil-for-food vouchers, supplying Hussein the power to destroy innocent Iraqis could presumably be sanctioned, as long as they profited from the deal. Their hands were clean; Iraqis were presumably expendable. After all, they were a civilizationally different people with another set of values.

The basic theme that we hear from the developed world: let the so-called leaders of the Third World work the suffering of their people as they can. Our policy is to maintain the given material standards of living of our own citizens, no European soldiers, except for the British, to die for foolish wars. The status quo must be protected. Up until now the immigration policy of Western Europe was the same. Welcome cheap labor. Give our citizens their thirty-five-hour work weeks, eight weeks vacation, retirement at full pay at age 55.

In the U.S. and Canada it is little different. Illegal immigrants are pouring over our borders (*Time Magazine* estimated three million in 2004). Cheap labor means high profits and low-cost services and goods. Robert Samuelson noted in October, 2004, that the increased poverty levels of the U.S., the swelling numbers of those without health insurance, consequent decreased median income for families and individuals, can all be put at the door of legal and illegal immigrants who are arriving in the U.S. without a high school education.[5] The prediction that our current population of c.300 million people will grow to between 400-450 million people by 2050, mostly new entrants, and uneducated, does not resonate with the leadership or the intellectual community.

The orthodoxy sees no correlation between the influx of poor from the Third World into the developed societies and the waning civilizational *élan* we ostensibly want to achieve. All people presumably can achieve the same levels of Western competence, if only we can soak the rich of their taxable wealth. If progress does not happen, sayeth the cultural relativists, we will all become Pakistan, Zimbabwe, or Honduras. So what!

Deep Fear

Underlying this unwillingness to examine comparatively the derived lifestyles and competencies of the peoples of the world, family, nationality, ethnicity, or race, is the great fear of variable intelligence. For, if all behavior is culturally derived, from tradition, and all cultures are relative and equal, then the claim about intelligence variability as a biological explanation of behavioral differences becomes the great moral turpitude.

Question: Why would anyone attempt to argue for such comparisons, of individuals, nationalities, religions, races? Is it not a ploy to denigrate and subject the seemingly at-risk groups to more segregation, discrimination, prejudice, indeed, even subjugation and slavery?

This is the implicit, often explicit response to those who would propose a biological explanation for such differences. This is why the issue of intelligence differences in social and educational behavior, cultural traditions is under interdict in the West. The biological explanation is prelude to a demonization of intent.

The tension arises from the fact that these groups are our neighbors, fellow citizens, members of the world community, neighbors in international organizations. We are not yet a homogenized humanity. Our biosocial heritage still haunts us. We need to find a way to be both objective and humane.

Yet, few realize that the entire Asiatic continent is inhabited by peoples and nations that are racially mixed. From the Northeast Asiatics, Korean, Chinese, Japanese, who are tri-racial hybrids, to the Indonesians and Thais, likewise hybrid variants of Australid, Caucasoid and Mongoloid racial strains, this human intermixing goes back to the most ancient periods following the original Diaspora from Africa some 2-1 million years ago.

In order to have a full understanding of the relationship between high intelligence and civilization, we must recognize that intelligence as an animal adaptation defines our special and powerful vertebrate adaptive zone. We are the products of this evolutionary progression, all *Homo sapiens*, yet with distinctive heritages when it comes to these momentary physical and intellectual differences.

In the scientific community, only the most extreme ideological leftist egalitarians would claim that human intelligence is homogeneously distributed, even within the narrowest and inbred ethnicities.[6] If this were the case, all aptitude testing would be banned. Colleges, corporations, the armed services, government would all be precluded from testing and choosing who should be chosen for training on the job. The theory of potential intellectual parity would mandate as explanation that such differences originate in previously existing social and familial inequalities. This same individual would in theory have equal potential as compared to an individual of privilege. Equal training would realize equal capabilities.

But clearly, experience argues that such explanations are mythological. We need to make careful choices of our astronauts, our scholarship applicants to medical school, the Air Force Academy, applicants for managerial or research positions at IBM. All require testing for basic general intelligence that will insure mastery of the course of study. This evidence for the factuality of biosocial causes of intellectual difference, recognized by the educated as well as the commoner, can only be communicated in shaded, veiled discussions. This, to avoid any possible policy institutionalizations that recognize intelligence as a differentiating factor in social behavior.[7]

Empirical evidence argues for group as well as individual differences. The latter apply to same-sex full siblings. I.Q., educational, vocational, professional, sociological, national profiles of people of the southern ethnicities, in Africa, South Asia, the Islamic world, all reveal lower intelligence achievements than Europeans and Northeast Asiatics.[8] There are evolutionary reasons for these differences.

On the other hand, it is also true that individual members of all these groups often have scores and achievements that lie within the general profile of the higher intelligence ethnicities. This is predictable in terms of the probability curve for any attribute, height, weight, or intelligence. Considering the vast and relatively recent admixture of ethnicities and races, in Latin America, Asia, even Africa, one cannot draw hard-and-fast divisions or distinctions between individuals and peoples. The test lies in behavior of individuals as well as nationalities.

What has happened to our globe since the beginning of the industrial revolution is an explosion of knowledge and technological/military power in the Eur-Asian complex. This dynamism has now been passed into Northeast Asia. These ethnicities seemed to have responded as the environmentalists predict all people would when faced with sufficient social opportunity. However, intelligence is a factor that has to be considered also. Yet, Iraq, Pakistan, Indonesia and the Muslim world had opportunities not too dissimilar. Their evidence is not unequivocal.

It is enough to say that the Chinese, Koreans, and Japanese were expected to counter the European Caucasoid challenge. The Japanese have given sufficient evidence of their readiness to challenge European hegemony in their leap into the Western world, symbolized by their defeat of Czarist Russia in 1904. The three Northeast Asian ethnicities as highly intelligent tri-racial hybrids had the genetics to respond in education, social discipline, science and technology. They are now the equals of the old West, if not on the way to besting their teachers.

The great growth of wealth in the twentieth century led to a view of the conspiratorial nature of temporary industrial class divisions. Communist and fascist ideology displaced the laissez faire optimism of the eighteenth to nineteenth century. The world moved too fast for sober evaluation. The result in Europe and Asia were the great aristocides of the twentieth century, in which literally hundreds of millions were destroyed in a vast conflagration of political and intellectual ineptitude.

This emotional misjudgment continued in the liberal redistributionist model of economic and social assistance to those non-European minorities that had not made the move into the modern scientific/technological world. The rising bar of required educational competencies and technological productivity pushed them inexorably to the bottom of the social scale. This distributionist vision of equality, which argued that the inequalities were due to a racist institutional structure dominated by the white male, turned the factual problem of non-achievement and social disorganization into a moral crusade.

It worked as long as the intimidated white male middle classes of North America and Europe had enough wealth to pay up. As we have argued in earlier books, and in the following chapters, the expansionary demographics of our international scene will continue to undercut egalitarian expectations.[9] Just as the communist ship sank, commissars instantaneously transformed into oligarchs, so, too, will our liberal zealots seek their own salvation.

There can be no turning back from a religio-ideological moral system that has taken hold in the educated West. As Sir Peter Bauer once stated ironically, we should try to forego "taxing poor people in rich countries to protect the life style of rich people in poor countries."[10] Sadly, in order for such a reexamination to occur, the ideological glue that holds the present system together today will have to weaken and the system collapse before reason can hope to gain hold of our international policy-making institutions.

Fear and ignorance have a way of paralyzing the mind. A real life problem arises, a seemingly simple solution presents itself. It is tried, fails, causes immeasurable harm to humanity. Myopia, tunnel vision, whatever, we try the same superstitious policies again and again until we are broken. In reality there was always another humane solution. Fear and ignorance precluded its consideration.

Eugenics was a *liberal* ideal until the late 1930s. From the end of the nineteenth century to the above timeframe, eugenics was linked with the new psychological testing movement and the clear understanding that low non-coping intelligence was rooted in families. The ideal was the improvement of the human race; socialists and feminists endorsed its utopian goals.[11]

Then came Hitler, with his screed directed mainly against the Jews. Read carefully, it was the typical anti-Semitic caricature, often directed toward poor Jews of East European origin, their Semitic appearance and their economic struggle for existence. The incubus of ethnic-religious prejudice and discrimination mandated their supreme efforts for economic survival, the supposed "sleazy cleverness" by which the Jews surmounted the various forms of prejudice, ghettoization, and the pogrom.

Esteemed thinkers such as Immanuel Kant (1780s) and Francis Galton (late nineteenth century) had engaged in such historically acceptable stereotyping.[12] With Hitler, the political import was more contemporary. The Jews had by then emerged from their ghettoes. Hitler feared them as much as he demonized them. Their "slimy" intellect was the threat to his plan for world domination. As such they were condemned to annihilation in Germany and Europe. Once Hitler attained power, all of Europe, with a few exceptions, participated in the *Holocaust*, a millennial exemplification of the twentieth-century war against intelligent minorities, ethnic, religious, social class.

Thus was born the great myth that this and other genocides were examples of eugenics at work. *WRONG*. When one examines each of these events of the twentieth and now into the twenty-first century, from Turkish Armenia to Rwanda/Burundi, it is clear that we have witnessed the application of *dysgenics*.

The resultant extermination of such competent minorities has led to the demeaning of the biosocial (intelligence) potential of the human species. The brewers of evil may have used the word *eugenics*. It once connoted science and humanitarian help. The truth, regrettably rejected by the world, was that the barbarism of Hitler, Stalin, Mao, and all the other "egalitarians" knew what they were about in clearing the deck of reasoning opponents.

Realism

The word *eugenics* is too tainted for adoption in any future program of human betterment. When the bank of redistributionary benevolence runs dry and the will languishes sometime during the second half of our century, there may be hope. Far-seeing intellectual and political leadership may be able to translate this long-existing scientific message and utilize it. What will need to be accomplished is the transformation of the current anti-biological view of human intelligence into a new philosophy of human betterment.

Our concern must be more than merely handing needy humans a temporary welfare bone. It must involve a commitment to the permanent uplifting of such groups without regard for irrelevant racial patterns. These are unimportant uncorrelated human externalities. The fact that large numbers of individuals from such ethnic and racial groups are intellectually, economically, educationally competitive argues strongly for the scientific fact that high intelligence can come in a variety of human dresses (Chapter 4). Witness the dark-skinned Indians from South Asia or the sallow-skinned Northeast Asiatics.

The concrete genes for high or low I.Q. when they are discovered will clarify this already well-established empirical fact. Were we able to introduce the biochemistry of high intelligence genetics into any population that is presently "undeveloped," the cultural transformation would take only a few generations. How can this be done? In Chapter 5, we will discuss the different contemporary programs that are already taking us down this road. All we need to do is to face reality, and engage in a great educational campaign against the demagogues of the political and religious right as well as the pseudo-Marxist left.

What would happen were we able to identify in the fetus or the fertilized egg the specific complex of genes for high and low "g" (general intelligence)? In this case, humans could be empowered by such knowledge to choose the intelligence and other profiling characteristics of their future progeny. Contrary to officialdom's imprecations, free humans would "vote with their feet." The current pseudo-ethical prohibitions on such knowledge and choice would quickly wither.

The reality of human awareness of the inborn nature of human intelligence differences would here end the debate questioning the link between civilization and high intelligence. The modern advance of science given the dissolution of illusionary sociopolitical policies would proclaim a new hope for humanity's future. A free citizenry would continue to educate us.

Our Civilizational Goal

Merely searching for high competency in intelligence is not enough. Evil individuals often have high I.Q.s, *e.g.*, the Nazi leadership, excluding Hitler and his originating thugs.[13] To avoid the corruption that can come even within a species of uniformly high "g", we must articulate the substantive nature of such a world, the concrete institutional structures, the constitutional protections of individual freedom, the fascinating and necessary cultural differences that produce a Leibniz within one ethnicity, a Newton in another a few hundred miles distant. We must build our species into an international system of smart, thinking people. Thus, we need to understand the nature of the high civilizations that humans have created spontaneously in the past, here if only to avoid the worst of their mistakes of ignorance as well as of intent.

In this case it is not enough to go back to that first proto-civilization that revealed the spontaneous flow of high technology, refined art, as it issued from an extraordinary hominid brain, *i.e.*, the Cro-Magnon Eur-Asians of 45,000-10,000 BCE. Theirs was largely a non-literate civilization of small groups, human bands or tribes in the dozens or low hundreds, hunting, gathering, and living in close proximity in caves and shelters, spread over a thousand-mile expanse of tundra-like plains.

We need to study how a fully modern, literate, civilizational enterprise was consciously constructed by groups of people, descended from these Cro-Magnons, as they migrated south into the warmer climates. This migration was first stimulated by the alteration of their autumnal, northern paradise by a long-term and major change into modern continental climatic conditions. The formerly halcyonic way of life disappeared.

Out of this search for survival, our mysterious human nature was able to produce the civilization/culture that epitomized the needs of our brain. We hunt, sow, plough, procreate, first to survive, to live. Then emerges an even deeper human inclination, the freedom for our minds to play cognitively. [See Appendix, "Western Civilization Begins at Sumer."]

Endnotes, Chapter 1

[1] Quoted in Herrnstein, R. 1989. "I.Q. and Falling Birth Rates," in *Atlantic Monthly*, May.
[2] Huntington, S. 1996. *The Clash of Civilizations*, N.Y.: Simon and Schuster.
[3] Boas, F. 1911. *The Mind of Primitive Man*, N.Y.: Macmillan; Boas, F. 1940. *Race, Language, Culture*, N.Y.: The Free Press.

[4] Benedict, R. 1934. *Patterns of Culture,* Boston: Houghton Mifflin; Mead, M. 1963. *Sex and Temperament in Three Primitive Societies,* N.Y.: William Morrow; Mead, M. 1964. *Continuities in Cultural Evolution,* New Haven: Yale Univ. Press.
[5] *The Washington Post,* 10/13/2004.
[6] Gould, S. J. 1981. *The Mismeasure of Man,* N.Y.: W. W. Norton; Lewontin, R., Rose S., Kamin, L. 1984. *Not in Our Genes,* N.Y.: Pantheon.
[7] Santy, P. 1994. *Choosing the Right Stuff,* Westport CT: Praeger.
[8] Lynn, R. 1996. *Dysgenics,* Westport CT: Praeger; Lynn, R. 2001. *Eugenics,* A *Reassessment,* Westport, CT: Praeger; Lynn, R., and Vanhanen, T. I.Q. *and the Wealth of Nations,* Westport, CT: Praeger.
[9] Itzkoff, S. W. 2003. *2050: The Collapse of the Global Techno-Economy,* Ashfield, MA: Paideia; Itzkoff, S. W. 2003. *Intellectual Capital in* Twenty-First-*Century Politics,* Ashfield, MA: Paideia.
[10] Bauer, P. 1972. *Dissent on Development,* Cambridge, MA: Harvard Univ. Press.
[11] Pearson, K. 1901. *National Life,* London: Methuen; Haldane, J. B. S. 1924. *Daedalus,* London; Gray, M. 1979. *Margaret Sanger,* A *Biography,* New York: R. Marek.
[12] Galton, F. 1869. *Hereditary Genius,* London: Macmillan; Galton, F. 1909. *Essays on Eugenics,* London: Eugenics Society"; Kant, I. (c. 1788) 1978. *Anthropology from a Pragmatic Point of View,* trans. by V. L. Dawdell, Carbondale, IL: Southern Illinois Univ. Press.
[13] Gilbert, G. M. 1947. *Nuremberg Diary,* N.Y.: Signet, p.34. The Wechsler-Bellevue I.Q. Test was used.

Chapter 2

Reason's Defeat, Civilization's Fall

Revolutionary Conditions

An intellectual and social revolution is lurking in the wings. It is global. As with all important historical transformations, in thought as well as in social consequence, it is feeding on the ruins of the previous and failed intellectual and social paradigm. This precursor condition of failure, a consequence of the twentieth- and twenty-first-century global abnegation of reason and leadership, has dissolved our dream of a middle-class life for all. For us, the living, the victims will be our grandchildren and great-grandchildren. They will live through generations of chaos, authoritarianism, economic and social collapse, then, stagnation. The seeds are now sprouting. We know the cause: the hardened ideologies of the present ensconced power structure.

Be prepared, it will begin to suffocate us sometime around mid-twenty-first century, two generations hence. And as always, the turnaround in re-thinking, re-planning, the putting into place of new institutions of social life and their tangible political, economic, and social policies will, we can hope, come later, probably much later. First, the full realization that our world society can no longer advance as a result of the consequences to which ideology has brought us. Then, new thoughts will have to germinate in a wholly new generation of leaders. The taboos of the past, as always, will have to become principles for the future.

The rebuilding of the best that Western Civilization has given to the human species is not foreordained, for the end of this century or the next. A century of outright irrational religious obscurantism could follow, building on the resentments of the many. Reform will require obstinate leadership, educating the masses regardless of their intellectual incapacity, to put into place reasoned reform. This leadership will have to beware both of a demonological search for scapegoats as well as of unscrupulous nirvanas, of which the twentieth-century exemplar had its surfeit.

The current taboo, and the future fulcrum of reform? Simply, the variability of cognitive, educable intelligence in the human community high enough to move us into policies that would lead to human enhancement rather than tragedy. This variability of human intelligence was once hidden from historical view by the seeming advance of civilizational knowledge, enhanced power to protect ourselves from the unpredictable events of nature. This massive variability stares us in the face now. It is a byproduct of this self-same power of human knowledge, science, medicine, and agriculture. It is an ironic success, flowing out of the advanced nations of the world. Our "success" has allowed for the philanthropic protective blanket of birth and life that has resulted in the flood of those formerly hidden poor now enveloping our world.

This global tide of humans, from c.1 to 1.5 billion, between 1850 and 1900, to 6.5 billion in 2005, is a millennial inundation. Adding to the current and building clouds of crises is the continuing demographic explosion of humans that augurs to choke the planet with at least 3-4 billion more impoverished, hopeless, and desperate souls, 9-10 billion by mid-twenty-first century. Will the same science that created for humanity such anti-civilizational trends be able to turn back this flood?

Is there any half-educated adult today in the West, here including the Northeast Asiatic triumvirate of developed ethnicities, the Chinese, Japanese, Koreans, that is not aware that the global conditions for long-term human prosperity are silently draining away? As we witness natural pandemics, never before experienced, esoteric and undefeated bacteria, can we doubt that even modern scientific medicine may at some point fail? Why is it, as we witness our hopes for a global egalitarian civilization crumble before our very eyes that these day-to-day factual realities do not register as meaning? Perhaps the answer lies in the opiated utopian pronouncements of the powerful? The down escalator increases in speed. Upward scurry the international "liberals" and agencies. Soon, exhaustion and triage.

Brainwashing would be too extreme a term to use for our inability to understand what is happening in our world. Even if many do perceive this oncoming barbarism, they cannot entertain the thought. Our ideological expectations as to how to improve the condition of humankind is in reality a propagandistic menu of politically convenient policies, policies that continue the self-interested perceptions of reality that the well-ensconced want us to accept. Conveniently, this miasma of ideology has the "beneficent" outcome of maintaining the power of the presently satiated. Marx would have recognized and rued this turn in ideology and its new form of oppression by the powerful.

The taboo against considering that individuals, no less ethnicities, religions, nationalities, races, are unable to learn and take hold, profit from and contribute to the institutions of traditional civilization, militates against public discussion.

For example, no one dares to speak about Africa south of the Sahara, or the Arab and Muslim world, even, and especially, Latin America, at our doorstep, in terms of the causes of poverty, degradation, the few powerful forever oppressing the many.

History is replete with attempts to stifle free thought. Revolutionary ideas threaten more than old beliefs. They burrow under the foundations of the established moral and civil order. They undermine existing power arrangements. Marx taught us that the beneficiaries of these exploitative power structures that dig in their heels at all truly new ways of thinking, especially any that concern human institutions, eventually lose this power. New ways of production, or lack of production, dialectically intercede to cut the ground from under the foundations of the status quo.

Indeed, the twentieth century was hardly immune from this dynamic of change. Marx would have been surprised at the totalitarianisms that were placed into political domination bearing the slogans of his own vision of "socialism." Here, too, the socialist euphemism still bedecks the banners of many statist political parties. The Western democracies are gentler in this respect, else these words could not see the light of day. Yet, the so-called free institutions, educational, political, communications, are lined up in unanimity. The interdict is total for any consideration that human biological intellectual capacity or incapacity may be central in the drama of our twenty-first century descent into chaos.

My argument is both critique and, then, utopian proposal. It is hardly mine alone, but based on this simple and always seminal fact: The basic policy dilemmas of the twentieth and twenty-first centuries arise from the enormous differences in human intellectual capacity, biologically and genetically rooted, among the inhabitants of our planet.

This claim is based upon an enormous accumulation of scientific and factual evidence. There has been virtually no contestation of this evidence, because there are no data to argue against it. Individuals and communities of high civilizational intelligence will prosper under all productive systems, if given a chance. Societies where lower levels of intelligence dominate will reduce civilizations to mere subsistence. Those today in power, in government, the media, academia, in the business world, think this reality of international decline will just go away.

Wait. There is no happiness in discussing this widening gap of the developing *versus* the unraveling world. Rather, there is the ardent hope that enough stubborn humans will study this issue and create a climate of judicious, if dissident opinion.

In our world today the facts are exploding the mythic claims and efforts for the long-term efficacy of the mere redistribution of wealth. For example, affirmative action, now two generations in place in American education, has only resulted in the degradation of the institutions subject to this institutional experiment. The only answer presented by the purveyors of this failed myth of supposedly pre-ordained equality of outcomes is a never-ending demonology, usually aimed at the white colonial male. Eventually, given the ubiquitous failures of these attempts at redistributing trillions of dollars of material and social aid, giving special privilege to the underachieving, the institutional system that is the object of this ideology will fall apart.

The success of high I.Q. individuals and their respective ethnicities and nationalities should be instructive. The confidence of the Chinese nation, now released from the imprisonment of Mao, with its advantage of close to a 2/3 standard estimated deviation over average American I.Q.s (105 to less than c.95) constitutes the ground of their confidence. Unfortunately, not our fear. High I.Q individuals and their nations become the leaders in the literate arts, entrepreneurship in business, science, and technology. They are the creators of the high arts. On the other hand, they also reap great wealth in producing the dross that satisfies the American mind.

So far, the ideologists have not yet focused their obloquy on the Northeast Asiatics, in their recent emancipations, as they have on the Americans. Even a fatted nerveless Western Europe still sees the American educated classes as enemy, in terms of productivity, but also international moral idealism, its energy past. We American have a few decades of relative prosperity and social calm before we will have to face our social and ideological antinomies. The West Europeans, however, in more near-term decline than we, are beginning to see the opacity of their attempt to absorb non-Europeans of differing intellectual/cultural aptitudes. There, as with our own immigration policies, the race is between rationality and social chaos.

In the material, technological world, if, for example, an airplane is designed or fabricated incompetently, it will not leave the ground, sputtering into a ditch. Even in the Soviet Union such technological failures in theory and in application were acknowledged, and new instrumental pathways pursued. In the human social and cultural realm, today, as so often in the past, there are too many vested institutional interests to allow for a secular reconsideration of the evidence. That will continue until, with all aboard, the plane goes down.

Ideology: Effaced Rationality

Perhaps if we understood better why societies cannot see through their failure of aim and realization, doomed to dry up in energy, wither, and be brought down by more dynamic challengers, we might be able to look more objectively at our own date with civilizational history. The issue comes down to being able to look at social reality in clear instrumental terms. Here we have to apply the same scientific standards as we do with physical experience. We have to back off from our knee-jerk mammalian emotionality. This can only be done by rising up out of our flesh and bones, so to speak, and looking at ourselves and humanity, as if from Mars, always with intellectual skepticism. Of course, it is tough to admit to the fallibility of our most treasured beliefs about self and society. Ironically, we forever need an alternative perspective, just to compare.

With regard to the intelligence issue, the irony is that we are practically forced to recognize individual differences. In most functions of society, whether they be civil service exams, SATs, personality and I.Q. tests that corporations give to evaluate prospective hires, testing is a given. The entire world is suffused with auditions, grades, evaluations, competitions, prizes, awards, medals, remedial classes, techniques, institutions, telling us in loud, clear terms that we are different: in talents, abilities, yes, perhaps, in intelligence.

Ask any mother of two or more sons or daughters, from the same father. They are born with differing abilities, personalities, talents, loves and hates; they are different from their first moments in the crèche at the hospital. We see these little arms and legs flail out, cries of irritation and need, the smiles of content after the nursing and the warm milk, all expressed differently.

Similarly, we glory in cultural differences that arise from different ethnicities, nationalities, religions. We travel to see different mountain ranges, tropical islands, but not only for their flora and fauna. We want to experience the differences of culture arising from people in differing geographies. French, Italian, Chinese cuisine fascinate in their differences. The music and art, the languages of different nations have intrinsic values that we recognize and intellectualize as part of our vision as to what the world is about.

We travel to Nigeria or Kenya, and can compare the lives of these people with the different racial and ethnic cultures we find in Korea or Taiwan, no less Sweden or Norway. Perhaps the historical or contemporary causes for differences in architectural styles in Thailand, as against Russia, are beyond our intellectualization at this point in our knowledge. Yet the mind still searches for the reason why people in Nairobi and Lagos have such different standards of life as compared to other humans of differing racial and ethnic backgrounds in Singapore or Brisbane. But here we speak of culture as cause. Rarely does the thought that bio-genetic reasons might account for some of the behavioral diversity of peoples enter our minds.

In an article in *The New York Times*, music columnist Anne Midgette writes about a music festival in La Jolla, California, that for once will not be devoted to the domineering aggrandizement of "white" male composers, and will now feature music by several talented Chinese ("yellow") male composers.[1] This was not irony, merely *The Times*' own inclination toward the vulgar politicization of the arts. What's the big deal about Bach, Fauré, Vaughan Williams? Their art, so implies our music critic, is a product of the Western persecution of all non-white, non-male human beings.

In the same newspaper, one day later, a detailed article outlined the ongoing loss of American superiority in the sciences to the Taiwanese, Japanese, and Koreans. Soon, mainland China. No one ponders the Northeast Asiatic I.Q.s of 105, in comparison with collapsing American educational achievement, large percentages, especially in the expanding African-American, Hispanic communities where 9th and 10th grade high school students are doing 4th and 5th grade work, prelude increasingly to their dropping out of school.[2]

Another, perhaps most inexcusable repression of reason, is our taught intellectual understanding of the many twentieth-century genocides. Here, not merely the destruction of indigenous social classes, but also the raised achievement and economic levels of ethnic minorities. The *Holocaust* of the Jews in the twentieth century is the prime example. The rationale for these exterminations was, of course, the supposed exploitation and oppression that these minorities had exercised over the majority. We remember Hitler's *Mein Kampf*, written well before his ascent to power, a discrete contribution to the contemporary river of anti-Semitic slime about "clever Jews" dominating Europe. His own screed against the Jews was overlain with fears of their take-over and control of Germany and then the rest of the world. He was speaking about a politically impotent 1 percent of the German population. To Hitler, the Jew was the filthy, morally degradable symbol of a twentieth-century exploitative ethnicity that would have to be effaced.

The twentieth-century stain of shame had begun with the scattered destruction of Turkey's Christian Armenians. It concluded with the attempted obliteration of the Amharic-speaking Tutsi of Rwanda and Burundi, and, lately, the urban Muslim Slavs of Bosnia. This ideological madness does not have to war against an ethnic minority. See the Kulaks of the Soviet Union, the "landlords" of Maoist China, the eyeglass-wearing middle classes of Pol Pot's Cambodia. These were all social class successes, whose intelligence and enterprise had added to the wealth of their nations, and the civilizational advance of the entire world.

Does one hear a word about the envy and hatred that underlay these destructions of humanity? The root cause, envy of, revenge against the higher intelligent classes is repressed because we are not free to understand the nature of human progress and failure. And because we are blinded, we may be enticed yet again to repeat these horror events.

This poison of envy, frustration over failure, causes the leadership of the Muslim world, hundreds of millions strong, to spew out a cacophony of hatred against a few million Jews who are accused of controlling the world (*viz* Mahathir bin Mohamad of Malaysia). In this they follow the inspiration of Adolph Hitler. The real cause of this hatred of "international Zionism" is that there is an Israel of five million souls among these hundreds of millions of Arabs. Israel is democratic politically, technologically and culturally advanced. It is also capable of defending itself against their hordes, despite an ocean of Arab oil wealth.

The euphemistic explanations obfuscate the root cause. Examples of getting it wrong as to fact and explanation: the inexcusable killing of small numbers of Gypsies in the *Holocaust;* the anger over Hutu economic and political subjugation by the Tutsi; the over-educated Cambodian middle class. If we are ever to move onto a wiser road of understanding concerning the human factual condition, we must confront the lure of ideology, the blind resistance to reality that has contaminated this last bloody century.

Ideology and Theology

Ideology: "visionary theorizing." *Theology*: "The study of God and his relationship to the world" (Webster's *New Collegiate Dictionary*).

Ideology and theology have much in common. It is the desire to believe, and to act in society on the basis of such beliefs. These beliefs are not necessarily based upon factual evidence. We want to believe, down deep. Theology develops out of the self-consciousness of establishment religion. It is rooted in the need to explain, the desire to know. Usually philosophically interpretive, the place of humans and knowledge in relation to a higher often supernatural power, theology can be intellectually rich and thought provoking. This is especially true as it moves away from socio/political doctrine into metaphysical discussions of the human condition, the moral imperatives of social life.

If theology expands beyond its particular religious institutional focus, and out into society, in terms of dictating economic, political, social policies, it transforms itself into ideology. Ideology can exist without the religious dimension. It takes its motivating juices from the universal mammalian search for meaning, a home from which to organize intellectual and social policy in a very dangerous and tenuous historical environment.

When religious or other political authority systems begin to fail, the search for a new fulcrum upon which to plan our existence becomes necessary. In times of revolutionary ferment, political, economical, technological, this search for a secure homeland of thought and action can exceed the limits of fact or circumstance, beyond the anchor of scientific knowledge. It can create mythic policies for nations and continents. These will purport to lead us away from the confusions of the moment, to secure utopia.

But because these visions are largely emotional, leadership needs to exploit the insecurities of the masses, to lead them down the road toward blind obeisance. The power agenda of such leadership groups, as in the communist world, will necessarily require the heel of tyranny.

Enfranchisement and Empowerment

The modern Enlightenment was constructed from the disintegrating intellectual institutional framework of Catholic Europe. The dominance of the Church, and the relative social, political, and economic stagnancy of the Middle Ages, 400-1400 CE, were themselves consequences of an earlier cultural emancipation, this from the skeletal remains of Roman imperial power. Once the universal political eminence of a long-enduring Hellenistic civilization, Rome gradually wasted away in political violence and cultural exhaustion. The dominance of a supplanting theologically-ruled universal culture took centuries to form, gradually embedding its symbols of meaning and guidance deep into the human psyche.

It took over 300 years from c.1400 CE to free the enquiring human mind. This process, encompassed by the Renaissance and the Reformation was not without much bloodshed and travail. Humans of high intelligence eventually find their means for the freedom to think and create. We have had to learn this again from the experience with the totalitarianisms of the twentieth century. The push to recreate civilizational institutions always takes place with much hesitation and conflict, and, yes, blood.

The Renaissance and the Reformation periods necessitated an enunciation of new moral and political values to accompany this thrust of the human mind in search for power over nature. Inevitably the quick to anticipate this new structure of knowledge in science, technology, and social life benefited. They inevitably pushed the earlier feudal/agricultural system into oblivion. *Laissez faire* was a concept statement about the inherent freedom of individuals and their immediate social, religious, and political communities to be able to loose the arbitrary historical restraints, church and divine right monarchies.

The democratic franchise had to expand. First from England and North America, then to France, eventually all of Europe moved erratically but inevitably toward removing the political barriers. Even the retrogressive Ottomans by the middle of the nineteenth century, following Russia and the emancipation of the serfs, 1862, attempted to stamp out slavery within its domains. The Arabs, protectively, fell into revolt, and the Turks stepped back.[3] The United States fought its own bloody and divisive Civil War, in part to eliminate the enslavement of African Negroes, the Emancipation Proclamation, 1863.

It should be remembered that as early as the last decade of the eighteenth century, during the debates over the new constitution for the fledgling United States of America, the assumption of legitimacy for African slavery was being challenged. Gouverneur Morris of New York condemned the incorporation of Negro slaves in the population statistics to be used as a basis for representation in the House of Representatives and the Electoral Congress, while the slaves themselves were not eligible to vote:

"The admission of slaves into the representation, when fairly explained, comes to this: that the inhabitant of Georgia and South Carolina who goes to the coast of Africa and, in defiance of the most sacred laws of humanity, tears away his fellow creatures from their dearest connections and damns them to the most cruel bondage, shall have more votes in a government instituted for the protection of the rights of mankind than the citizen of Pennsylvania or New Jersey who views with a laudable horror so nefarious a practice."[4]

The implicit belief behind this broadening of suffrage was that the expanding horizons of knowledge and power, the new industrialism, combined with the ability of scientific medicine to fend off diseases and thus shrinking death rates in all segments of the population, could expand the reach of the new scientific/industrial civilization. The world, indeed the universe, was opening itself up to the scientific search for the causes and consequences of natural phenomena.

Next came an intense effort to search through the practical consequences of this naturalistic understanding. The spate of inventions, the growth of the physical sciences and then the biological and medical sciences, greatly expanded our awareness of the relationship of humans to the biophysical world around them. With all of this came an enormous *hybris*, a sense of the unlimited power of human intellectuality to work within this nexus of knowledge, to obtain power and control, power and control not merely over the material and physical externalities of human experience, but the seemingly indelible social and cultural arrangements handed to us by history.

Here is where we should understand the coming of socialism and its critiques.[5] Even in the late eighteenth century, the *volonté générale* of J. J. Rousseau's *Social Contract*, 1762, intuited that the *laissez faire* explosion of creative energy emanating from the bourgeoisie middle classes would inevitably engender revolutionary countermeasures imposed upon them by the multiplying masses at the bottom of the existing social structure.[6] Rousseau intuited this even before the blood letting against the *ancien régime* and the revolution of 1789. The socialists followed this theme into the next century, culminated by the influential conceptualizations of Karl Marx (1818-1883).[7]

Karl Marx himself sought to harmonize his view of the economic basis for historical evolution with Darwin's biological theory of evolution, 1859.[8] An entirely new conceptualization as to the form of society had inserted itself into nineteenth-century life. Medicine and expanding economic horizons had exploded populations, people had been torn from their farms and villages and given an entirely new cast to the prospects for humanity living within the nexus of a revolutionary expansion of knowledge, industrial production and urban existence.

"{Marx} wanted to proceed, and to a very great extent did proceed, scientifically. Nothing was to be deduced from preconceived ideas; from the observed evolutionary laws and forces of modern society alone were conclusions to be drawn....The great scientific achievement of Marx...[lies] in the *method* and *principles* of his investigations in the *philosophy of history*. Here he has, as is now generally admitted broken new ground and opened new ways and new outlooks. Nobody before him has so clearly shown the role of the productive agencies in historical evolution; nobody so masterfully exhibited their great determining influence on the forms and ideologies of social organisms....If he has been justly compared with Darwin, it is in these respects that he ranks with that great genius..."[9]

Socialism and Marxism caused to give an aura of inevitability to the idea that social differences created in the wake of the anarchic vitality of scientific industrialism and the class divisions that grated anew, would produce the ultimate revolution, one social unity, the proletariat, including all previous classes. It envisioned the harmonization of all inherent vocational and professional differences that modern society required. The scope of Marxist theory was akin to the many great scientific unifications, in the tradition of Newton and Darwin, both in thought and practice. The social world was now ordered, and in Newtonian harmony with itself.

Marx' vision was directed toward the Europeans, with a caveat toward the still evolving Slavs. These burgeoning masses of European workers and farmers suffering exploitation anew, on the land, in the mills, mines, factories, were essentially, wage slaves. Their desire for social justice needed to be enunciated and addressed.

We must remember that the nineteenth century was already an expansive urban, demographic cauldron. Cities were exploding with people, Paris, 1796, 536 K, 1850, 2 million; London 1800, 1 million, 1850, 2 million. In 1800, there were 23 cities with populations over 100,000. By 1900, there were 135.[10]

From the days of Disraeli (1804-1881) and Gladstone (1809-1898) in Britain and Bismarck (1815-1898) in imperial Germany, government now acted to intervene, to mitigate the conditions of work, retirement, housing, medical care, public education. The old institutional structure had no intellectual response to socialist theory, except to attempt to defuse the revolutionary impetus of socialist agitation. As the franchise spread throughout Europe, and monarchy and autocracy tottered, a new *Weltgeist*, as Marx' tutor, the philosopher of history, G. W. F. Hegel (1770-1831), had outlined, began to shape the mind of the civilized West.[11]

True Belief

Where there is moral certitude, no questions can be asked. It is the rock upon which our energies are formed, and from which they spring forth to engage the world.

By the end of the nineteenth century, it was clear that special political privilege would have to give way to popular government. All economic advantage would come under the taint of illegitimacy. As this world lurched forward in wealth and power, the masses led by socialist intellectuals explored a vision of egalitarianism. All humans, being equal in their potential for advancement, should in outcome be equal, socially and economically.

The transition was from the seventeenth- and eighteenth-century vision of a world of opportunity to be gained by individual creative effort and enterprise. The nineteenth-century criterion for a humane social existence was now to be tested on the anvil of achievement. Lack of progress by individuals, nations, continents carried with it an implicit taint that the system was saturated in exploitation.

The solution was to be far more cataclysmic than Marx' opaque prediction, an inevitable proletarian victory made possible by the internal contradictions inherent in the current system of class domination, industrial capitalism. This classic Marxist prediction should have come about through the inevitable collapse of capitalism even as the bourgeoisie fought ineptly to retain its privileges.

With the turn of the twentieth century, instead of a struggle against mere "big capital" the enemy began to be redefined. Those at the top of the ladder were no longer the recipients of an imperfect and immoral system. Rather, they the individuals, as well as the institutions of capitalism were now marked. No longer innocent bystanders of the declining *Weltgeist*, themselves awaiting incorporation into the universal proletariat, as Marx saw them, they were now condemned. In large sectors of the changing twentieth-century world, the radical left and the opportunistic fascists viewed these classes of the successful as candidates for extirpation.

The reach of government toward the end of the nineteenth century, given electronic communication, steam railroad and water transportation, soon the airplane, no less the armaments of mechanized warfare and poison gas, presented a new focus for revolutionary agitation. Gaining the reins of national power through the mobilization of the working and middle classes created the possibility for a wholly new pattern of political life, totalitarianism.

To accomplish this goal of overturning the old order, even that of Western bourgeoisie representational democracy, a new application of reason had to be promoted throughout the lands. Here, reassembled facts had to be disseminated to the masses. Control the new instruments of communication and transportation. Propagandize semi-literate populations and gullible middle-class "humanitarians" into becoming the servants of these revolutionary social truths. Reason, the new socialist/communist/fascist argument went, demanded that we recognize that even so-called scientific truth was a tool of class oppression. Equality of outcome now could only be guaranteed by the state.

What held innocent humanity back were the purported injustices of the old order. In one way or another all social, cultural, economic differences needed to be effaced through controlled educational, political, and economic means. The first order of government, democratically if possible, autocratically and with force and bloodshed if necessary, was to level the playing field. This supposed factuality (ideology) mandated the harshest punishments for those who had profited from the exploitative injustices of monarchy, bourgeois mercantilism, and capitalism. Whatever stood in the way of achieving the tangible uniformity of the twentieth-century social order had to be swept away.

Intransigent Belief

We have, as a world, endured two phases of the ideology of egalitarian redistribution. (A) The first involved the bloody totalitarian populist ideologies of such as Stalin, Hitler, Mao, and too many others which pointed the finger of genocide on a variety of ethnic minorities, from the days of the Armenians, the *Holocaust,* the Igbos, Tutsi, Bosnian Muslims. Other genocidal events were directed at indigenous elites, the Russian Kulaks and *intelligentsia*, Mao's landlords, Pol Pot's middle-class Cambodians. The recent history of *aristocide* may now be beyond the horizon. The wars instigated during this time of troubled change, the twentieth century, also added to the loss, these several hundred million of our most intelligent fellow humans.

Following the destruction of the various fascisms of that century, the deaths of Stalin and Mao, the explosion of technology, democracy, economic expansion, now including democratizing Japan and Germany, the developed nations could no longer look away from the rest of the world. It was not pretty. Ideology now demanded a self-imposed beneficent spread of this surplus wealth around the world, now to the newly de-colonialized and enfranchised "Third World."

(B) Fifty years of internationally-organized efforts, literally trillions of dollars spread out across foreign domains as well as targeted to the internal proletariat (U.S.A.). The fear of a return of totalitarian egalitarian ideology partially explains the eagerness of the West to dole out this wealth to the poor of the world. But there existed an indigenous liberal imperative to now bring the entirety of humanity into the circle of western, free enterprise democracies. The sixty-four-dollar question: Has this most recent ideological wager with history worked?

There should be universal agreement, sadly, no. The nations of Northeast Asia, Eastern Europe who have abandoned the model of dictatorship or central planning are now eager to search for the brains that will propel them forward. Unfortunately, these nations had the ability to go forward in a civilizationally competent manner before the twentieth-century horror. That is why the struggle to destroy totalitarian hate was so epic. And that is why under new ideological auspices they have roared back to central positions in the economic and social life of the democratic developed world. There is much educated intelligence in those nations. And we Americans recognize this, but in a whisper.

One need not expatiate on the condition of the failed "nations" of the world, after so many trillions have been spent, nor on the condition of the underclass people of southern hemisphere origins within the wealthy nations, the U.S.A., and now Europe, even after this enormous redistribution. We have inoculated populations against disease. We have not been able to teach them about the opportunities that birth control presents to their futurity. Pandemics such as AIDS may well destroy nation after nation of the poor.

Yet, the powers-that-be still believe that redistributive equalization of the races, ethnicities, nationalities, religions of the world is possible. The call is out to "fine tune" the aid, always conditional upon the addition of a few thousand more "peace-keepers," here, there and everywhere.

Why is there not more curiosity over other possible scenarios for understanding this descent into purgatory? Whispered by thousands of scientists over the past century, *the cause of non-development, and the eruption of a wide rainbow of social pathologies may not necessarily be externally induced, by society or history.* Such hypotheses are viewed as unfriendly. Thus we toil, with ever waning resources, up this ever more rapidly descending social escalator of dissolution.

It is a "no-brainer" as to why ideology triumphs over factuality. We humans are mammals, deeply emotional, our minds equipped for ultimate sacrifice for the "other." Over time these dynamics of feeling implode, invest our ethnicity in epic patriotic struggles for survival or conquest. Sometimes, in more expansive and universal eras, we project these feelings outward, toward our fellows.

The past 150 years have seen the most explosively unifying period in the history of the human race. This is, of course, a product of science and technology. It is not incidental that the extinguishing of slavery and serfdom around the world took place as a matter of humanitarianism and justice in the mid-nineteenth century, parallel with this broadening of human perceptions, beyond our local communities and discrete nations.

It is doubly ironic that this sense of all people living on one planet earth should have, under the aegis of ideology, turned the twentieth century into such an extended killing field, supposedly to attain this condition of justice and equality for the multiplying masses. We still have it in our hearts that we want the poor around the world on board, especially those races and ethnicities of color who were once subject to our domination, then largely beyond our system of justice. Now they are front and center in our concern.

There are only two ways that the current superstitions of redistributionist egalitarian ideology will be countered. All ideas run their course, losing power over our minds as the realization eludes the promise. Fortunate for us, the walls of communist ideology both in the West and the East came down softly. The disillusionment with official lies in both geographic domains of pseudo-Marxism, led to increasing inefficiencies and hardship for the people. And there was another alternative beyond the Wall, a criterion as to how humans might live. This was a soft landing.

The other denouement might and will probably not be soft. The overflowing destitute from the "failed" world will probably not allow for such a radical and easy political/social turn. Even Russia, more than happy now to close its borders to the world of travail, has within its domains, Chechnya and Ingushetia.

Can the West, where the wealth for the moment is, turn a different cheek toward this global human tragedy, and say: "From now on, castor oil"?

The Moral Hurt

Let's not forget the potential hurt that this message of intellectual inequality sends. How do we speak to our American minorities, soon to be a majorities, those for whom we have spent trillions to bring to social and economic parity with the dominating Europeans? How can we say to our neighbors, fellow employees: "Folks you are now out on your own, show us your real stuff? Instead of the 'evil whitey' being at the crux of these surface inferiorities, slavery, then segregation, discrimination, prejudice, and the rest, it is really an in-born intellectual inadequacy that today holds you back. That is why all of our efforts, reverse discrimination, affirmative action, quotas, are to no avail."

The answer is that we can't say these things, at least not in public. Our supposed factual derogation of the intelligence/genetic argument has been enveloped in a haze of pseudo-moral egotism. Supposedly, we know the truth: It is right to strive in our way to make all people socially and economically equal. But remember, in our way. The present course of policy must be maintained. And it will be maintained, no matter the results. Know this, the sole cause of social/economic inequality is oppression by the dominating class.

And because we cannot speak openly and humanely about possible biosocial causes for civilizational failure we are in effect paralyzed. The only expectation, that splash of ice-water awakening that comes after the fierce taxation on the waning middle classes no longer supports this ideological fix. The tragedy of promises made, never delivered, a world in social collapse.

Plato tried to conjure up a parable about the diverse souls of humans. Here he spoke to the brilliance of his own Greek citizens. The "lie of words" would help soften the blow, that humans were born with different temperaments, different capacities. The irony was that his gold-souled leaders would live as did classic Spartan generals, on gruel, but here, for the love of knowledge. The iron souls below would enjoy the material pleasures, but not the power to make decisions, nor to rule, politically. In our own time the education of high intelligence often leads to wealth as well as power. Plato anticipated this potential for corruption, and rejected it for his *Republic* (Books 5-7).

Eventually we will develop moral, humane, gently philanthropic policies to raise socio-economic standards worldwide, and in a deeper, more permanent manner. The policy needs be two-fold: 1. Raise intelligence levels worldwide; 2. Balance our demographic/ecological profile with the discipline of nature and culture.

There is no real moral perspective, no humane social policy imperative that can exist apart from factual reality. True morality takes its power from its ability to predict the consequences of our social policies. If our moral jeremiads are real, humans should as a consequence live better. If this morality is part of a spurious ideology, we will feel the pangs. We should have learned something from the fascist and communist pronouncements of the twentieth century. Regrettably for our civilizational prognosis, we still have a long way to go.

Endnotes, Chapter 2

[1] Midgette, Anne, *The New York Times*, 5/02/2004.
[2] see Itzkoff, S. W. 1994. *The Decline of Intelligence in America*, Westport, CT: Praeger.
[3] Toledano, E. 1997. *Slavery and Abolition in the Ottoman Middle East*, Seattle: Univ. of Washington Press.
[4] Philadelphia, The Federalist Papers, 1787; Mintz, M. M. 1970. *Gouverneur Morris and the American Revolution*; Burer, S. 2000. *The Doctors of Revolution*, N.Y.: Thames and Hudson.
[5] Brians, P. 1998. *An Introduction to 19th Century Socialism*, St. Louis: Washington Univ. Press; Distante, P. 2001. *Evolutionary Philosophy in the Late 19th Century*.
[6] Trans. by G. D. H. Cole, 1913, Adelaide, Australia: *The Constitution Society*, 2000.
[7] Wheen, F. 2000. *Karl Marx, a Life*, N.Y.: Norton; Berlin, I. *Karl Marx*; Mazlish, B. 1984. *The Meaning of Karl Marx*, N.Y.: Oxford.
[8] Smith, J. M. 1982. *Evolution Now: A Century Late,* San Francisco: Freeman; Tort, P. 2001. *Darwin and the Meaning of Evolution*, N.Y.: Abrams.
[9] Bernstein, Eduard. "Marx," *Encyclopaedia Britannica*, 11th ed., 1911, Vol. XVII, pp. 810-811. Bernstein, a prominent socialist, and a Jew, was a member of the German *Reichstag*, 1902-1906.
[10] Population Reference Bureau, 2000. *World Population Growth, 1750-2150*.
[11] Plant, R. 1983. *Hegel, An Introduction*, Oxford: Blackwell.

Chapter 3

Cassandra's Revenge

Final Swing

We use a baseball metaphor. The modern redistributionist ideology is at bat, possibly for the last time. There are two out; it is the ninth inning. The score, 200+ million killed in retributionist wars and genocide over the eight and one half innings of the last century. Three and two, one more swing to decide the fate of the 7 billion impoverished humans who will be in the stands by mid-century (plus 2 to 3 billion middle-class holdouts).

The first class warfare revolutionists at bat were the late-nineteenth-century socialist utopians, led by Karl Marx. The Bismarcks, Disraelis, Poincarés of Europe defanged this early challenge by the end of the century.[1] Second came the nationalist fascist and communist hate-mongers, the Lenins and Stalins, the come-lately Ottoman recidivists, then Hitler, Mussolini, Mao, Pol Pot, Franco, and the rest. By the end of the century they and their ilk had had their bloody hands and noses pushed into the quicksand of history.

Out of the bench, third at bat, the democratic, economically-developed, philanthropic West. The Western nations had learned to change the character of the lives of their own indigenous populations, creating virtually classless societies, societies that would certainly have received a nod of approbation from Karl Marx. And they had developed welfare society safety nets ensuring that no citizen would have to suffer the hazards of social chance, consonant with the ancient Babylonian and Biblical concern for widows and orphans.

Look again at what the Northeast Asiatics had achieved in just a few generations, having suffered atomic and fire bombings in Japan, risen from the swamps of Singapore, suffered through the genocidal madness of a Mao, Koreans having seen their nation destroyed from the communist north. Millennial achievements by peoples who had lived, just a few decades earlier, under the most abject political and economic conditions.[2]

If here, why not everywhere, solemnly queried the gurus. The pitch would be fast and high. A hefty swing subsidized by middle-class tax calories and the ball could go over the fence and into the South Bronx, a home run. Seven billion potentially destitute souls would, by mid-century, be able to stand tall and straight, as newly enfranchised members of the global middle class. Redistribute the wealth, but wisely, and the masses will create their mini-Paris, even under the palm trees.

Wait! Something has just happened to this confident utopianism. There is a murmur of suspicion among the middle-class intimidated. It's not working. But, they can't think further, no less whisper about the cause of failure. No matter. Out of the soft chairs at the U.N. in New York the ideological explanation sirens forth in frustration at the injustice of it all.

The poisonous residue of the regnant ideology, however, still remains in the minds of the intimidated. The pontifications of the power classes: media, academia, international bureaucracies, regnant national politicos still command policy and money. One would think that serious reconsideration of the use of this wasting wealth would be in order, middle-class sweat and taxes pouring out impotently into this infinite empyrean of suffering. Progress toward making the poor equal and independent? Unacknowledged failure, ever more poor, AIDS, irrationalism, terrorist violence by the failed, a tidal wave of crises, without end.

A systemic if skeletal structure still holds the perverse mythology in place. Mammalian empathy plus the wealth, if waning, of the guilt-ridden West.

The system? The bureaucratic national and international political institutions that have been put into place over the past fifty years. It has transformed rational policy adjudications and debate into superstitious obeisance, no matter failure or success. Marx's oppressing classes: the U.N. WTO, IMF, World Bank, the "do-good" churches and their morally eager volunteer organizations, the cynical demands to the *have* nations for unending handouts.

We can't change this slide, for, as with the communist system, the only surcease from repetitive crises, and more demands for middle-class salvation will be collapse; the *haves* are no longer.

The ink in Karl Marx' quill would have over-flown with bitter irony at this new form of ideological social class exploitation. We have again missed his message. A wholly new productive system is even now waiting in the wings of history. Necessarily, only after the revolution. But what a revolution, what a possible turn in our perceptions of human function and destiny!

We must think of our human species as one, all good folks participating in a rational, scientific world community. To survive in this oncoming internationalist world our species must be one. Now, in terms of intellectual capacity, not in terms of racial or ethnic homogeneity. Why, because ultimately, we will be unable to help those who cannot help themselves to rise to this standard.

A new moral and political vision of equality and modernity awaits its moment. But not before the present irrational order has seared history.

Scenario of Collapse
Demography

Bureaucratic Optimism: The fact that the developed world has achieved demographic equilibrium—often feared—shrinkage of population, argues that the same principles can be applied to the "Third World" and with it a slowing of global population growth. In this way conditions will be created for economic growth, educational and health progress, ultimately to balance numbers against resources and ecological carrying norms.

Put succinctly, the European nations, and the European minorities throughout the world, now including upper caste India, are in demographic balance. The Northeast Asiatics, Japanese, Koreans, even mainland Chinese populations have their numbers under control. In fact, the official lament is that Japan and Western Europe are in rapid population decline and will not be able to support their aging retirement populations with diminished workforces.

Mainland China still mandates an extra child allowance for non-Han Chinese, but its overall rate of reproduction may now be below replacement levels. These child bonuses will eventually be withdrawn and the Chinese will continue to enforce a one-child-per-female policy. Given a rising standard of living, the need for education and health services, the penalties for additional children may dissuade all but the most isolated Chinese populations. China has vast underdeveloped geographies that need water to support transported populations. This transfer of water resources, and then people, is being vigorously pursued by the Chinese government. By mid-century, overpopulation in China should be a concern of the past.

Realism: Does it seem reasonable, for example, to predict a damper on the population explosion in the Islamic world, given the existing servitude of the female? The developed world dares not intervene, cultural relativism, sayeth the anthropologists. In the rest of the Third World, populations are exploding with philanthropic health care attempts to lower death rates. Forget birth control. AIDS is a tragic counter to this demographic trend. Western health workers cannot establish quarters in the bedrooms of these people to distribute condoms. Would they use them?

The irony is that except for the Catholic Church, *e.g.*, Latin America, birth control has no stringent religious blockages from any but the most orthodox religious centers, for example, Judaism. The American right-wing religious establishment has been, at the least, unhelpful, about these issues of birth control and abortion.

The call of the establishment: If European birth rates declined, couldn't birth rates around the world also level off? A global population of only 10 billion might be manageable, even reducible over time.

The present explosion of people derives from the impoverished south. In Europe and North America, these immigrants from the south with their extremely high birth rates create ever more social problems and economic travail for their hosts. Undeniably, terrorism has its origins in human degradation. The causes are not, as the establishment would have it, a recidivistic cultural clime. Rather, the roots of terrorism lie in the home population's inability to learn and work at an international technological middle-class standard. Thus, a reactionary drift downward that not even oil can intercept. The consequence, hatred of those who are able to master the new.

Immigrants from south to north are lured by the welfare bandwagon, even the minimum wage structure of work in the north. It is an irresistible magnet, given the conditions of tyranny and social degradation under which these humans live at home. They now and will add to the demographic disequilibrium of the developed nations of the north.

Are we really serious in believing that the ongoing demographic explosion of this global underclass will be stanched by present policies, these surging masses of the impoverished, rising up and entering the global techno-economy? Consider again: J. V. Borges quotes the U.N. Statistical Yearbook as predicting 8.04 billion humans on earth by 2025.[3] The Population Reference Bureau in 2004 predicted that by then more than 5 billion of these humans would be packed into mega-cities, *i.e.*, populations of more than 10 million persons.[4]

Democracy
Bureaucratic Optimism: The war in Afghanistan against the Taliban and Al Qaeda, and in Iraq against Saddam Hussein and his Baath Party by the United States and a number of half-willing allies reflects a benign hope. The forced establishment of democratic forms by the U.S., placing small, usually exile elites into power will turn such nations away from fundamentalist religious and other tyrannical forms of political brainwashing. This endeavor will result in a domino effect, wherein autocratic cliques will yield to indigenous democratic systems. Qaddafi's Libya is a well-advertised exemplar.

The optimistic fallout, among other beneficent outcomes, will be economic progress in an open, free-market society, secular outlooks in education and morals among the populations, eventually demographic stability. Democracies rarely need to secure their power by resorting to external expansive aggression. Thus the pro-active push for democratic institutions in the "Third World" and the raising of these societies into a true United Nations of free self-governing progressive peoples could augur a long period of world peace.

Realism: The results of these military, political, and economic efforts around the world have been less than 100 percent effective. Even in Central Europe, the fates of Albania, Macedonia, Kosovo, Bosnia, are still murky. These ethnicities, as with Byelorussia and Ukraine, (now hopeful), along with the other peoples of Eastern Europe, have never had a democratic experience. Similar to China, they are making hesitant steps toward economic development, the productive foundation of the possible in any political system.

The European nations of South America, Uruguay, Argentina, Chile, are candidates for stability, economic growth, and then the building of real democratic community life. The key lies in the level of educational uplift for which the citizenry can be mobilized, their willingness to push back the ethnic and religious particularism that prevents them from joining the democratic pulsations of modern life.

The rest of South America, for example, is divided between small European minorities who rule and dominate economically, and a vast mixed ethnic population, exploding in numbers, that seeks to expropriate the wealth of the rich and the middle classes. The push for social revolution, rather than the level market place is clue to their perception of the possible.

Is there hope for massive public education investment, an economy that expands indefinitely, and will lift all boats, end class warfare? See Bolivia for a look into tomorrow's democratic politics and economics in Latin America, *e.g.*, populist self-destruction.

Few nations of the Third World have the oil resources that still give hope to Iraq. Certainly free cash flow will not result merely by lifting agricultural tariffs and allowing a cocoa or sugar plantation farmer in the Ivory Coast, on his two acres of wealth to export his products freely. The poor are pouring forth. They will sub-divide and then sub-divide this little garden of possibility. And what about the so-called democratically elected power people, guess who—the military? Will they not, as always, skim off their take leaving the citizenry the chaff?

If we send in the mercenaries to protect these "democratically"-elected thieves, will this satisfy the U.N. as to the state of democracy. We seat the Sudan on the U.N. "Human Rights Commission." All the while these same leaders back in Khartoum are figuring the next step in their multiple genocides of black people in the south and west of that nation.

By now we should understand the locus of possibility, where and where not truly representative, constitutional democracy might function. Democracy, in the European/North American sense, did not exist in the emerging tribal world over the past hundred years. Is it merely a case of groups being overlooked by history, exploited by the stronger? They *have* lived upon this planet for as many eons as those who worked so diligently in Philadelphia, over two hundred years ago.[5]

This dawning awareness of reality now spreads unease throughout the middle class world. The Japanese in the spring of 2004 shunned Japanese citizens returning to Japan after their kidnapping in Iraq by terrorists. The hint was, bad enough to have to contribute several hundred soldiers to this unsavory task, but volunteers? Leave the frustrations for the Americans.

Ivo Daalder of the Brookings Institution and James Lindsay of the Council on Foreign Relations, two relatively independent think tanks, recently put into writing the murmurings of the few enlightened. In "An Alliance of Democracies," written for *The Washington Post*, they express the growing dissatisfaction with the workings of the United Nations, now epitomized by the corrupt "Oil for Food" program that enriched many a French bank working for U. N. functionaries. (The beneficiaries included Kofi Annan's son.)[6] A figure of $21 billion is rumored to have been the over-all take including those U.N. opponents of an "illegal" war. Naturally, the Iraqi people received little. "It {the U.N.} treats its members as sovereign equals regardless of the character of their governments."

And, of course, most of these "governments" are gangs, often able to fool the gullible with their charade/veneer of democratic forms. In the long run, the intellectual impotence of the masses allows for that just barely smarter group of the unscrupulous to exploit the hapless many.

Dalder's and Lindsay's solution is the formation of a group of truly democratic middle-class societies that will band together to preserve the peace, negotiate equitable and fair trade agreements, "combat terrorism, curtail weapons proliferation, cure infectious diseases, curb global warming..." all of which the U.N. has failed to achieve.

Curbing global warming and curing infectious diseases is on their table! Why not the slowing of the demographic explosion from below? Clearly they aren't pushing this mission impossible.

Economic Development
    Bureaucratic Optimism: At the end of World War II, the developed West, including the now democratic nations of the former Fascist world, but excluding the expanding communist bloc, set out on a campaign to free the colonial peoples of the world, to raise them up as equals on the international stage. Partially, in response to this communist threat of revolution and subversion, partially through ideological guilt over the variable state of humanity, the now wealthy and expanding West took upon itself and its newly-created international organizations this philanthropic process of development.

The good fortune was the explosive expansion of the economies of the developed world including the former Axis nations. New technologies, ever more efficient production expanded the pie of wealth in the West. The press of competition eventually blessed the world with the peaceful collapse of the communist hegemonic challenge. Naturally, the Western theology of belief in the uniformity of human intelligence was the fuel that fed the political engine for the handouts of remorse. Indeed, there were failures, now say the bureaucrats in

Brussels. Let Brussels and New York make sure it gets done. Careful diligence would be ever necessary.

Wait a second, says the World Bank, the WTO, the U.N., what's with all this twenty-first-century economic pie shrinking, humans expanding, scare stuff? Some of the most demographically over-packed economic entities, Singapore, Hong Kong, Switzerland, Germany, Japan, Great Britain, still have majority middle-class populations. They are prosperous economic entities either with democratic institutions or participant populations agitating incessantly for the purification of these institutions.

This international elite predicts that India, Pakistan, Nigeria, Mexico, Indonesia, Brazil, Iraq, will likewise rise up to majority middle-class techno-prosperity. All we need is that the present institutions of international economic development be allowed to flourish, with the help of the middle-class taxpayers of the world. The major international organization and the prosperous national entities behind them represent the road toward the future of economic and social development on a global level.

The global bureaucrats must argue that only if we can stimulate the underdeveloped peoples to join the global open market trading system will their cultural perceptions change beyond the parochial. They will then practice birth control, seeing that their own and other's uncontrolled proliferation is the open door to impoverishment, tyranny, and the abandoned dream for self-governance and individual freedom.

Their new outlook and accomplishments will enable them to join with the rest of the humankind in creating a universal technological culture having similar educational skills and cultural outlook. The perverse controls by pseudo-religious zealots in Saudi Arabia, the United States, in Nigeria and elsewhere will be neutralized. The natural wealth offshore, on or under the earth will provide for the possible.

The international organizations strive for this goal. Even Sudan—the White Nile streaming through its countryside, rich loam as thick as Illinois on its lands—recently mired in its ancient dogmas, but now guided politically and economically by the moderns, could become wealthy and modern. In fact, the Islamic world, much of it nourished by ancient seas of petroleum, could rouse itself from its religious torpor and join in the liberation and empowerment of its masses. We must try.

India, exploding in a burst of modernization by dint of its highly educated and dominant high castes, has seen the threat. Its agricultural production from its hinterlands has barely kept pace with a 2 percent population increase per year. In 2004 a political explosion of resentment erupted from these hundreds of millions who remain behind. Yet the newly empowered Congress Party remains modernly rational. The emphasis on the higher education of the upper caste Indians has certainly paid off. Next, intone the optimists, build schools without thatched roofs, roads and water wells for the yet "untouched."

Thomas Friedman of *The New York Times* weeps with joy in noting this possible emancipation of untouchable caste Indians. A philanthropic Indian technologist opens a private school for these children, who at four years of age were still urinating and defecating randomly around the countryside. Now, at age eight they are learning to use computers. Soon, says Friedman they will all fulfill their desires to be physicists, astronauts, nurses, teachers.[7] This is the dream, a world coming together, parochialism dissolving under the nurturing juices of globalization.

A 2004 report reveals the extent to which South Korea has so opened its economy to globalization (foreign investment). Almost 50 percent of the value of the Seoul stock exchange of Korean companies is now owned by foreigners. Mission accomplished; next, Pyongyang.

An international scientific culture is realizable. Wealth and power still lie with secular, democratic, free enterprise societies, all open to scientific research, technological innovation, and a commitment to allow for the free evolution of cultural values. Globalization will isolate and dissolve parochial nationalism, and theological fanaticism. Given that the West created this new global system, as a product of at least 500 years of cultural and intellectual evolution, transmitting these values and skills to the still underdeveloped will need persistence. Because of their former colonial subjugation, the most recent fifty years of extremely slow, frustrating, often retrogressive progress will need time and money.

Realism: After fifty years of largely unsuccessful developmental efforts for those populations, which have documented lower I.Q.s, educational, and social/behavioral profiles, huge differences as compared to the developed ethnicities and nations of the world, the burden of proof for this optimistic scenario is with the establishment bureaucracies. How long the fecundity of this middle-class treasure vault? Will the controlling institutions of the world ever admit the impotency of the dream?

We can point to the developmental successes of the Northeastern Asiatic nations. But their intelligence and civilizational levels have always been extremely high, at times in the vanguard of the West. So, too, with the Indian and perhaps Persian upper classes. The test lies with the three or four billion humans on their way to be added to the existing impoverished billions. And it is not merely an issue that can allow of cauterization, isolation by the West. The germs are now international; transport and communication place the plight of these masses, if not in our living rooms, then on our streets, and forever.

Can a world economic system devoted to the maintenance if not the enhancement of the civilizational traditions of history maintain itself in the face of an expanding miasma of pathology around the world? We cannot return to the great unturned plains, the nourishing primeval forests. Subsistent humans, distant from each other, living off the fruits of nature, are today a chimera.

The question comes down to the production of wealth. First come agriculture, basic needs, clothes, shelter, sanitation systems, schools, medical support, prevention and treatment. Great revolutions seem to be taking place in Northeast Asia, Japan, South Korea, the offshore Chinese, including Malaysia. Mainland China, seriously overpopulated in terms of development, is rapidly neutralizing its old deficiencies, in the process stimulating the world economy in a dynamic unseen since the end of World War II.

Consider our most optimistic target date for the onset of the global malaise, first economic, then political and cultural, 2050. By then, at the latest, the Western civilizational way of life will be in quicksand. The most conservative predictions range between nine or ten billion people. In terms of productive middle-class standards of living, how many will qualify?

Hypothesis: 225 million of the 500 million in the U.S. and Canada, another 500 million in Eurasia, including Western Europe, Russia, and Eastern Europe. Perhaps 200 million out of 1.5 billion Indians (remember India, including Bangladesh and Pakistan had 300 million people in 1947). Northeast Asia, including China, perhaps Viet Nam, Malaysia, and Thailand, 500 million out of c.1.7 billion. Australia, New Zealand, parts of South America, 100 million. Let us be generous and estimate another 300-400 million living as besieged middle-class minorities in the rest of the world. This totals up to about 2 billion humans living independently out of the at least 9-10 billion on this earth predicted by 2050 Pessimistic caveat, AIDS, and its ever unknown successor pandemics. These middle classes will be required to pump trillions of tax dollars, at the least, to keep this global tragedy from investing their borders.[8]

Note that the definition of middle class will undoubtedly change. There will be slave labor in various parts of the world, making sandals, growing tobacco, cocoa, opium, possibly putting together cell phones. The old North American and European wages for the high-tech, unionized upper-class standards of living will no longer be $15.-20.-per-hour with benefits, once dreamed of in the U.S. and Europe.

Today, the standard of impoverization in half the world, *i.e.*, three billion people, is a family income of two dollars per day, seven hundred thirty dollars per year. Question, how many more millions, maybe billions, are living on less than three dollars per day, eleven hundred dollars per year? The international bureaucrats presumably view this additional one-dollar-per-day as the entrance hall to middle-class life.

The formerly "rich" working classes will be competing with the middle class of the future, workers earning in the range of $.50-$2.00-per-hour without health benefits or frills. The 700 million smart, hopeful, Chinese and Indians industrial/technological workers, now and to be, cannot but undercut the present wage scales, and possibly even corporate dominance of the current labor/business structure in the West. Simply, much of today's middle class will decline.

For example, India is graduating 75K information technology workers per year who speak English. They will earn between $5-12K per year. China will graduate at least 50K IT workers, in addition to many thousands of engineers, earning between $4 and 8 thousand-per-year, all a fraction earned by middle-class American IT specialists.[9]

Taxes derive from the labor of individuals and businesses, their surplus wealth. Will the global technological corporations still be headquartered in the United States, what with its precipitous fall in intellectual/educational profile? Will there be enough corporate productive wealth in the West to support the current lifestyles of the middle classes? Look now, and then ahead. Will we be poorer or richer in fifty years? The writing on the wall is sharp and clear.

The Chinese can be both poor materially as well as middle class in behavior, even with salaries in the $2.-per-hour range. These are a highly cognitive people who will one day assert their political and cultural human rights. It took revolutionary internal leadership to turn this nation free from its Maoist slave encampment. But it needed, as few nations have in order to so benefit, a highly intelligent, morally rigorous, and most important, a leadership with a respect for its own people, the desire to benefit and not to exploit them.

Deng Xiaoping and his followers had to have had the clarity of mind to throw off the opium of communist ideology and set their nation on a course consonant with Chinese potentiality. The common people in spite of the inevitable corrupt post-communist bureaucracy were respected in terms of their capacity to labor for their personal/family benefit.

This is not too different from the American post-revolutionary war leadership. These Franklins, Jeffersons, Hamiltons, considered themselves as one, members of a political community, responsible to this incipient nation's ordinary citizens. The average American, c.1790, was relatively poor in material things. Some may have had large homes. But they built them by hand from the trees that they felled.

There is a harmonization in the intelligence that creates a free constitutional system of political life, and the people who can respond with an heroic and progressive work ethic, having imagination and educational openness to boot. One sees this in the stone fences deep in the New England forests, once pasture lands or fields for grain and potato. These were the products of human sweat and persistence.

Only a few zones of twenty-first-century possibility remain in the world today. Eastern Europe, especially Russia, is demographically empty. Along with the former Soviet Central Asian colonies, it has the natural resources and a history of intelligent achievement. But it, too, will have to bend to the competitive demands of a world economy.

Western Europe is already burdened by a rapidly growing underclass from the Third World. This will add to the drying up of free cash flow as they attempt to maintain welfare benefits for an aging indigenous population and the newcomers. For these immigrants there is only negative evidence for educational and intellectual parity with the productive old Europeans. There is likewise no positive evidence from Latin America, South Asia (possible exception India), the Islamic world (possible exceptions Turkey, Kurdistan, Iran, Afghanistan).

Does anyone believe that Africa can extricate itself from congenital poverty and degradation? To survive, this continent of despair will always need Western wealth, bi-lateral and international philanthropy, yes, autocratic military, police, and medical supervision from without. Colonialism revisited?

Philanthropic wealth has to come from somewhere. Technological innovation, rapidly moving free trade, financial, and market exchanges, and the willing cooperation of its citizens to believe in the future of growth, might keep things going before the burden falls heavily. As the middle-class locals become poorer, don't expect them to ante up tax monies except in their own defense.

Think of the enormous economic drain on the U.S. precipitated by the Iraq war, in the hundreds of billions of dollars at last count. Consider the international cost to all nations, Russia, France, even China, of the struggle against nihilistic Islamic terrorism. What about AIDS and the next pandemic, the need to fund mercenary armies in Africa, the Caribbean, Indonesia, and elsewhere to calm the chaotic waters of cultural dissolution. What can we expect after the 2005 Tsunami, and the billions of dollars of reparations it required from the outside world? Now add three or four billion more inept humans to the present sad international stew, c.2005.

As the horizons of promise begin to be foreclosed on our grandchildren, will the indigenous middle classes of the West be stimulated to buy the Lexus', Mercedes', DVDs, picture cell phones, and whatever else will be invented as toys for the once free of heart? In a world ever on the brink, every economic and emotional passion that was once focused on the "good life" will be directed toward keeping global horrors from crossing our borders, our shores.

Consider the rusting tin architectural extravaganzas of a Frank Gehry, the Andy Warhol cartoons at $40 million a pop that decorate glass-walled corporate offices, the $90. *prix fixe* dinners without wine, coffee, or tip, at *Jean Georges*, the middle-class waters off of Cancun and Nice, now patrolled with minesweepers and searchlights. When one is warned not to get any closer than five feet to a Rembrandt at the National Gallery, when children have to pass through metal detectors to go to school, when armed guards regularly patrol playgrounds, we already feel the chill of history.

Prosperity is a state of mind. Slow up the growth, the expansion, the allure, the effort winds down. Next, the taxes dry up. Triage, in terms of social services becomes the norm, first we save the police and potable water. The resident impoverished, presently the focus of fatted guilt, fade from the mind's eye, egalitarian ideologues dispersing, securing their own hides.

United States: "Hegemonic Decline"[10]
Portent

No question but that the U.S. owned the twentieth century. It is natural that those living at the end of the century envisaged this power to be both universal, inevitable, and foreordained long into the future. This is to be expected. The Romans had no real appreciation of the fact that by the time the Goths took Rome in 410 CE, the empire was already split into two and was slowly dissolving. The long-enduring internal absorption of the Roman legal system, Hellenistic literature even in its mystery religion Christian cloaking, undergirded their educated perceptions of social reality. As such, this historical tradition held both intelligent barbarian and Roman in a bond of civilizational continuity, yes, through the aegis of the Church.

We in 2005 realize that something is now amiss. The Chinese loom large. But so did the Japanese in the 70s and 80s. Today, they are good but not omnipotent. China will be another story, 1.3 + billion highly charged and hungry humans. Underemployment in China is pervasive, the divide between rich and poor growing, a state bureaucracy still fights for its perks and employs many at a vast cost to the nation. They will come apart at the seams, say our optimists.

Vast wealth still sloshes around the fifty states. As with Britain before Thatcher's revolution, we can hold our heads high, enjoy a semblance of international wealth, for our own corporations are now largely global, and small business with a domestic focus still employ many at decent wages. Of course, with another revolutionist such as Thatcher and Reagan, the U.S., might as with Britain surge forward again for a time, regaining a modicum of balance of trade parity at least with its European rivals.

For those Americans sensitive to the great tidal movements of history, China is not merely a burr to be picked off as the U.S. proceeds toward its manifest destiny. Our primary worry remains, jobs, high-paying American industrial jobs. Over two million new job seekers enter the market each year, 629K in the three months ending June 2004.[11] A legitimate concern. Ever since the origins of NAFTA, a treaty that allowed for the migration of many American industries over the border to Mexico, to the *maquilladoras*, at $2.-per-hour, we have been uneasily preparing for that "great sucking sound." For a decade or so in the

1980s Mexico prospered, and the American economy led by its technological and higher education leadership continued to expand.

In the 1990s the industries and the jobs started to migrate from North America, including Mexico, to Asia, especially China, now making its turn into state-sponsored capitalism. These Chinese jobs were at the $1.-per-hour rate, max, the workers educable and industrious. Mexican workers make less now than when NAFTA was proposed. More Mexican entrants into the labor force, less educated workers, competition of smarter people across the seas. Mexico's population, c.120 million, continued to explode. U.S. industries were now packing up, and factory jobs that paid $2-4-per-hour in Mexico were going to China at that seemingly slave wage of $1.-per-hour. Mexico has lost 500,000 manufacturing jobs in the last several years.[12] How many of these unemployed have surged, illegally, over our borders?

If U.S.-based global corporations didn't shift production to a low wage high skill environment, the Japanese and the Europeans would certainly continue to do so. Could we close our doors to *their* Chinese-made products along with those American companies that had fled? The choice: a), a full-fledged trade war, else b), lower the corporate costs of production, now an international mandate. It has truly become a corporate struggle for the survival of the solvent.

Some declared, give it time, the Chinese workers will demand more and the costs of doing business in Asia will rise. But with 1.3+ billion people, and at least 200 million people scheduled to enter the Chinese work force over the next 10 years, off the farm, or off the decayed state-run industries, salaries and conditions of work are irrelevant, no unions in this "socialist" society would interfere with "Yankee (Wal-Mart) exploiters." One estimate is that since 2000, the U.S. had lost three million very high-paying industrial jobs to Asia.

Unfortunately there is no longer a civilizational glue that will soften the landing, as it did for Rome over a period of several centuries, and many more additional centuries for Constantinople. There are those who write about this incipient slide, and wonder why. The explanations are often suggestive, the decline of religious morality; the opulence and corruption of our media myth-makers; rapid and unabsorbable immigration of non-English-speaking, non-Anglo-Saxon types.

A serious exemplification of this type of thinking is given in a book by Samuel P. Huntington of Harvard University, *Who Are We? The Challenge to America's National Identity*.[13] Huntington had previously, in 1996, written *The Clash of Civilizations, and the Remaking of the World Order*, the thesis of which was that conflict in the world would no longer involve national states nor the type of ideological conflict epitomized in the "cold war."[14] Rather it would be between large blocs of nations representing diverse civilizational ethos.

In the more recent book, Huntington views the United States as undergoing a cultural transformation from the older Anglo-Saxon Protestant ideal. Multiculturalism in the schools as a new ideological transformation of the American identity, linked with an almost unrestricted legal and illegal immigration reality are at the core of his concern. These new immigrants preponderantly from Latin America have altered the shape of American life. What with enormous welfare benefits to these and our other indigenous and immigrant poor, not characteristic of nineteenth- and early-twentieth-century support systems for new immigrants in a then-growing economy, these new immigrants need continued massive governmental assistance. Medicaid, special education, police protection, emergency room care, affirmative action programs are needed to carve out positions for them for which they cannot compete with traditional assimilated Americans.

The result is a nation culturally, economically, and racially divided, fundamentally at a loss for an identity strong enough for the challenges of history. Add to the worsening conditions at the bottom of the social ladder, contrasting with the increasingly cosmopolitanism and internationalism of our elites, Huntington fears for a nation coming apart at the seams. Undigested resident millions, a cultural value system dissolving before our eyes, a nation whose identity, ethnically, politically, philosophically is shredded. This is a national profile much weaker than the economic and military statistics featured by the leadership.

Cause and Reality

The prosperity and power of the U.S. was revealed in the final years of the twentieth century and the first decade of the twenty-first. However, in the latter time-frame, the seeds of dissolution sown in the final half of the twentieth century were already sprouting. No question but that the power of the American military dwarfed anything available to other nations, mostly unwilling to surrender the American shield and build a military machine for themselves. The wealth to engage in a campaign to oust Saddam Hussein from Iraq and rebuild the country was available. If it took a 2003, 375 billion dollar deficit, and a 2004, 477 billion dollar deficit to do it, the United States was still credit worthy, even given its over seven trillion dollar cumulative debt to its own people and the world.[15] In early 2004, the International Monetary Fund warned the United States that if it continued to spend beyond its means, annual deficits of the above levels, a cumulative debt of 47 trillion dollars, could be expected over the next 70 years![16]

The problem was, of course, the disappearance of much of the American productive industrial and technological machine. We were becoming a "service" economy, swimming in the corporate wealth of Wall Street. This to a great extent being international wealth brought home, it benefited the stock-, capital-holding classes in the U.S. The ongoing production of middle-class wealth through the manufacture and export of goods was waning, those three million or so jobs lost since 2000. Of course the investment by international corporations in the U.S. still was ongoing. In 2005, an American middle class perdures, still plenty of money around to be spent.

However, taking a longer view than the next election, it is clear that the clouds on the horizon are not ephemeral in what they augur for American wealth and power. The intelligence levels of this population are lowering, the ability to produce what no one else can at a cost level that sustains a middle-class American lifestyle are disappearing. The proportion of the population that needs to be supported by this capital-owning middle class is growing larger proportionately. Note, the Germans, even with their waning indigenous ethnic population, high 11.4 percent unemployment, rich retirement welfare perks (some once lived in Florida on their unemployment benefits) still have a positive balance of payments, producing for export what other nations cannot, at least for now.

The only way that the U.S. could escape its inexorable balance of payments deficits, for the moment supported by the purchase of American currency and bonds by eager Japanese and Chinese, they protecting the low value of their currency and low prices of their goods, is to produce more of what others cannot. This requires a tight union between the technologist classes coming out of the MITs and Stanfords, and the service classes right down the hall, graduates of our fine colleges and universities, finally the old-fashioned productive American high school graduate who at one time could read.

A paradigm of what these fragile sprouts of American destiny will look like a few decades down the road is given in the great California collapse of 2003. This led to the recall of Governor Greg Davis and the election of the Austrian born weightlifter and actor Arnold Schwarzenegger.

Recall, in 1999, the height of the so-called technological/internet bubble, in which California's "Silicon Valley" was the center, wealth poured into the state's tax coffers. Thirty-two thousand individuals and couples were millionaire taxpayers. They paid nearly one third of the total tax revenues for the state, while constituting .0025 percent of the population. The spending by the state for a variety of public works and social programs, education, welfare, police, soared.

In 2002, after the bubble had burst and the 32,000 were no longer in the tax clover for the state, California was sporting a $38 billion dollar deficit. Cutting a variety of programs and taking on massive bond debt, California is saddling its citizens for decades. Inevitably this crisis, emblematic of our 50-state future will permanently reduce the lifestyle of the vastly increasing percentage and numbers of poor.

George Will reports that by mid-2004 this debt had risen to over $50 billion.[17] California had become a poor state, and was destined to remain so as more and more high tech was going overseas to find educated people who would work at a pittance compared with current U.S. labor costs.[18]

The national scene is little different. Economist Robert Samuelson marvels at the philanthropic character of the American people, when in 2000, U.S. federal spending, after deducting defense and interest payments on the then-modest $5 trillion debt, 81 percent of $1.6 trillion tax receipts, went for social programs, Social Security, Medicare, Medicaid, and food stamps. The richest one percent of taxpayers paid 37 percent of the taxes that doled out these social benefits; the top 10 percent paid 70 percent of the taxes, double their share of received income, and the top 50 percent paid over 96 percent of the taxes. Forty-three percent of Americans paid nothing in federal taxes receiving these and other national and local benefits.

Clearly, at that moment in time much surplus wealth was available to fund these expenditures, as was the political/ideological willingness.[19] Senator Kerry, and the Democratic Party, in his election bid, 2004, hoped to hike taxes on the top $200,000+ incomes in order to find more monies for the out-of-luck. Given the Swiss cheese character of our tax laws, good luck!

In the U.S., the free-wheeling capitalist system has created its own share of shameful corruption at the top. The political destiny of the middle classes does rest on the veneer of legitimacy in the wealth accumulations by the independent capital-holding classes. There can be no middle class when everyone works for the government. However, the differences between worker on the line and top CEO, rewards in the U.S. have been sharply accentuated in comparison to other developed societies.

The average chief executive of a U.S. corporation receives c.531 times what the hourly workers earn. In Great Britain = 25x; France = 16x; Japan = 10x. Even Brazil where the differentials in wealth and poverty are Grand Canyon-like, the Brazilian CEO ratio to line worker is lower than the U.S., at 57x.[20] The latter comparison is partly explainable by the fact that many foreign corporations are located in Brazil, bringing with them international standards of remuneration for the same type of labor as in the home country. Not included in this Brazilian calculus are the enormous numbers of people surviving on welfare, agricultural scraps, essentially invisible to the statistical labor market.

Prospect

The United States will over the next two generations fall victim to the stagnant economic impasse of the West, in general, but with its own unique qualitative economic, social and cultural malaise.

1. Even a short-run peek at the economic future of the United States invites skepticism. The huge trade deficit, and the 2004 decline of the value of the dollar against other currencies was precipitated by the doubts of foreign investors in what they saw to be an inflated currency and an economy on the edge. As noted above, it would have been worse had it not been for the support of the dollar by the Northeast "troika," China, Japan, South Korea. This they did in order to maintain the competitive pricing of their exports, the Chinese now having accumulated over $400 billion dollars in surplus in their current account. Given continued budget and trade deficits of one trillion dollars per year, the dollar could collapse over time, huge inflation and depression cycles exploded into reality.

2. The ongoing generational decline in educational achievement levels, for example, places U.S. 12th grade achievement at the bottom of the West. Even worse, this 12th grade represents only 74.4 percent of the eighth graders of four years earlier, meaning the weakest students have already disappeared from 12th grade. The declining standards of higher education are exemplified in affirmative action, racial, ethnic, gender profiling so that even the least prepared students can be admitted to college, often on scholarships, thence to receive their degrees. The drying up of indigenous scholars in the sciences and engineering, less than 50 percent of Americans in our own graduate schools, will have a culminating impact.[21]

3. In 2004 the Computer Systems Policy Project in Washington D.C. asserted that to add to the off-shoring of low-skill factory jobs, the outflow of highly skilled computer programming and engineering jobs, as well as white collar banking and financial services jobs is increasing. These job requirements can't be filled in the U.S. Add to that, those high-skilled jobs that are paying c.$150,000 per year can be equally accomplished by Indians and Chinese, for example requiring maximum salaries of $15,000-$20,000 per year. This trend will continue, especially as these previously undeveloped nations grow economically, eventually requiring the actual transfer of high tech corporate facilities to these buyer nations. "There is no job that is America's God-given right anymore. We have to compete for jobs": Carly Fiorina, former CEO of Hewlett-Packard Corp, soon to be headquartered in Beijing?[22]

4   The population of the United States as we go forward into the twenty-first century will be increasingly minority shaped, non-European and non-Northeast Asiatic. The educational and professional/vocational skill levels of record are lower that the traditional Western and Northeast Asiatic achievement levels. Adding to the approximately 300 million Americans are an additional approximately 18-20 million illegal immigrants, now in low-skilled slave/menial work. The expected increase in our population level by another 100-200 million people by 2050 will surely be made up of additional low educationally skilled persons. California is predicted to have 50 million people in 2025, most new immigrants from Latin America.[23]

5   The retirement of post-war "baby boomers," their reproductive rate at barely replacement levels, will ensure this transition. Needed to be mentioned, are the millions of educated and emancipated feminists who exchanged family life for careers.

By 2050, it is inconceivable that the United States will be in the forefront of scientific/technological, productive innovation.

The unskilled are even now dependant on the trickle-down affluence of the wealthy. For the moment these unskilled services are needed. When this trickle-down wealth dries up, heavy redistributionist taxes, the flight of industry to lower-cost climes, the surge in official and unofficial unemployment, will create much instability and travail. In mid-2004, with an official unemployment rate of 5.6 percent, the U.S. Bureau of Labor Statistics said that 66.6 million people who could work are not looking for jobs, up 4.4 million in the past four years. Of course, someone is supporting these people with food and shelter.

6   Without an expanding high-margin economic base, in technology and industrial production, that would be able to pay for vast amounts of imported energy, the U.S. will not be able to maintain the consumer buying binge, 65 percent of the economy, and the consequent free flow of tax monies, $1,325,000,000,000 (one trillion, three hundred twenty five billion dollars) in 2001, from an ever declining percentage of the affluent to support the great infrastructure of the welfare state, nor its military and international political presumptions. All of the above listed benefits, Social Security, *et al.*, will have to be radically scaled down. If not, the collapse of the dollar, soaring inflation will lay waste to the economy. Either way, the poor are going to suffer. Neither law nor historical precedent, past or present, guarantees or testifies that governments can/will fulfill their promises.

7   Government is as potent in redistributing the national patrimony as it has in hand tax funds to so do. The danger is that a semi-Maoist fascist

revolution could be put into place, blessed by a voting, impoverished, "democratic," populist putsch. The rich, then under siege, would quickly flee, the middle classes absorbed into a state-run command economy. The poor would be promised their jobs and middle-class standards of life. However, the promise would be rapidly succeeded by forced labor. Such a radical coup could take power as the independent middle classes diminish in number and voting power. Next, the failures of a Stalinist or Maoist enslavement.

A Tense, Stagnant World

High intelligence produces the new. The new takes hold only in the context of a receptive population and social environment. Fifteenth-century Europe was one context of readiness and eagerness to throw off tradition and opt for a Renaissance of thought and practice. Fifteenth-century China took on another perspective. China, the home of much intellectual and practical advance, during the Middle Ages, under the Manchu leadership launched a fleet to explore beyond its borders, to look again at the outside world. This may have been Marco Polo-inspired curiosity, since with its c.70 million population China then was in demographic balance with itself (410 million in 1850).[24]

Europe was barely awakening, enclosed within its own domains. To the Chinese leadership listening to the reports about the southern and western lands adjoining China, and over the seas to the coasts of East Africa, barbarism seemed to be universal. The Chinese burned their transcontinental fleet, closed their doors to protect the rich intellectual and esthetic culture that they had developed. Weakened over time by this suppression of change and progress, they finally succumbed to western power and exploitation, until today.

What the world will look like *vis à vis* scientific and technological innovation, the flourishing of a supportive esthetic, legal, and moral middle class, is predictively chancy, even a decade into our future. And perhaps one should not make substantive forecasts. What we can only know is given by the trends of today. But we know the power of ideology to interdict rational reform. The current trend thus seems irresistible.

The Northeast Asian "ethnics" will be roaring forth with ever new productivity enhancements that will require ever fewer workers. Compare their achievements with the exploding demography in the Islamic world. Today, of the 100 million Arab youth between 15-24 years of age, almost 20 percent are unemployed, many of these among the 15-20 million Muslims now comprising Europe's new dependency class. Is it any wonder that among the nine leading Arab economies, several hundred million people, having tremendous amounts of oil revenues to support higher education, between 1980 and 1999, almost twenty years, only 370 new patents were registered with the U.S. Patent Office. In the same period South Korea, with a much smaller demographic profile, 45 million, but with much higher I.Q.s, registered 16,328 patents for inventions.[25]

Even given the movement of the great technological and industrial corporations and all their home office requirements to the growth nations, where people will still have the monies to purchase and/or to trade among these desirable goods of modernity, how much movement, how much trade, how much profit from mass production, will wash over the West? On our global horizon is an economic and social profile wherein over three-quarters of the world must be taxpayer-supported by the one quarter that has the educational and productive capability of living a civilizational existence.

Growth is the key for prosperity and optimism, growth even in the non-tangibles, of culture and the arts. So, too, there is gratification in seeing expenditures spent for renewal and improvement. The vision of the in-power optimists is that this growth will occur more so, given the nine or ten billion "happy customers" that will occupy our planet by mid-century. Is this a sober extrapolation of reality or opiated mythmaking?

Once upon a time the Roman elites retreated to the countryside, walled off their estates (*latifundia*), hired their Gothic protectors. Hopefully, the random chaos would remain outside the gates. Then, the land was still empty of humans, and fruitful. Today, we have our own gated communities. But the air, the water, the land that we need for survival are subject to contention.

Endnotes, Chapter 3

[1] Feuchtwanger, E. 2002. *Bismarck*, N.Y.: Routledge; Kent, G. O. 1978. *Bismarck and His Times*, Carbondale, Il.: The Univ. of Southern Illinois Press.
[2] Stiglitz, J., and Yusuf, S. 2001. *Rethinking the East Asian Miracle*, N.Y.: The World Bank; Amsdan, A. H. 2003. *The Rise of the 'Rest,'* N.Y.: Oxford Univ. Press.
[3] International Studies Association, Hong Kong, 2001.
[4] Washington, D.C.
[5] see A. Barker, *Financial Times*, 7/14/2004; *The Washington Post*, Editorial, 6/20/2004; P. Healy, *The Boston Globe*, 7/16/2004; "Crimes of War Project," *The Magazine*, April 2002.
[6] Ivo Daalder and James Lindsay, "An Alliance of Democracies," in *The Washington Post*, 5/23/2004.
[7] *The New York Times*, 5/21/2004.
[8] "Scientists Warn of Flu Epidemic" 21st *Century.Com*, 12/25/2003; *NAID* "Planning for the 21st Century—Executive Summary, 2004." Governments give the cost of such pandemics as $120 billion per year.
[9] *Deccan Herald* (India), 9/03/2003; "Outsource to India or Die," *The Economic Times Online*, 7/02/2004.
[10] Bond Mutual Fund Manager, William H. Gross.
[11] Economic Policy Institute, 7/02/2004.

[12] *Arizona Daily Star*, 4/03/2004.
[13] 2004, N.Y: Simon and Schuster.
[14] 1996.
[15] *The Denver Post*, 7/22/2004; *Bureau of the Public Debt*, 7/21/2004.
[16] *The New York Times*, 1/08/2004.
[17] *The Washington Post*, 7/15/2004.
[18] Weintraub, Daniel, *Sacramento Bee*, 1/15/2002.
[19] Samuelson, Robert, *The Washington Post*, 12/17/2003.
[20] Morgenson, Gretchen, The *New York Times*, 1/25/2004.
[21] *The New York Times*, 6/19/2004.
[22] *The Wall Street Journal*, 2/12/2004.
[23] U. S. Census Bureau.
[24] Ho Ping Ti. 1959. *Studies of the Population of China, 1368-1953*, Cambridge, MA:
[25] Arab 2003 Human Development Report.

Chapter 4

Civilizational Intelligence

The Core
Speak to a classroom of 18-year-olds about human intelligence variability, and you will immediately be aware that this issue burns. They shuffle, look away, become silent. They know, by this moment in life, that it is at the core of their life probabilities. More than good luck or good works, even drive and ambition, such students will be judged by how bright they are. We should not be surprised at their unease, their unwillingness to acknowledge this issue, only to speak in euphemistic terms about social "causes" for intelligence differences. Deep down, they know that they have been and will be judged by their "smarts."

The world pivots on the functional intelligence of individuals working together. Intelligence and the drives that lie at its core, is central to civilizational advance or retrogression. This is difficult to prove, as we cannot judge ourselves from above. There is no Martian circling the earth to evaluate for us the works of *Homo*. Our civilizational journey will be judged by ourselves alone.

We can see in civilization a mere concatenation of ancient and derelict monuments. Obviously they lived out there, and are now gone. We alone are here, today. And if we do not wish to evaluate, compare, analyze the works of other people, we can float with time, whatever comes forth into experience is no better or worse than what has come before. This in a nutshell is where most of the critical commentary on life in the United States or in the West devolves. For the middle classes, things are yet not too bad; just don't shake the tree.

This is *Homo*'s perennial error. Overriding the typical laissez faire attitudes of the commonwealth of the living, leadership so-called, should be looking critically at the evolving state of world affairs. It is getting worse. Believe it or not there are *reasons* why it is getting worse. But because of ideology, the core issue of human intelligence variability in the human species, and the consequent differences in individual, national, ethnic, racial behaviors, constitute a "no-no." This, they say, is the most abusive kind of profiling. Consider any other social/historical cause, but not *this*.

Indeed, there are many individuals, and around the world, for whom these issues burn with concern, and thus the study and analysis, as within these pages, continues, shrieks out for a few who would read, look, consider, perhaps murmur a few public words. Instead we have the leadership glorifying "diversity" Of course, this is a pose, an assumed ignorance of the deep sources of this diversity.

Hopefully, there is little diversity when it comes to choosing pilots, or other applicants for jobs critical to the life of humans. There was a time when the study of intelligence differences became a passion of analysis. It was in a context of European ethnic uniformity, as within the British, French, or American populations. It is different now. The power forces say, *don't discuss*. In this globally integrated world, however, the intelligence diversity map is critical for understanding our united future.

The Human Mind Examined

Interest in the scientific study of human intellectual variability can be traced to Charles Darwin's cousin, Francis Galton. Starting in the 1860s, Galton, became curious as to why some individuals rose up socially, intellectually and financially, here filtering out social class privileges. Others, often of similar background fell back. Galton set out to study genealogies to see if he could establish patterns of consanguinity. He devised experiments to see if achieved social positions, and implicitly native ability could be correlated with sensory and physical acuity and dexterity. These experiments were largely unproductive. But he did satisfy himself that intellect and achievement were in some way passed down through the generations.[1]

At the very inception of the twentieth century, Alfred Binet in France was asked by the French government to see if he could develop a series of tests that could predict in young children about to start school which might become fragile learners. These might benefit from additional preparation before embarking on the traditional and demanding French school curriculum. These tests marked the beginnings of I.Q., using a metric of grade level. This was established by surveying the average achievement of children at each grade level, to be divided by chronological age.[2]

With a mean of 1.0, or 100, as the central judgmental mark, this scoring, developed by the German psychologist Wilhelm Stern, about the same time, would distinguish those who were more advanced than same-aged cohorts. The more advanced received scores for their age above 100, those below would need extra resources, hopefully helping them to catch up to their peers. These tests in and of themselves were predictive of future school achievement in children, and thus the practice of I.Q. testing spread throughout the West.[3]

Lewis Terman in the United States starting in the 1920s set off to attempt to correlate extremely high scholastic achievement and I.Q. with a variety of personality traits and future vocational achievement. His gifted studies, of children with I.Q.s 140 or higher, with a few exceptions, were carried on at Stanford University by himself and his students over a period of fifty years. The result was to validate commonsense opinion that high academic achievers turned out to be high social and economic achievers as well.[4] Correlated with high educational and professional achievement were seemingly positive personality and family traits, mental and physical health and stability, family structure, *e.g.*, low divorce rates.

By the mid-twentieth century, the use of I.Q. tests in various forms including so-called aptitude and achievement tests, the SATs for college admission, military intelligence tests to weed out those who would fail in service as well as those fit candidates for officer's school—including rigorous screening of the astronaut candidates in the 1960s and '70s—all reflected the fact that these tests did have predictive value. Today, aptitude tests and I.Q. tests turn out to be the most powerful instruments for predicting educational and vocational success.[5] These tests still tell us much more about individuals than would their family profiles, and, of course, commonsense evaluations. Most important, I.Q. tests often revealed talents in socially deprived youngsters, ordinarily undiscovered, who thus might flourish with a bit of additional societal assistance.

Understanding Intellectual Differences

The study of I.Q. differences, as we have noted above, was originated as part of the search for a method for predicting educational and vocational achievement. This method arrived at the cusp of the twentieth century. Many thinkers had anecdotally given expression to this belief in earlier periods, including the scientific approach of Francis Galton during the latter decades of the nineteenth century.

We now have a period of one hundred years during which millions of persons throughout the world have been subject to a variety of I.Q., achievement, aptitude tests both for educational as well as vocational prediction. These have proved extraordinarily prescient tools for understanding a large class of human behaviors. And today, in 2005, they are ubiquitous, measuring every area of human behavior.

Minorities   Controversy occurs when certain recognizable groups, racial, ethnic, religious, gender, or national, reveal test scores that are comparatively negative in competition with others. Then, claims that the tests are biased, and should be overridden, arise. The appeal to government, and the flourishing of so-called anti-discriminatory laws, affirmative action, and quotas in contracts, school or job admission and retention create a veritable social battlefield among all groups. Naturally, laws that are placed into practice that disqualified one group on the basis of external racial or ethnic characteristics will motivate all decent humans to go to the boards, fighting it out in the courts and at the ballot box. In the United States since the Supreme Court ruled in *Brown vs. Board of Education*, 1954, that government should get out of the race business, pro or con, the attempt to override such race/ethnic neutral governmental arbitrage has been effortful.[6]

Achievement, I.Q. Tests   The tests of I.Q. as they have developed over the century have been broken up into two segments, verbal and numerical, along with spatial and figural tests. The reason for this is that both verbal and numerical tests give different predictive results. A test taker who does very well or very poorly on the verbal may achieve opposite results in the other. Yet both parts of the traditional I.Q. tell us much about the aptitude for critical kinds of learning in school, and often out into the vocational and professional worlds of adulthood. This difference in performance on tests is still mysterious, because both parts reveal skills necessary for cognitive reasoning. Also, test-taking skills and other personality factors often blur these results.

It is in the area of the ability of a person to think symbolically through word, sentence, paragraph meaning, and then in manipulating numerical or other non-verbal relationships, that we create the concept of cognitive intelligence or "g", the general ability to be able to reason. Here the ability to account for relationships beyond the particular sensory inputs of life lived on the public avenues of experience often lands I.Q. testing in controversy. In the world of testing, certain tests inter-correlate in their results, reveal similar attainment levels. When aptitude tests go beyond sensory acuity or design recognition to probe into more active inter-relational analysis on the part of the test taker, they are said to be weighted heavily in the "g" factor, general intelligence.[7]

General intelligence is increasingly interpreted as the ability or non-ability to probe different areas of learning, skill acquisition that require thought and analysis. It touches on an increasingly wide spectrum of professional skills. Often high general intelligence individuals show an aptitude for being able to move from one profession to another. It is usual for an individual doing well on the math portion of the I.Q. to do well on the verbal, and vice versa. Poor achievers likewise stay within a moderate range of variation in both parts of the I.Q.

Occasionally, one will find a whiz in math doing only modestly on the verbal. More often, high verbal achievers will do more poorly on the math side of the test. So-called savants can achieve on a mysteriously extraordinary level in verbal and arithmetic rote skill testing. They often have surprising musical or artistic skills, as well. Usually their low intelligence will be revealed on general I.Q. tests, especially those sections that require active operational manipulation of concepts.[8]

The Mean In order to systematize the variation in the expected norm on achievement on I.Q. tests, the concept of the mean I.Q. and the standard of deviation away from the mean has been developed. In the Caucasoid populations of North America and Europe who first came under the scrutiny of I.Q. this mean was established at 100. Clearly the meaning of this "mean" can vary with the type of tests that are utilized, as well as changes in the demography of the population under study.

The mean, as a concept, is not static. It is not surprising that European creative leadership has descended significantly since the early parts of the century before the great World Wars and genocides of European populations, Armenian, Russian/Ukrainian, *Holocaust* victims. Not only were high ability ethnic minorities and successful social class minorities butchered in the tens of millions, but some of the most talented young men of Europe were destroyed before they were able to form families. It is, however, difficult to evaluate this shifting nature of the *mean*; even populations in place have changed over time.

Standard Deviation The concept of "standard deviation" was introduced as a way of managing the significance of those either above or below the mean, 100, in their I.Q. score.[9] That number was to be the pivot from which variance in I.Q. could be compared. The conventional spread of 15 points on each side of 100 seemed to be significant in both signaling ability levels, as well as for comparative study of differing populations besides Europeans. Thus, from the practical educational/behavioral standpoint a score of 115 or 85 seemed to point to specific skill/intellectual constellations. The use of a 15-point differential on each side of the mean seemed to include symmetrically reduced numbers of individuals. The highest probability of scores in the European populations came in at 100, and fewer and fewer scores appeared at each standard deviation of scores higher or lower.

The use of this 15-point variance in I.Q. scores revealed that men had a greater statistical variance from the mean, about 18 points, while women ranged more tightly in the 12-point range. Thus we would expect that males would be more widely distributed over the I.Q. spectrum, more males at the extreme highs and more at the extreme lows, women concentrated more densely around the mean of 100.

This explains the dominance of men in high abstract vocations. Where the intellectual levels of a nation are high, men will tend to dominate in the sciences, business, and in the arts. But as is commonly noted men will also dominate the numbers of the prison incarcerated, the educational remedial programs, autism, asylums for the insane and debilitated. And, of course, they will be over-represented in the flag-draped coffins returning from wars.

In contemporary societies of lower average intelligence, because they dominate the intellectual center, women will be found to be the most employable in basic non-skilled factory employment. As the intelligence levels of developed societies begin to recede, the extremely high male I.Q.s disappearing, women will increasingly move into those now-vacated slots.[10]

I.Q. and Social Competence The results from the longitudinal study of extremely high I.Q.s started by Lewis Terman, at Stanford University, in the 1920s has predictively borne out the commonsense view that a high I.Q. results in higher social, economic, intellectual and personal/psychological achievement over the timeline of individuals, in those several-thousand California youngsters chosen by Terman, these all with I.Q.s over 140.[11]

Conversely, individuals with I.Q.s 85 and below revealed not only meager educational achievement but they suffered from vocational, economic, and personal debilitation. Some of the I.Q. and social debilitations of racial and ethnic minority students were attributed to the discriminatory environment of living among dominating Europeans. Results from the testing of criminals of all racial/ethnic backgrounds, in prison, revealed that large percentages of them scored below the normal range of 85-90 I.Q.[12]

Ethnicity and Race Inevitably, testing, identifying the ethnicity and race of the test takers for comparative analysis revealed much interesting and, often, extremely controversial data. American blacks scored in the 82-85 range; African blacks, from below the Sahara, when given the opportunity to experience European-type educational programs, invariably scored in the 70-75 I.Q. range.[13] Clearly, some impact of the very different cultural traditions had to have been reflected in these scores. Yet, Northeast Asiatics, Japanese, Chinese, and Koreans, whether at home or as migrants into new cultural traditions, scored in the 105 range. Here, social, economic, and familial profiles regardless of past social and racial privation patterns culminated in similar or superior I.Q. profiles as compared to Europeans. The difference in I.Q., c.85/75, between American blacks and Africans in the home countries is generally explained by the added percentage of European genetics in the African/American heritage, usually estimated to be around 20 percent.[14]

Ashkenazi (European) Jews scored at the highest average level of any ethnic group in the world, 115-118 I.Q., one standard deviation above the traditional European mean.[15] Interestingly, as the discrimination against Jews began to abate in Europe and North America in the nineteenth century, and Jews were allowed to compete freely with their national compatriots, they moved disproportionately into positions of influence, power, and wealth.[16]

The psychologist Ellis Batten Page exemplified this seemingly causal outcome of I.Q. differentials by noting that a population of c.180 million people with a mean I.Q. of 100, the American European community, as compared to a 3 percent sub-population, the Jews, with a mean I.Q. of 109, would at an I.Q. level of 180 throw off an equal number of such powerfully intelligent individuals. This was the logical conclusion using ordinary statistical principles. However, Page missed the even more powerful point that Jews with four Ashkenazi (European) grandparents, factually, have I.Q.s in the range of 115-118. Here 4+ million Jews would throw off an equal number of high I.Q.s in the then-majority population of 176 million, at about I.Q. 160.[17]

Power of "g"   The "g" factor of general intelligence, a concept originated in the early twentieth century by the English psychologist Charles Spearman (1904) defines this integrating deep-structured intellectual element of achievement. It is the common factor which is statistically extracted from a variety of tests all searching for cognitive organization of the testing material. The "g" factor discovered in the testing materials separates itself from other special sensory or motor skills, *i.e.,* surface-structure abilities such as short-term memorization, rapid physical dexterity, and others not requiring evaluative processing.[18] This ability to reason, to find patterns of meaning is seen as a necessary pre-condition for highly demanding professional achievement over a wide variety of civilizational endeavors. This research has been borne out over the past fifty years at the least, especially in the work of Hans Eysenck, Arthur Jensen, Richard Lynn, Thomas Bouchard, Volkmar Weiss.[19]

One might understand the role of "g" as follows: In order to attain high intellectual, creative achievement in a modern society, a high I.Q. ("g") is a necessary pre-condition. Hans Eysenck has placed this point at one standard deviation, 115 I.Q., above the European mean. And, indeed, I.Q.s of medical students in modern university programs rarely reveal I.Q.s lower than 115.[20] On the other hand a high I.Q. by itself has not turned out to be a sufficient condition for social success.[21]

Another baseball metaphor: To score a run, the batter has to pass first base. The run will not be scored, however, until he reaches home plate. High achievement must start with high natural intelligence, ("g"=first base). It cannot be fulfilled as a sufficient condition until education, personality, social opportunity, are all mobilized to maximize this significant biological potentiality (home plate).

The Gene(s) for Intelligence

The original failure of Francis Galton in searching for basic physiological correlates of cognitive intelligence led in the work of Binet and Spearman, and their followers to the use of so-called "paper and pencil" correlates of later educational and vocational achievements.[22] I.Q. tests and their various brethren, including academic achievement tests, the SAT, aptitude tests, all tried to link skills in verbal and mathematical achievement with this deeply mysterious entity we call "g".

As such, these tests, even when used and adapted for international use, all having similar predictive value, remained under the cloud of cultural and educational relativism, *i.e.*, women, people of color, ethnic and linguistic minorities, people living in underdeveloped nations without traditions of literacy, would fail tests designed for people of a European background. The fly in the ointment of this argument was the very high achievement levels on similar I.Q. tests for Northeast Asiatics, Japanese, Chinese, and Koreans, wherever in the world they took these tests.[23] Certainly these were peoples of different historical and cultural backgrounds, as compared with the Europeans, yet they were outdistancing the Europeans in their I.Q. scores.

So-called reaction time experiments as developed by Arthur Jensen have attempted to come closer to the Galton ideal of raw physical or physiological differences being used as a criterion for measuring intellectual ability. In these experiments, for example, a subject sits before a bank of bulbs, with an on/off buttons in front of the console. The most correlative of these experiments with high achievements in other areas of behaviors occurs when an individual holding the home button down, then hearing a buzzer which announces that one of the bulbs in the bank will light up, responds when this light goes on by releasing the home button and pressing the button in front of the lit bulb in the bank. The speed and accuracy of this so-called "choice" reaction time, meaning the subject must anticipate which bulb will light up and then speedily close down the light, correlates very highly with traditional IQ tests.[24]

Yet such experiments are still analogical.

All researchers into the measurement of intelligence (psychometrics) through these correlational techniques acknowledge the obliqueness of such knowledge. After all, human behavior is a product of our bio-genetic structure. In this we join with other living things. Thus, the search has continued into ways of finding the genes for cognitive intelligence, perhaps identifying the biochemical, metabolic pathways that distinguish a higher "g" from a lower.

As studies of the human genome have developed over the past decade, and we are more aware as to the number of human genes, as well as their relationship to the structure and function of phenotypic (surface) behaviors, the theoretical understanding of the genetic relationship to cognitive intelligence has taken a major step forward.

One of the consistent criticisms of the polygenic view of I.Q. that there are hundreds, if not more, genes that make up a blending of our intellectual behaviors, has maintained itself because of the puzzling fact that the variance within a family of full siblings, and a larger, similar ethnic population (Europeans), is little different.[25] In a blending theory of many genes involved in intellectual function, full siblings should be more similar than unrelated individuals in the larger population. They are not; the variation between brothers is just as large. See the siblings of most of the recent Presidents of the United States.

Led by Robert Plomin, Thomas Bouchard, and Volkmar Weiss, a new view of cognitive intelligence has begun to evolve.[26] Here, "g" is the product of a major gene locus of up to four or five genes. Classical Mendelian relationships can be observed in familial settings over the generations. Even in improbably high intelligence parents, tracing their genetic impact one or two generation beyond, it is quite often found that one descendant is of extremely high intelligence, then two modestly bright and successful individuals, and a "relatively black sheep."[27]

Terman's longitudinal studies of "genius" revealed that youngsters who scored in the 150-160 I.Q. range marrying individuals of sometimes equally high intelligence would find that their own children vary widely in I.Q. scores. These would have high I.Q.s often averaging in the 130s, thus not improbably high, although a minority of the offspring would equal the parental I.Q.s.

We could conceive the process as that of a pin ball machine, where the iron balls (sperm), surge forth to seek out a resting place (egg-slot) in the machinery (individual genome), once taking up a very high I.Q. position, other times, other babies, lower or intermediate, but not the averaging blending that the polygenic theory had heretofore described.

The theory of Volkmar Weiss was developed since 1972 in East Germany, as part of a secret attempt by the government to identify potential genetic candidates for both athletic and academic distinction (GDR Central Office for Genealogy, still in Leipzig). Weiss argues that in the relationship of profiles in traditional ethnically homogeneous societies, Germans and by implication all Europeans, have an I.Q. balance between individual genotypes, M1M1=130 I.Q., M1M2=112 I.Q., and M2M2=94 I.Q., ranging from small percentage of I.Q. 130, M1M1, larger grouping of M1M2=c.112, I.Q., and the majority population at M2M2=94 I.Q. Naturally, correspondingly smaller populations of lower I.Q.

One of Weiss' concerns is how to explain the relative paucity in percentage of population of M1M1 high I.Q. types with all the power that M1M1 connotes, and why, given the positive selectivity of high intelligence, only a relatively small number of leaders in society arises.[28] Seemingly, Weiss argues, society has no room for them. By implication there is less reproductive opportunity for this sub-population of the talented. It does explain however why it is that even with the birth into this class of the talented who tend to intermarry with each other, the so-called regression to the mean is never regression to the mean of the larger outside population but regression to the mean of the intra-breeding group, here M1M1, or 130 I.Q. types.

What this shift in theory toward the major gene locus approach to intelligence has released is the push to map the human genome for what is today a censored endeavor in the sciences. If we can search the genome to find gene loci for a number of human diseases, genetic disabilities, why not search for a major gene loci for human intelligence? Why not? First, it has to be recognized that there is such a thing as genetically-rooted general intelligence differences. Officialdom, however, will not lower the blessed wand. Thus the research is largely hidden in Europe and North America, perhaps now in Asia, in obscure research laboratories.

The three scholars, Plomin, Bouchard, and Weiss, are in the vanguard of an attempt to find metabolic and hormonal pathways that differentiate individuals of seemingly opposing I.Q. profiles, thence to trace these enzymatic differences in function and brain/neurology energies to their sources in a specific gene locus, the human genome.

Weiss, in a recent series of correspondences, explains it as follows:

"Enzymes responsible for the regulation of brain energy metabolism and correlated with IQ and social status should be the target of further research."[29] Here the focus is on serum homocysteine levels of different families as pointing to variances in brain energy metabolism, thence the surface attributes in learning and behavior that we identify for individuals. Weiss believes 40 percent of variance in I.Q. is attributable to a major gene locus, plus other minor loci—dyslexia is an example—including other small contributions from a large number of other gene loci.[30]

We may not find over the next several generations the exact constellation and locus of the genes determining high or low intelligence in humans. But there is a real probability that the biochemical pathways that are sent forth into the nervous system and brain will be measured and correlated with I.Q. scores, thus becoming an even more determining and predictive factor in assessing human potential. Already we can predict on the basis of pre-natal testing, often very early in the embryo's developmental, factors that may cause serious debilitation in the neonate. Such predictive flags may also show up in the greater subtleties of sub-normal, normal, and high intellectual potential.

Given today's ideological climate, what this will means on the sociological, political level of decisionmaking is hard to predict.

The Societal Challenge to the "g" Factor

The intellectual discord induced by research into the relationship between intelligence, genetics, and social amelioration has been as epochal as that which greeted Copernicus and his followers of the heliocentric theory in the sixteenth and seventeenth centuries. Then the victims were often burnt or underwent the Inquisition. The same happened in the Soviet Union when a number of noted

Russian geneticists were sent to the gulags. They died because of their research into the importance of genetics in assessing human and biological inheritance and behavior.[31]

In the West, a softer, kinder form of expulsion and cauterization was practiced. This was especially evident in the publication of a series of books, epitomized in *The Bell Curve* by authors Herrnstein and Murray.[32] Although they accumulated massive evidence to show the relationship of I.Q. to genetic inheritance and its impact on social/economic success and failure, behavior contributory to personal, familial and community life, and behavior both dysfunctional and destructive, the furor and condemnation from officialdom, academic and political, was resounding.[33] Such ideas were under interdict. After all, the entire Western establishment had mobilized its wealth and moral authority to equalize middle class and poor through the redistribution of the wealth produced by the European and North American middle classes.

The issue of human intelligence variability could not be subject to a secular search for understanding, given the political commitments mandated by the regnant ideology.[34]

It was clear that the massive efforts of years of investment in programs designed to effect such equalization were not succeeding. There were few scientific minds, specialists in these areas of psychology, genetics, or sociology who could point to long-term positive results in these efforts. The redesign of the SATs in the mid-1980s was effected so that they would be normed upward, reinterpreting the grades such that higher marks were assured for the majority of students now taking the test. This re-norming of the scores was explicitly attributed to a newer kind of student then applying to college as compared to the late forties when the results were still consonant with the proportionately fewer students applying to college.

The explanation for this dumbing down of the SAT, an I.Q. ("g" factor) equivalent aptitude test, was that the larger numbers of students taking the tests was unable to reach the scores of their peers of several decades earlier. The larger cohort was weaker intellectually and educationally. The solution was to call a 500 math score 580, a verbal 500, now to be 600. Same difficulty of test, but more esteeming grades. Here was an example of the masking of a changed *mean*.

Yet, taking a test is a cultural act. Success or failure can be laid to antecedent familial, social, or educational experiences, especially when students are involved who are not of European, Caucasian background, leaving aside the special circumstances of the Northeast Asiatics. One could argue that making college available for many more young people of diverse social backgrounds could unleash talents potentials heretofore unrecognized.

After all, the so-called pure correlation between testing success and worldly achievement has not shown tight causal predictability. Long ago, Lewis Terman and his Stanford University associates realized this with regard to the young geniuses. Worldly success was not strictly correlated with their I.Q.s. For example, students of 175 I.Q. did not live especially superior lives, economically, professionally, or socially to those with I.Q.s of 140, a significant "g" differential.[35]

Volkmar Weiss, responding to this evidence with his own analysis, also wondered why persons with I.Q.s of 175-196 do no better in life, socially and economically than do those with 135 I.Q.s. To Weiss, this argued for the reality of the AA major gene locus (130 I.Q) being a core dimension of high intelligent individuals, and that 170 I.Q.s may only indicate anomalous specialized achievements.[36]

His admission that the major gene complex accounts for no more than a 40 percent variance, significant in itself, reveals that other dimensions of human behavior, besides the major gene complex for "g", general intelligence, may be influential. After all, even the most advanced societies reveal mean population I.Q.s of 100-105, Europe/Northeast Asia. The persistence of these lower I.Q. levels may be telling us something about the need for a hierarchy of intelligence achievements in order for a society to function.

Recent academic research in the United States buttresses Weiss' intuition. The job/economic advantage of college graduates over high school graduates, and therefore their presumed family formation possibilities, has fallen between 1990 and 2005.[37]

A Broader Perspective on Intelligence

Avoiding "g" The above ambiguities have led to proposals for an alternative theoretical view of human intelligence and achievement. Some of these views purport to neutralize psychometric concentration on the "g" factor. Howard Gardner, of Harvard, promoted a vision of human intelligence as qualitative and plural. Here, the talented basketball player, the dancer, the artist, the mathematician, would have scored high on tests akin to their vocational superiority. One could summarize such views as an extrapolation from the vocational diversity of a culture into psychology.[38]

Indeed, basketball players have highly-developed talents. Clearly, however, in the classical I.Q. correlational structure of "g", great basket ball players did not score especially high. The implicit position of Gardner was that human intelligence was infinitely varied in its expression in complex cultures. Thus, the "g" factor would here be an irrelevant abstraction. The "g" factor did reveal certain differences in cognitive functioning, but was not a significant determiner of human achievement. Clearly, Gardner has argued, the diversity of talents exhibited along a wide rainbow of human excellences had to be evidence for a needed reinterpretation of human intelligence, less reductive to the biological.

Robert Sternberg of Yale University also gained some recognition with his attempt to go beyond "g", with an additional element on the path toward human success. This he called practical intelligence.[39] He built his persuasive views on the commonsense realization that many high I.Q. types did not achieve mundane success in the world, and by contrast many less formally educated, non- cognitive types were greatly successful and contributors to their communities. Admittedly, the predictive search for the germinating seeds of this practical intelligence was hard to come by.

Another approach to broadening the definition of intelligence beyond "g" was the popularization of the concept of emotional intelligence developed in a book of that title by Daniel Goleman, a science writer for *The New York Times*. Goleman made use of the research by a neurologist, Antonio Dimasio, of the University of Iowa, on the relationship of emotional drives and brain structure.[40]

Pre-frontal Cortex   Goleman's use of Dimasio's emphasis on emotions as an independent factor in human behavioral makeup argued for the nondefinitive importance of "g" by itself in the panoply of human behavioral experience. In other words, a person could lose emotional control, ambition, relatedness to oneself and others, sometimes through accident and illness, that would still maintain the integrity of the cognitive element. These humans became completely dysfunctional even while their "g"-factored intelligence seemed unimpaired.[41]

Dimasio amassed evidence that revealed a relationship between specific areas of the brain and consequential patterns of behavior. His work concentrated on physical damage to the pre-frontal cortex. This was part of a rich and varied set of researches into brain structure often reconfirming the nineteenth-century view that the brain while guided by a central controlling system contained sub-areas, hippocampus, amygdala, hypothalamus, *i.e.*, the limbic system, the ancient mammalian and primate brain inheritance, that gave shape to specific sensory, emotional, memory, elements. These elements, all adding to the overall meaning of cognition, gave it color and affect. The scientific basis for Dimasio's work was contributed by the path-breaking mid-twentieth-century research of A. R. Luria, Roman Jakobson, and Kurt Goldstein.[42]

Four Factors   Perhaps the most theoretically suggestive broadening of the concept of intelligence beyond the "g" of I.Q. was offered in the 1940s by the American psychologist Ward Halstead, and developed by his follower, the Australian evolutionist David Stenhouse. This theory consisted of a four-factored view of human intelligence: A=Abstract/Cognitive/I.Q.; S=Sensory Motor; C=Central Integrative/Memory; P=Postponement/Persistence, referring to the interdicting of instinctual drives. These factors must in some way be seen as acting as a semi-independent, non-correlative element in human mental behavior, perhaps reflecting differing genetic elements.[43]

S: For example, we know from a variety of so-called talent dimensions of cultural behavior that highly intelligent individuals seem to have special sensory skills. From basketball players to violinists, and sculptors to painters, unique visual, auditory, neurological, even culinary, enological (wine making and tasting) skills, when linked in tandem with adequate cognitive skills, can result in civilizational greatness. The semi-independence of such talents is seen in the existence of savants, people with special skills—math calculation, word memory, musical and artistic—that are accompanied by extremely low cognition. These tragic humans are more freaks than they are talents. These skills, however, reveal a brain/neurological/genetic connection. Without cognitive correlates, they become meaningless glosses on the full development of these individuals. The special skills and talents are real in that they reveal themselves in cultural behaviors. Without the buttressing of "g", they are empty talents. We do not know genetically or neurologically from where they arise.

C/M: Memory is an interesting dimension of the human palette of knowledge. On the surface one would expect that memory abilities are linked to cognitive skills. We remember best when we can relate one event to another. The richer our structure of factual relationships—a map of the universe inside our skulls—the more we will be able to recall, to pull remembered information out of the deep structures of our brain.

On the other hand, psychologists have long been able to distinguish between the ability to remember strings of unrelated information and the concomitant ability to organize things into a theoretically useful fund of information. There seems to be a definite disconnect between this ability to remember random information and the information that successful businessmen, historians, medical doctors, and others working in the knowledge areas accumulate. Here, too, we see hints of this factor of memory in the savant talents of retarded persons.[44]

P: This is the most suggestive and perhaps most mysterious dimension of seemingly "g"-independent mental factors in humans. One of Lewis Terman's most important longitudinal findings among his 140+ I.Q. geniuses was that, over the decades, the lowest 5 percent of the social achievers, the "failures," if you will, described themselves in terms of their inability to persist, concentrate their efforts, focus on a goal, shove aside momentary distractions in pursuit of long-range ambitions. From a brain structure perspective, as Antonio Dimasio has chronicled, building on almost a century of awareness of the "P" factor in human behavior, the frontal areas of the cortex have been implicated in these brain and personality functions.[45]

People of great drive, persistence, even zealotry, are not necessarily the most intelligent and cognitive of individuals. Often, ruthless political personalities seem to be endowed with powerful "P"-factor drives and capabilities. Other driving, ambitious individuals reveal mental skills and emotional sensitivity of below-normal qualities. It is not rare to find highly intellectual persons with little drive, ambition, forcefulness of personality. No matter their potential ability, they languish in their chosen fields.

High "g" in itself, it seems, needs to be accompanied by a constellation of other biological factors both in talent and personality in order for an individual to flourish in all social contexts. On the other hand individuals with established I.Q.s below the 100 I.Q. Caucasoid mean will rarely rise beyond the unskilled levels of human civilizational performance.

Male and Female Perhaps the most intriguing hints about the possibility of other gene loci in the impact on the purely cognitive dimensions of "g" goes back to the work of Harvard Medical School neurologist, Norman Geschwind. Geschwind's work was largely focused on the study of male/female differences both in learning disabilities as well as in special talents. Here the statistical reality of a much larger variance in male intelligence, a standard deviation of 18 points either side of the mean, as compared to a female variance of 12 I.Q. points (15 points average), needed interpretation. This statistical analysis explained in mathematical terms what social experience placed before our eyes, males were highly over-represented at both the lower and upper levels of I.Q., retardates as well as genius.[46]

Geschwind, here stimulated by the work of John Money and Steven Goldberg, focused by way of biological explanation on both the levels of testosterone as well as yet unclear hormonal production of auto-immune reactions as having a strong bearing on male intellectual performance.[47] Geschwind followed this pathway of intra-uterine and neo-natal development into real difference in brain hemispheric structures between males and females.[48] Not merely social conditioning, as the ideologists would explain away sexual differences, but real biologically separated pathways from conception to mortality. What else but genetically-linked sex hormonal developmental linkages could account for the historical and contemporary reality of male superiority in mathematics and chess?

These theoretical considerations were taken up by Julian Stanley and Camille Benbow of Johns Hopkins University, who profiled mathematically precocious youths, as evidenced by achievements on the classic SAT exams. This was a study of the top precocities in math, those *7th graders* scoring above 700 out of a possible perfect score of 800 on the math portion of the 12th grade math SAT. Using a research base of 10,000 young males and females of great math abilities, they found that 20 percent were left handers, twice the normal proportion. Sixty percent showed evidence of auto-immune disorders, asthma or allergies. This latter disorder was five times the general average. Seventy percent of these youngsters were myopic (near-sighted), an affirmation of the folk lore for brainy types.[49]

As the researchers went down the list from the highest scorers to lesser achievers, they found that the incidence of these seeming defects fell toward the natural population average. The proportion of males over females in this cohort of high math achievers (700 Math SAT or higher at 7th grade level) was 13 males to one female.[50]

Significance   It is fair to say that these other contributions to our knowledge of human cultural behavior support the view that a high "g" factor is a necessary pre-condition for success in any human vocation of worth. And that while evidence argues for a major gene locus for cognitive intelligence, "g", clearly other genetic elements contribute to the expression of "g" and thus to the richness and diversity of creative, dynamic civilizations.

There are, operating out of the human genome, genetic linkages of extraordinary subtlety. These account for the full civilizational expression of human intelligence. We are a product of an evolutionary development that connects us to a history of primate and human adaptations. There is in human civilization, its correlative underlying genetic/morphological/behavioral structure, a huge evolutionary revolution to be reckoned with.

Origin of Intelligence Variability[51]

What we call intelligence in its animal embodiment, including humans, is the ability to deal with complex sensory-induced stimulation, to sort it out and to make a consequent adaptive response. This response should, as with all other adaptive animal reactions, lead to the reproductive survival of the individual, often, in consequence, to the survival of the species in general.

The significance of intelligence as an adaptation of vertebrates is that it is behavior bound. And as such its selective value arises in an environment of change. If an animal and its kin, behaviorally, cannot adapt to external (and even self-induced cultural) changes within the reproductive generation, they and their genes disappear from the face of this earth, becoming fossilized memories. In the more ancient traditions of animal life, the variability within "species" is usually so great, and the external challenges usually so gradual that a portion of the variable group will survive, shaping the genes and environments in consonance and leading evolution on its way forward, here a few survivors, most others relegated to oblivion.[52]

A few scientists, most with an ideological prejudice against the idea of genetic natures somewhat independent of environmental shaping, see *Homo* as a great evolutionary accident. These are mostly sociological egalitarian ideologists of the pseudo-Marxist school.[53] There are few real creationist events in scientific evolution, only our ignorance which masks an understanding of cause.[54]

As long as our world is changing, both in genomic species variability and the ability of animals to alter behavior within the generations as a consequence of new experiences, intelligence will command a selective premium.[55] The primates of which we humans are members carved out their ecological niche at the time of the great placental mammal breakthrough some hundred million years ago. It took almost that long for the challenges of that niche, land and tree roaming, defensive, often nocturnal creatures to nurture that added bit of brain power against the rapidly multiplying mammalian opportunists who rushed forward under the noses of the increasingly specialized dinosaurian dominators during this evolutionary period, called the Cretaceous.[56]

The dominance of the mammals of the late Cretaceous came not because of a catastrophic comet that purportedly destroyed the dinosaurs, c.65 mya, but not all the other reptiles, including birds (Georges Cuvier's "castrophism," c.1800), but rather because of the positive selective environments in which mammals grew larger and developed more brain power. This process was a plus both to their aggressive omnivorous search for food, a penchant for animal eggs, but also a woe to the young of the long-regnant, now-decadent dinosaurs.[57]

We humans are the inevitable articulation of this primeval adaptive tack. *Homo* by itself should have been satisfied to dominate this land surface, wandering and predatory, in its basic *Homo erectus* (Peking Man), *Homo neanderthalis* (Caucasoid Eurasians) forms, thus settling into a tentative and rugged balance with nature. But, an outlier human form came out of the mists of the glacial cool.

To understand the uniqueness of this "sport" in the evolution of *Homo*, a taxonomic (defining who is a *Homo*) challenge over at least the past 3-4 million years, we need to refer briefly to the controversy over "out-of-Africa Eve." Using hypothetical rates of change in mitochondrial DNA of modern humans, some scientists have thus estimated the time of origin of modern humans. In testing modern humans throughout the world, this hypothetical projection-in-time of an "out-of-Africa" migration of modern humans is estimated to be from two hundred to four hundred thousand years ago. These scientists unfortunately seem to disregard the possibility of an in and out migration from Africa during this broad time span.[58]

The argument is that an African human is the modern ancestor of us all. The so-called recent and modern five races of man are products of this late migration throughout the world. In addition, this late migration of modern humans is supposed to have resulted in the genocide of all other extant hominids throughout the world, a massive genocide. Supposedly no genes from the more ancient fossil humans found and documented throughout the world have insinuated themselves into modern humans. Most scientists now disagree with this well-advertised politically-correct hypothesis. No factual, evidential support for what is basically a laboratory concoction has come forth. By contrast, there is now enormous factual geological (fossil) support for the continuity of the evolving line of humans in situ in the various Eur-Asian and African ecologies.[59]

Such abstract laboratory-developed hypotheses concerning human origins are not new. The famous DNA timetables show the separation of the chimpanzees and hominids, australopithecines, plus others, and *Homo*, supposedly taking place about five million years ago. The fossil record is increasingly pushing the dating of hominid fossils back toward the eight million years ago mark. The human genome is not that different in number and structure from other animals.[60] One can predict, on the basis of evolutionary timetable sequences for all advanced animals (mammals), that this timetable of primate/hominid separation will continue to recede into evolutionary history.[61]

The point of this analysis is to argue a case made first by anthropologist Carleton Coon, against much political condemnation, that the five races of humans found in recent historical experience—Caucasoids, Mongoloids, Capoids (Bushman), Australids, Negroids—originated much earlier in human evolution, perhaps before or shortly after the primeval migrations out of Africa between two and one million years ago.[62] The paleontological evidence for continuity seems ever more decisive with regard to the origin of these now five interbreeding sub-species of *Homo sapiens*.[63]

It was in the north, Eurasia, not too far from the Caucasoid Neanderthals, morphologically and culturally primitive, that an epochal revolution in one small group of ancestral migrants out of Africa took place. For as-yet unknown causes (Darwinian in nature), a rapid reconstruction in human morphology occurred. This explosive expansion of brain power took hold north of the Mediterranean. The skull and iso-cortex of the brain expanded like a balloon as part of this revolution in human morphology.[64]

Modern genetic analysis argues for a tiny evolutionary bottleneck out of which a very small genetic profile expanded throughout the world, *but not necessarily from Africa*. This basic alteration in human morphology does not suggest the introduction of any new physical specialization for internecine warfare and/or competition with either other forms of life, mammals, else in the struggle with fellow humans. Except for language, humans have no real adaptive specializations, no hooves, wings, or razor canines.[65]

This modern form of humans, *Homo sapiens sapiens*, Cro-Magnon, the first fossil exemplars, now date to c.45,000 B.P.. The Neanderthals, by contrast, inhabiters of the apparently colder tundras of northern Eur-Asia do seem to have evolved a number of cold-weather physical adaptations, hairiness, short and stocky builds, heavy bones, large noses to warm the cold air. This argues, in the case of the Cro-Magnons, for an originating point in more temperate domains, perhaps the Caucasus or the Mid-East.

Physically, the Cro-Magnons were and are the modern peoples of Europe and Western-Asia, as they gradually come under the scrutiny of human history some 10-12,000 years ago. Much migrating has, of course, changed the racial and ethnic mix in the millennia leading into the twenty-first century. The Cro-Magnons had huge thin skulls and brain power within. Their cultural work was both revolutionary in time and unique to the history of *Homo*, rich pre-literary technological and artistic remains, clearly transcendental innovators of human economic and thus mental life.

This new brain morphology and its genetic underpinnings probably appeared first in peripheral human mutants. The mutations away from the gross human boniness of body and skull became extraordinarily selective for life and procreation under the ever-changing stresses of glacial change. These brain structure changes became crucial for advanced symbolic thinking. We see this broadened gradient of psychological intentionalities: of the Cro-Magnons far beyond the simple tool scrapers of the Neanderthals, their closest competitors. Now, modern art, technology, domestication (horses, reindeer), chronometrical symbols probing the meaning of the sequences and regularities of natural events. They even took care to create garbage dumps well separated from their living quarters.[66] What a contrast to the behavior of modern humans in the favellas of the urban morass.

The revolution in brain morphology and then in brain cultural function of the Caucasoid Cro-Magnons sprinted across an intellectual Rubicon far in advance of the existing classically defined races of *Homo*. This is especially true of the then more isolated southern races, Negroid, Australids, Capoids. The Neanderthals disappeared from these northern geographies about 27,000 B.P., probably not without contributing some of their genes to the Cro-Magnons and thus their descendants.

The great revolution in Northeast Asian morphology and cultural competency took place after 2000 BCE when waves of Caucasoids moved East into India and China, Korea and Japan. The languages of the Koreans and Japanese, for example, are related to Finno-Altaic language family of Eastern Europe and Central Asia.[67] The culture of China from the first dynasties of the Yellow River near Sian, reveal a strong Persian Indo-European affinity. It was then that these indigenous peoples, more similar to contemporary mixed race Khazaks than Han Chinese, gave China its literacy.[68]

The Japanese and Koreans finally settled into their respective territories after picking up a strong admixture of ancient Mongoloid genes as they traveled east and bred into the indigenous Malayo-Polynesian peoples already settled on these lands, c.300 BCE. It could be that these now Japanese and Korean migrants carried with them a strong component of the revolutionary major gene complex of M1M1 (130-plus I.Q.) of the Cro-Magnons.

Outcome and Perspective

Within the current international system of peoples, cultures, nations, is that high intelligence arose in the north settling within the Eur-Asian Caucasoids, no earlier than c.100,000 years ago, later to be transferred to the Northeast Asiatics, themselves of hybrid Caucasoid/Mongoloid/Australid biological heritage.[69] The biogenetic civilizational potential represented by these peoples has flourished in large urban constellations.

The other, mostly southern races/ethnicities of *Homo* had during this period, c.100,000 B.P., been impacted by the above aggressive expansive intelligence profiles. The world of subsistence hunting, gathering, and farming was gradually enfiladed by the genes of the north. For example, except for the peripheral New Guinea Australids, and the remnant aboriginals of Australia, no other pure-blooded Australid peoples exist, even as they speak their ancient tongues.[70] In fact morphology and fossil evidence hints that the both Australian and some New Guinea aboriginals were moved over the sapiens line by migrating Caucasoids and their genes.[71] From Polynesia to Indonesia, to Thailand, Cambodia, and even into southern China, Taiwan, Andaman Islanders, Tungiks from Siberia, early Australid exemplars, received samplings of northern genetics.[72] Carleton Coon argued that the Negroes of West Africa are most similar racially to the Caucasoids, and may have been impacted by such wanderers from the north after 100,000 B.P.[73]

Such migrations that blurred ancient racial lines, and possibly genetic barriers, up until today have served to diminish differences in the overall intellectual/cultural profiles of the human species. Before the twentieth century, the populations in Latin America, the Caribbean, Africa, South Asia, were relatively small, and sadly inconspicuous to the aggressive cognitive Eur-Asian and "Mongoloid" tide from the north. But soon, Western medicine, hygiene, communication and transportation exploded their survival rates and we are now ever more submerged in a mass of struggling humans around the world.

These populations have now been fully impacted by the literate civilizations of the north, but largely unable to emulate and absorb the internal intellectual dynamics of the twenty-first century. Certainly the twenty-first century is not the end of the human evolutionary story.

The power of high vertebrate/mammal/primate intelligence has imprinted itself on the evolutionary process for at least a billion years. Our solar system may well continue in its present rhythmic fluctuations such that the Earth will remain climatically habitable for another billion years. The challenge for the advanced nations of the world now centers on their ability to understand the meaning of the present international dynamic. Our human world no longer can be anything but *one*. The sadly intractable proletariats of the poor and uneducable must be transformed into a middle class, in balance with nature and civilization.

To make this a humane transformation over the generations, there are and will come to exist rational social and political pathways for the willing. Intelligence will eventually make itself fully felt throughout our globe. To achieve this goal a truly revolutionary alteration in our thinking is required. The facts are there, and conclusive. The will is weak. Unhappily, before we will be able to achieve this new world community, we will experience rough days of reckoning.

Endnotes, Chapter 4

[1] Galton, F. 1869. *Hereditary Genius*, London: Macmillan; Galton, F. 1888. "Correlations and their measurement, chiefly from anthropological data," *Proceedings of the Royal Society of London*, 45:135-145.

[2] Binet, A., and Simon, T. 1916 (1905). "Upon the Necessity of Establishing a Scientific Diagnosis of Inferior States of Intelligence, from *L'Année Psychologique*, xi:163-190, in E. S. Kite, tr., *The Development of Intelligence*, Baltimore: Williams and Williams.

[3] Stern, W. 1914. *Psychology of Early Childhood Up to the Sixth Year of Age*, tr. A Barwell, New York.

[4] Terman, L. 1925. *Genetic Studies of Genius*, Stanford: Stanford Univ. Press; Fincher, J. 1973. "The Terman Study Is Fifty Years Old," *Human Behavior*, 2:8-15; Stanley, J. C., *et al.* 1973. *The Gifted and Creative: A Fifty Year Perspective*, Baltimore: Johns Hopkins.

[5] Gordon, R. A. 1980. "Research on I.Q., Race, and Delinquency," in *Taboos in Criminology*, E. Sagarin, ed., Beverly Hills, CA: Sage, pp. 37-66; Gottfredson, L. S. 1986. "The 'g' factor in employment," *Jrnl. of Vocational Behavior*, 29:293-450.

[6] Moynihan, D. P. 1965. *The Negro Family*, Washington, D.C.: Dept. of Labor; Rainwater, C., and Yaney, W. L. 1967. *The Moynihan Report and the Politics of Controversy*, Cambridge, MA: MIT.

[7] Jensen, A. R. 1998. *The "g" Factor: The Science of Mental Ability*, Westport, CT: Praeger; Spearman, C. 1904. "General intelligence, objectively determined and measured," *American Journal of Psychology*, 15:201-293.

[8] Clarke, L. 1973. *Can't Read, Can't Write*, N.Y.: Penguin; Wing, L. 1978. "The Autiology and Pathogenesis of Early Infant Autism," *Trends in Neuroscience*, July; Lindsley, O. R. 1965. "Can Deficiency Produce Specific Superiority—The Challenge of the Idiot Savant," *Exceptional Children*, 31:226-231; Scheerer, M., Rothman, E., Goldstein, K. 1945. "A Case of 'Idiot Savant'," *Psychological Monographs*, 58:4.

[9] Pearson, K. 1904. "On the laws of inheritance in man," Biometrika, 3:131-140. Standard deviation first discussed in 1893 by Pearson, see Jensen, *The "g" Factor, op. cit.*, p. 14.

[10] Itzkoff, S. W. 1985. *Why Humans Vary in Intelligence*, Ashfield, MA: Paideia. Chapters 15, 16; Geary, D. 1998. *The Evolution of Human Sex Differences*, Washington, D.C.: American Psychological Assoc.; Baron-Cohen, S. 2003. *The Essential Difference*, London: Allen Lane.

[11] Terman, *Genetic Studies of Genius*, op. cit.; Fincher, "The Terman Study Is Fifty Years Old," op. cit.; Stanley et al., *The Gifted and Creative*, op. cit.

[12] Wilson, J. A., and Herrnstein, F. J. 1985. *Crime and Human Nature*, N.Y.: Simon and Schuster.

[13] Lynn, R., and Vanhanen, T. 2002. *I.Q. and the Wealth of Nations*, Westport, CT: Praeger, Table 7.7, pp. 100-103.

[14] Reed, T. E. 1969. "Caucasian Genes in American Negroes," *Science*, 165:762-768; Chakraborty, R. et al. 1992. "Caucasian Genes in American Blacks: New Data," *American Journal of Human Genetics*, 50:145-155.

[15] Storfer, M. D. 1990. *Intelligence and Giftedness*, San Francisco: Jossey-Bass, pp. 315- 321. Vincent, Paul. 1966. "The Measured Intelligence of Glasgow Jewish School Children" *Jewish Journal of Sociology*, 8, 92-108.

[16] Nathaniel Weyl estimates that between 1901-1962, 225 Nobel prizes in the sciences have been awarded. Sixty-three Nobelists were born in English-speaking countries, including Jews. 36.5 of all the Nobel prizes were Jews. In the period from 1960 to 1985, 29 of 89 Americans were Jews, or 33 percent. Jews then comprised about 2.5 percent of the population. Many of these Jews were refugees from Hitler and Stalin. In Germany, the Jews were about one percent of the population, producing 10 out of 32 Nobel prizes between 1905 and 1931, over-represented despite discrimination, by thirty times. Weyl, N., and Possony, S. T. 1963. *The Geography of Intellect*, Chicago: Regnery, pp. 140-144; Weyl, N. 1989. *The Geography of American Achievement*, Washington, D.C.: Scott-Townsend, pp. 85-86; Gordon, S. 1984. *Hitler, Germans, and the Jewish Question*, Princeton: Princeton Univ. Press; Zuckerman, H. 1977. *Scientific Elites: Nobel Laureates in the United States* N.Y.: Simon and Schuster.

[17] Page, E. B. 1976. "A Historical Step Beyond Terman," in Keating, D. P., ed. *Intellectual Talent*, Baltimore: Johns Hopkins Press, pp. 305-306.

[18] Spearman, C. 1927. *The Abilities of Man*, N.Y.: Macmillan; Spearman, C. and Jones, L. W.. 1950. *Human Ability*, London: Macmillan.

[19] Eysenck, H. 1953. *The Structure of Human Personality*, N.Y: Wiley; Eysenck, H. 1995. *Genius: The Natural History of Creativity*, Cambridge: Cambridge Univ. Press; Bouchard, T. J., et al. 1990. "Sources of Human Psychological Difference: The Minnesota Study of Twins Reared Apart," *Science*, 250:223-228; Jensen, A. R. 1981. *Straight Talk about Mental Testing*, N.Y.: Free Press; Jensen, A. R. 1994. "Psychometric 'g' Related to Differences in Head Size," *Personality and Individual Differences*, 17:597-606; Lynn, R. 1987. "The Intelligence of the Mongoloids," *Personality and Individual Differences*, 8:813-844; Lynn, R., and Pagliari. 1994. "The Intelligence of American Children Is Still Rising," *Jrnl. of Biosocial Science*, 26:65-67; Weiss, V. 1990. "Social and Demographic Origins of the European Proletariat," *Mankind Quarterly*, 31:126-1521.

[20] Cattell, R. B. 1983. "The Role of Psychological Testing," in *Intelligence and National Achievement*, ed. by R. B. Cattell, Washington, D.C.: Cliveden Press, pp. 19-69. The mean for physicians and surgeons is I.Q. 128.

[21] Oden, M. H. 1968. "The Fulfillment of Promise," *Genetic Psychology Monographs*, 77:3-93.

[22] Galton, F. 1883. *Inquiries into Human Faculty and its Development*, London: Macmillan; Spearman, C. 1927. *The Abilities of Man*, N.Y.: Macmillan; Guilford, J. P. 1967. *The Nature of Human Intelligence*, N.Y.: McGraw Hill; Thurstone, L. L. 1938. "Primary Mental Abilities," *Psychometric Monographs*, Vol. 1, Chicago: Univ. of Chicago Press.

[23] Lynn, R. 1997. "Geographic Variation in Intelligence," in *The Scientific Study of Human Nature*, by H. Nyborg and J. Gray, Hillsdale, N.J.: Erlbaum.

[24] Jensen, A. R. 1998. *The "g" Factor*, op. cit., pp. 214-231.

[25] Guthke, J. 1988. "Intelligenz Diagnostik," in *Psychologische Diagnostik*, ed. by R. Jäger, München: *Psychologie Verlag Unum*, pp. 333-347; Propping, P. 1989. *Psychiatrische Genetic*, Berlin: Springer.
[26] Plomin, R, et al. 1995. "Allelic Associations Between 100 DNA Markers and High versus-low I.Q.," *Intelligence*, 21:31-48; Weiss, V. 1992. "Major Genes of General Intelligence," *Personality and Individual Differences*, 13:1115-1134; Bouchard, T. J. 1993. "The Genetic Architecture of Human Intelligence," in *Biological Approaches to the Study of Intelligence*, P. A. Vernon, ed., Norwood, N.J.: Ablex, pp. 33-85; Akesson, H. O. 1984. "Intelligence and Polygenetic Inheritance: A Dogma to Reexamine," *Acta Paediatr. Scand.*, 73:13-17.
[27] Marcus, G. 2004. *The Birth of the Mind: How a Tiny Number of Genes Creates the Complexity of Human Thought*, N.Y.: Basic Books; Weiss, V. 1992. "Major Genes of General Intelligence," *op. cit.*, reprint, 17-21.
[28] Weiss, V. 1992. "Major Genes of General Intelligence," *Personality and Individual Differences*, 13, 1115-1134; (Weiss p. 21, reprint).
[29] Weiss, V. 2003. www.volkmar-weiss.de/homocysteine.html, 1/05/2003. Discussion with Kozich (Prague); Barbaux et al.; Jee (Korea); Beaty on relationship of homocysteine metabolism as a clue to major gene locus of "g", p. 1.
[30] Weiss, V. 2003, *op. cit.*, letter to Dr. Jee (Korea), reprint, p. 4.
[31] Eysenck, H. J. 1982. "The Sociology of Psychological Knowledge, the Genetic Interpretation of I.Q. and Marxist-Leninist Ideology," *Bulletin of the British Psychological Society*, 35:449-451.
[32] Herrnstein, R. J., and Murray, C. 1994. *The Bell Curve*, N.Y.: Free Press; Itzkoff: S. W. 1994. *The Decline of Intelligence in the United States*, Westport, CT: Praeger; Rushton, J. P. 1994. *Race, Evolution and Behavior*, New Brunswick, N.J.: Transaction.
[33] Tavris, C. 1995. "A Place in the Sun," *Skeptic*, 3:3:58-93.
[34] Gottfredson, L. S. 1997. "Mainstream Science on Intelligence," *Intelligence*, 24:13-24; also reprinted in *The Wall Street Journal*, 1997.
[35] Terman, L. M., and Oden, M. H. 1948. *The Child Grows Up: Genetic Studies of Genius*, Stanford: Stanford Univ. Press., p. 18; Weiss, V. 1992. "Major Genes of General Intelligence," *Personality and Individual Differences*, 13:1115-1134, (using Terman,etc.).
[36] .Weiss, V. 1992. *op. cit.*
[37] Uchitelle, L. 2005. "College Degree Still Pays, but It's Leveling Off," *The New York Times*, Jan. 13.
[38] Gardner, H. 1983. *Frames of Mind*, N.Y.: Basic Books; Gardner, H. 1993. *Creating Minds*, N.Y.: Basic Books.
[39] Sternberg, R. J. 1988. *The Triarchic Mind: A New Theory of Intelligence*. N.Y.: Viking.
[40] Goleman, D. 1995. *Emotional Intelligence*, N.Y.: Bantam.
[41] Dimasio, A. R. 1994. *Descartes' Error*, N.Y.: Avon; Dimasio, A. R. 2003. *Looking for Spinoza*, N.Y.: Harcourt.
[42] Jakobson, R. 1971. *Studies on Child Language and Aphasia*, The Hague: Mouton; Luria, A. R., and Yudovich, F. I. 1956. *Speech and the Development of Mental Processes in the Child*, Baltimore: Penguin; Goldstein, K. 1940. *Human Nature in the Light of Psychopathology*, Cambridge: Harvard Univ. Press; Goldstein, K. 1934 (1963). *The Organism*, Boston: Beacon.
[43] Halstead, W. C. 1947. *Brain and Intelligence*, Chicago: Univ. of Chicago Press; Stenhouse, D. 1973. *The Evolution of Intelligence*, N.Y.: Harper.
[44] Fisher, R. A. 1970. *Statistical Methods for Research Workers*, 14th ed., N.Y.: Hafner Press, pp. 194-206; Jensen, A. R. 1989. "The relationship between learning and intelligence," in *Learning and Individual Differences*, 1:37-62.

[45] Dimasio, A. R. *op. cit*, f.n.; Jakobson, Luria, Goldstein, *op. cit.*, f.n. 39.
[46] Marx, J. L. 1982. "Auto-Immunity in Left Handers," *Science*, 217:144; Geschwind, N., and Bekar, P. 1982. "Left Handedness: Association with Immune Disease, Migraine, and Developmental Learning Disorder, *Proceedings of the National Academy of Sciences*, August.
[47] Money, J., and Ekhardt, A. A. 1972. *Man and Woman, Boy and Girl*, Baltimore: Johns Hopkins; Goldberg, S. 1973. *The Inevitability of Patriarchy*, N.Y.: Morrow.
[48] Kolata, G. 1983. "Math Genius May Have a Hormonal Basis," *Science*, 222:1312; Geschwind, N., Bekar, P. 1982. *Op. cit.* f.n. 44.
[49] Benbow, C. P., and Stanley, JU. C. 1983. "Sex Differences in Mathematical Reasoning Ability," *Science*, 222:1029-1031.
[50] Kolata, G. 1983. *Op. cit.*, f.n. 46.
[51] Itzkoff: S. W. 1983. *The Form of Man, the evolutionary origins of human intelligence*, Ashfield, MA: Paideia; Itzkoff, S. W. 1987. *Why Humans Vary in Intelligence*, Ashfield, MA: Paideia. See above books for the research evidence, both evolutionary and psychological.
[52] McMenamin, M. A. S., and MacMenamin, L. S. 1990. *The Emergence of Animals, The Cambrian Breakthrough*, N.Y.: Columbia Univ. Press; Long, J. A. 1995. *The Rise of Fishes*, Baltimore: Johns Hopkins; Radinsky, L. 1987. *The Evolution of Vertebrate Design*, Chicago: Univ. of Chicago Press.
[53] Gould, S. J., and Eldredge, N. 1977. "Punctuated Equilibrium...," *Paleobiology*, 3:115-151; Gould, S. J. 1976. "Biological Potential versus Biological Determinism," *Natural History*, 93:22-29; Gould, S. J. 1981. *The Mismeasure of Man*, N.Y.: W. W. Norton.
[54] Sepkoski, J. J. 1990. "The Taxonomic Structure of Periodic Extinctions," in *Global Catastrophes in Earth History* by Sharpton, V. L., and Ward, P. D., eds., Boulder: Geological Society of America; Raup, D. M. 1991. *Extinction: Bad Genes or Bad Luck*, N.Y.: Norton; Alvarez, L. W. 1983. "Experimental evidence that an asteroid impact led to the extinction of many species 65 million years ago," *Proceedings of the National Academy of Sciences*, 80(2):627-642; Stanley, S. M. 1988. "Paleozoic mass extinctions...," *American Journal of Science*, 288:334-352.
[55] MacLean, P. 1990. *The Triune Brain in Evolution*, N.Y.: Plenum; Jerison, H. J. 1973. *Evolution of Brain and Intelligence*, N.Y.: Academic Press; Colbert, E. H., and Morales, M. 1991. *Evolution of the Vertebrates*, 4th ed., N.Y.: Wiley Liss.
[56] Kemp, T. S. 1982. *Mammal-like Reptiles and the Origin of Mammals*, N.Y.: Academic Press; Simpson, G. G. 1952. *The Major Features of Evolution*, N.Y.: Columbia Univ. Press; Novacek, M J., *et al.*, 1997. "Epipubic Bones in Eutherian Mammals from the Late Cretaceous of Mongolia," *Nature*, 389:483-486.
[57] Cuvier, G. 1825. *Discourse on the Revolutions of the Surface of the Globe*, (Paris); Upchurch, G. R. 1989. "Terrestrial Environmental Changes and Extinction Patterns at the Cretaceous-Tertiary Boundary, North America," in *Mass Extinctions*, by S. K. Donovan, ed., N.Y.: Columbia Univ. Press; Colbert, E. H. 1986. "Mesozoic Tetrapod Extinctions: A Review," in *Dynamics of Extinction* by D. K. Elliott, ed., N.Y.: John Wiley; Itzkoff, S. W. 2000. *The Inevitable Domination by Man*, Ashfield, MA: Paideia. See Chs. 7, 8 for full research citations; Hu, Y., *et al.* 2005 "Ancient Mammals, 130mya, With Ingested Dinosaur Bones" *Nature*, January 13.
[58] Cann, R. L., Stoneking, M., and Wilson, A. 1987. "Mitochonrial DNA and Human Evolution," *Nature*, 325:31-36; Otte, M. 1998. "Comment on 'African Eve,'" *Current Anthropology*, June Supplement, Vol. 39; Groves, C. P. 1989. "A Regional Approach to the Problem of the Origin of Modern Humans," in *The Origin of Modern Humans...*" by Mellars and Stringer, eds., Princeton: Princeton Univ. Press; Wilford, J. N. 2003. "In Ancient Skulls from Ethio-

pia, Familiar Faces" (coexistence of African and Neanderthal humans, Richard Klein comments), *The New York Times*, 6/12/2003.

[59] Wolpoff, M., and Caspari, R. 1997. *Race and Human Evolution*, N.Y.: Simon and Schuster; Brown, P. 1993. "Recent Human Evolution in East Asia and Australia," in *Modern Humans and the Impact of Chronometric Dating* by Aitken, M. J., et al., Princeton: Princeton Univ. Press; Bar Yosef, O. 1993. "The Role of Western Asia in Modern Human Origins," in *Modern Humans and the Impact of Chronometric Dating* by Aitken, et al., op. cit.

[60] Stebbin, G. L. 1982. *Darwin to DNA, Molecules to Humanity*, San Francisco: Freeman; Goodman, M. 1990. "Primate Evolution at the DNA Level and a Classification of Hominoids," *Jrnl. Of Mol. Evol.*, 30:260-266; Gibbons, A. 1995. "When it Comes to Evolution, Humans Are in a Slow Class," *Science*, 3/31/2004, 267:1907-1908; Watson, J., 2003, has estimated the human genome as 22,000 years, an average animal structure.

[61] Itzkoff, S. W. 2000. *The Inevitable Domination by Man*, Ashfield, MA: Paideia, Chs. 11, 12, for the research; Boivin, M. 2003. Review of *The Inevitable Domination by Man*, *Contemporary Psychology*, October. Confirms the prediction on chronological separation of pongids and hominids in reviewed book; Brunet, M. 2003. "Seven Million Year Old Human Skull, 'Sabelanthropus tchadenensis' in Central Africa," *Nature*, 7/11/2003.

[62] Coon, C. S. 1962. *The Origin of Races*, N.Y.: Knopf; Coon, C. S., and Hunt, E. E. 1965. *The Living Races of Man*, N.Y.: Knopf.

[63] Klein, R. G. 1992. "The Archaeology of Modern Human Origins," *Evolutionary Anthropology*, 1:5-14; Klein, R. G. 1995. "Anatomy, Behavior, and Modern Human Origins," *Jrnl. Of World Prehistory*, 9:2:167-197; Bar-Yosef, O. 1996. "Modern Humans, Neanderthals and the Middle-Upper Paleolithic in Western Asia," in *The Origin of Modern Man* by Bar-Yosef and Cavalli-Sforza, eds., Forli: ABACO Edizioni.

[64] Klein, R. G. 1989. *The Human Career*, Chicago: Univ. of Chicago Press, p. 349, Fig. 72, p. 348, Fig. 7.3, p. 350; Schwartz, J. 1993. *What the Bones Tell Us*, N.Y.: Henry Holt, pp. 227-231.

[65] Davidson, I., and Noble, W. 1993. "Tools and Language in Human Evolution," in *Tools, Language and Cognition in Human Evolution*, K. Gibson and T. Ingold, eds., Cambridge: Cambridge Univ. Press, pp. 363-388; Marshack, A. 1976. "Some Implications of the Paleolithic Evidence for the Origin of Language," *Current Anthropology*, June, 17:2:2274-282.

[66] Leakey, R. 1981. *The Making of Mankind*, N.Y.: Dutton, pp. 193-196; Clottes, J. 1996. *The Cave Beneath the Sea*, N.Y.: Harry Abrams.

[67] Brues, A. 1977. *People and Races*, N.Y.: Macmillan, pp. 258-259; Coon, C. S. 1965. *The Living Races of Man*, N.Y.: Knopf, pp. 150-152; Murdock, G. P. 1964. "Genetic Classification of the Austronesian Languages," *Ethnology*, 3:117-126.

[68] Darlington, C. D. 1969. *The Evolution of Man and Society*, London: Allen and Unwin, pp. 613-618; Thomo, A. 1964. "Die Enstehung der Mongoliden," *Homo*, 15:1-12. Note: The terracotta soldiers unearthed as a memorial to a Chinese Qin dynasty king, c.300-200 B.C.E. still show their Kazakh-like physiognomy (recognized by current Chinese authorities). This is c.1,500 years beyond the Shang invasions c. 2000-1800 B.C.E. of probably Persian-like people.

[69] Littleton, C. S. 1985. "The Indo-European Strain in Japanese Mythology," *Mankind Quarterly*, 26:152-174; Darlington, C. D. 1969. *Op. cit.*, p. 618, note 62; Coon, C. S. 1982. *Racial Adaptations*, Chicago: Nelson Hall, pp. 156-157.

[70] Pearson, R. 1970. *Introduction to Anthropology*, N.Y.: Holt, Rinehart, Winston, p. 553; Roberts, R. G., et al. 1990. "Thermoluminescence Dating of a 50,000-year-old Human Occupation Site in Northern Australia," *Nature*, 345:153-156; Habgood, P. J. 1985. "The Origin of

the Australian Aborigines..." in *Hominid Evolution Past, Present, and Future*, P. O. Tobias, ed., N.Y.: Alan Liss, pp. 367-380.

[71] Theunisson, B., *et al.* 1990. "The Establishment of a Chronological Framework for the Hominid-bearing Deposits of Java," in *Establishment of a Geological Framework for Paleoanthropology*, by L. F. LaPorte, Boulder: Geological Society of America; Itzkoff, S. W. 2000. *The Inevitable Domination by Man*, Ashfield, MA: Paideia, pp. 302-303.

[72] Brues, A. 1977. *People and Races, op. cit.*, p. 295; Coon, C. S. 1965. *The Living Races of Man, op. cit.*, Plate 43; Howells, W. 1963. *Back of History*, N.Y.: Doubleday Anchor, p. 90.

[73] Coon, C. S. 1962. *op. cit.*, pp. 649-657; Coon, C. S. 1982. *Op. cit.*, pp. 149, 154; Wolpoff, M., and Caspari, R. 1997, *op. cit.*, pp. 267-268.

Additional Bibliography—Chapter 4

Burnham, S. 1993. *America's BiModal Crisis*, Athens, Georgia: Foundation for Human Understanding.

Butcher, H. J. 1968. *Human Intelligence: Its Nature and Assessment*, N.Y.: Harper and Row.

Eysenck, H. J. 1971. *Race, Intelligence and Education*, London: Temple Smith.

Flynn, J. R. 1980. *Race, IQ And Jensen*, London: Routledge and Kegan Paul.

Gould, S. J. 1981. *The Mismeasure of Man*, N.Y.: W. W. Norton and Co.

Guilford, J. P. 1967. *The Nature of Human Intelligence*, N.Y.: McGraw-Hill.

Jensen, A. R. 1980. *Bias In Mental Testing*, N.Y.: The Free Press.

Jensen, A .R. 1998. *The g Factor, The Science of Mental Ability*, Westport, CT: Praeger.

Loehlin, J. C., Lindzey, G., Spuhler, J. N. 1975. *Race Differences in Intelligence*. San Francisco: W. H. Freeman.

Modgil, S., and Modgil, C., eds. 1987. *Arthur Jensen, Consensus and Controversy*. N. Y.: The Falmer Press.

Pearson, R. 1991. *Race, Intelligence and Bias in Academe*, Washington, D.C.: Scott-Townsend.

Pearson, R. 1992. *Shockley on Eugenics and Race*, Washington, D.C.: Scott-Townsend Publishers.

Pearson, R. 1996. *Heredity and Humanity*, Washington, D. C.: Scott-Townsend.

Seligman, D. 1992. *A Question of Intelligence*, N.Y.: Birch Lane-Carol Group.

Spitz, H. H. 1986. *The Raising Of Intelligence*, Hillsdale, N.J.: Lawrence Erlbaum Associates.

Taylor, J. 1992. *Paved with Good Intentions*, N.Y.: Carroll and Graf Publishers.

Vernon, P. E. 1979. *Intelligence: Heredity and Environment*, San Francisco: W. H. Freeman.

Part II—The Possible

Chapter 5

Shaping Our Human Nature

"The other night, just before dusk, I walked across the pasture with a bucket of grain. Two dozen chickens followed me in a mob. Some came running toward me, wings flapping, as if with enough room they might actually take off. I led them into their pen, scattered the grain and closed the gate. Then I drove the ducks and the geese into their yard. 'Drove' is too strong a word. I hinted at the direction I wanted them to go, and they went. I opened another gate and led the horses down to the barnyard. When they had been fed, I stepped into the pigpen. The gilt came over for a rubdown, and the barrow flopped down beside her. They lay back to back, eyes closed, pale pink bellies available for scratching.

Some evenings I notice the haze that settles in the valley nearby or the big orange moon coming up over the trees. But that night I noticed how we all fit together, the animals and the humans. The piglets arrive pretty wild. Baby chicks clatter about the brooder house in fear. But time passes, and they all settle down. They seem to tame themselves, somehow.

That night I suddenly realized all the ways that they've tamed me. I never rush the ducks. It only confuses them. I never ask too much when herding chickens. The horses expect a certain presence from me, which changes with every situation. The pigs want joy and vigorous scratching.

None of the animals seem to want me to be other than human. But they want me to be a human who knows how the world looks to them and respects it.

All of our animals, except one, were raised among humans from birth. That one is Nell, the mustang. We bought her not far from our farm here in upstate New York, but she was adopted as a weanling in Nevada – part of the federal adoption program for wild horses.

I've seen other mustangs captured, so I have a good idea what it was like for her. She's 17 now and has lived the last decade with us. She's been trained, trailered, ridden and cared for. And yet it's always a tossup whether she'll let me catch her.

Our animals show their trust in us every day. But sometimes Nell trusts us, and sometimes she doesn't. The freeze brand on her neck isn't the only sign of that long-ago capture. All the rest of us, animal and human, live together in a single place. Nell lives in her own. She somehow reserves the right to withhold herself, to stand apart.

The chickens grow placid, the pigs learn to like us, and the other horses go on with their lives. And yet the most meaningful moments, after all these years, are when Nell crosses over from her world to ours. She walks right up, as if to ask where I've been, and settles her head in my arms. I feel the power of the choice she has made every time she makes it."

Verlyn Klinkenborg[1]

The Question

Is there such a thing as a human nature? Real enough query, when one considers the evolutionary facts. Is there any longer a vertebrate animal nature, unshaped by humans?

Clearly, by c.500 K B.P., there were no other animal challengers to human survival, if not dominance as a genus, *Homo*. But, the brain kept growing. This seemingly autochthonous, *orthoselective*, inertial process of brain growth and dominance had an inner dynamic that the outside world reinforced, in success. It was positively selective over many millennia, if not millions of years in clearing the savannahs of Africa of rival primates, even hominids such as the australopithecines and their kin. Eventually the neo-cortex exploded in size (as we noted in Chapter 4) some 200-100 thousand years ago in a new balloon-brained, baby-faced, strong but calcium gracile creature called *Homo sapiens sapiens*, Cro-Magnon. His bones and cultural effusions we now find in Eur-Asia, dating back to c.45,000 years ago.

What do these undisputed facts mean for an understanding of our fellow humans today, and tomorrow?

First, the instinctual grip of our mammalian genetics has been largely attenuated. We feel powerful emotions of nurturing protectiveness, hate, bondedness, as with all primates. However, there is no longer a mammalian directiveness of behavior transmitted from our genetic structure that cannot be cancelled by the thinking brain. We can violate every law of sociobiological survival seemingly passed on through this mammalian genetic heritage. Conversely, there is no evidence that the brain can discipline the vast reservoir of directionless emotions that have welled up, accompanying the growth of the neo-cortex. The new brain is as yet untutored so as to show us its way, and to limit the damage we do to our own species.

The environment that supposedly shapes us (the egalitarian dogmatists have never admitted to this) is the same culture that our brain creates. The environment into which we emotionally crave to inaugurate the *have-nots* is the creation of the *haves*. Those presently outside the dominant civilizational culture must provide the brain power that recognizes the meanings of advanced civilizational symbolic structures. Otherwise, they create their own world of unstable symbolic behaviors. That is, until the culture of the *have nots* dominates and becomes the symbolic norm. Barbarism or a new "civilization"? It all depends on one's definitions.

Understanding the Problem

The great brain and civilizational heritage of the descendants of *Homo sapiens sapiens,* both east and west, has created an unprecedented evolutionary and taxonomic situation. We are in a category of life unique to the past, not in violation of evolution's rules, but in a novel extension of these rules, as with all innovative developments in nature's unfolding scene on this planet, Earth. Mammalian instinct can no longer guide us. Nor can the mysticism of the theologians.

Our human nature lies in the mysterious reconstruction of the human brain in its developing incarnations over the past several million years. Our knowledge is incomprehensibly incomplete. But, so are the existing species-wide similarities and dissimilarities in brain structure and function. There are still many models of the human brain. Thus exist the myriad patterns in cultural symbolism, the meanings that human brains spew out that reflect its inner complexities.

At the most powerfully dynamic end of the range that the evolution of *Homo sapiens* has thrown up is the brain of *Homo sapiens sapiens*, a brain that knows *no* racial coloration or divide. This brain created literate complex, urban civilizations of high cognitive content and demand. Indeed, these civilizational achievements have not been accompanied by lessened bestialities roaring up over our prudence and onto the supposed civilizational scene. Clearly this brain, and its civilizational accomplishments, is a work in progress.

The other model stems from great populations of still incompletely evolved sapiens newly emancipated from subsistence hunting, gathering, and garden agriculture. In between is a universal blending of intellectual skills and cultural outlooks on the human experience. The travails of the twenty-first century already reflect this new challenge to the understanding and confrontation with that which we call "human nature."

Let there be no hesitation as to which model of human nature will emerge dominant. For hundreds of millions of vertebrate and mammal years, the larger and more complex brain has fed off the instabilities in Earth's ecology to triumph over lethargic genetically-leashed forms of vertebrate life. The learning and creating brain of *Homo sapiens sapiens* will eventually push the borderline intelligence of our fellows to the side, as it has over the last five million years.

By the middle of this century, when demography will tell its story of paralysis and chaos, these two models of human intelligence will have to confront each other in this global society. It will take a long time to bring this state of conflict to clear political and intellectual consciousness. Perhaps in a century or two beyond the inevitable debasement of middle-class life, the human community will be forced to cast an eye to the past. Then life in the *Homo sapiens sapiens* zone of the civilizational middle class will again define the criteria as to how we explore human nature. They may then demand of the leadership a universal political reconstruction that could bring enduring social peace and ecological balance, what we now purport to envision for our children and grandchildren.

Exploring Human Nature

Evolution has exploded onto our planet a new taxonomic class of living beings. Rooted in part to its mammalian and primate roots, a surging brain inside a delicate bony encasement, evolution has spawned upon this earth a wholly new character of life. The revolution is incomplete because this new form of man, *Homo sapiens sapiens*, was formed out of one of the many branches of this hominid surge. Other humans, living apart for most of the civilizational expansion of the northerners, created cultures consonant with their brain/intellectual possibilities. Recently, scientific knowledge and the power of this Cro-Magnon intelligence has itself created the current demographic hypertrophy from the south, of marginal human intelligence. This is the only way to explain the cultural degradation of so many billions of lives now upon our earth.

Eventually, if evolution is our clue, and it must be, the powerfully intelligent will shut down the demographic explosion of these civilizationally incapable billions. We must thus phrase our inquiry into human nature in terms of highest human intelligence, an intelligence that in the future will *not* have a recognizable racial or physical phenotype.

To the questions, who are we? what are we by nature?, the answer must be agnostic. We are what our brain and body will tell us in expressing themselves culturally over time. There is no given human nature when it comes to the concretia of cultural life or knowledge. In simple terms, we create our human nature daily. But not without limits.

There are those with the power to block off human creativity and innovation, even change. History, down to the twentieth century has shown us that pharaonic Egypt, medieval Catholicism, communist totalitarianism, contemporary recidivistic Islam can destroy and hurt, but never seal up the dykes. The question concerns the freedoms allowable in civilized, democratic, advanced nations. How far can both scientific and social explorations be allowed to run unfettered in a tightly dependent world, one in which so much today unseen, is possible tomorrow?

The great but unspoken example is the ongoing demographic explosion that modern science and medicine have unleashed around the world. In all earlier civilized societies there has been at the least an implicit understanding that the population of a city or nation had to be held within the limits of the resources, agricultural or ecological. This is one reason nations undertook the military road to expand the reach of their economic security by enveloping their neighbors and subjecting them to political and economic subservience.

Our demographic explosion, fewer children dying at birth, extending the age range of adults, inhibiting plague and starvation, all without conscious attempts to limit demography down the line into the next generation has become a moral as well as a physical disaster. How many good, often devout physicians went off to the underdeveloped world to fend off disease (nature), which held in balance the populations of the undeveloped world? They had little overt interest in the more problematic issues of birth and population control. So they sailed back to their tea and crumpets (gin and tonics), smug in a philanthropy that ultimately made victims of those they purported to help.

Why not even speak about the wholesale lurch into industrialization that in the nineteenth century opened the dykes to the demographic explosion of the industrial proletariat. Could this advance in material and scientific, industrial, technological capabilities have been more nuanced and guided, so as to not create this millennial crisis of urbanism and the environment?

Today, we seek to ban the cloning of humans, asexual reproduction, a seemingly Frankensteinian overshooting of the capabilities of science to do the new. Test-tube babies are already history. Screening the genome of the unborn to discover serious disabilities, then possible abortion, is also part of medical orthodoxy. So, too, the ultrasound sex selection by parents of the gender of their unborn, and, of course, possible abortion of the unwanted sex. We debate the use of gene therapies that will enhance *myostatins* for muscular growth, because while they may aid in developing greater muscular control for the aged or victims of muscular dystrophy, they are already being used to build muscles in athletes, possibly distorting what is natural in competitive sports, and its record keeping.

The possibilities for reshaping the human genome, broadening the definition of reproductive orthodoxy, even the nature of marriage, heterosexual and homosexual, can and is altering our vision of the natural in social life. But some innovations are as yet unacceptable. Rarely has the prohibition of innovation, by priests, mullahs, rabbis, commissars, kings, even a U.S. House of Representatives, not been overturned by subsequent generations.

We ask, what is a more rational form of human guidance over the shape of human cultural life? In the 1950s, we turned away from the deadly morning sickness palliative, thalidomide. We banned the use of DDT after its development and use. No more will a drug come to market without careful governmentally-regulated scientific testing. Hopefully, we have seen the last of poison gas used against soldier and civilian. The world condemns, as it should, the development and possible use of the atomic bomb. Someday, we may even obtain unanimity in the world community against state-sponsored terror, innocence purposely destroyed.

Clearly, we try things out, then reject, after the fact, given the evidence that it violates a human standard. In this way, we gradually discover human nature. Certainly the Sumerians, the creators of the first literate civilization, would have been outraged by the atomic bomb, terrorism against the innocent, perhaps even some versions of our own sexual "perversions," as contrasted to their own.

Here is the rub. We cannot and have not rejected new injections into the mulligan stew of human nature behaviors for all time. All things are to be reconsidered in the context of the new. Thus there are not absolutes, no linear directionality toward utopia, the real humanity discovered once and for all. The cultural relativists, at first anthropologists, now political haters of high civilization and educated intelligence, see in the universality of certain cultural institutions, a searchlight into the mystery. They view the fact that all human cultures as we found them in the nineteenth century engaged in technological fabrication, plastic arts, dance, ritual and religion, moral prohibitions, political structures, as signs of a universal humanity.

To this view literacy, urbanism, the high intellectual arts and sciences seem to be extensions only of a mass, quantitative rather than qualitative difference. Thus the cultural relativists' veneration for traditions of head hunting, polygamy, tribal autocracy, mutilation, free expressive nudity. What might seem morally pernicious to today's internet users, they reply by comparing the simple folks with civilization's dropping of atomic bombs, current female stylistic decorations, tyranny in the modern world. It is all relative, sayeth Margaret Mead.

They are outraged, viewing in perspective Western civilization, science, technology, literacy and abstraction, democratic law, rolling over these derelict cultures and pushing them into demographic and economic collapse. In reality, these folk are back, now packed into the stench of urban wastelands.

Both sides of the current intellectual spectrum, the relativists and the censors, seem to acknowledge the need for historical restraint. Suggestively, the restraints that the most advanced abstract cultures of our time are forced to place on the new do have their roots in something both historical and universal.

It may go back as far as the lives of the Cro-Magnons, 20,000 years ago, when there are indications that a tough series of centuries, extreme cold, and the gradual disappearance of the great mammals, forced them to face up to want, and the only animals who could survive the snow and cold, species of deer and elk. There are indications that they disciplined themselves in the hunt, and began to herd and tend these animals so as to preserve their food supply.

The ability to think ahead in times precarious, a not unusual characteristic of historic civilizations, argues that there may be an imprint left in our genes from those cultures that lived together to survive, and by contrast the Neanderthals, Patagonians, Tasmanians, the Bushmen, who did not This discipline ultimately transitioned into the literate, civilized life. It has served to shape our choices as to what will become our human nature in the future.

The Struggle to Understand

The model of possible understanding of this mysterious thing we call human nature begins within a context of human self-discovery and the free evolutionary development of that as-yet mysterious creature inside our brain and body. This model of *Homo sapiens sapiens* can only exist in a harmonious social setting, itself created by its own high intellectual achievements. There is another model or context for human life that is also being played out in those vast urban *favellas* of human degradation. Say what you will about the possibilities of human redemption from these life circumstances. Those who are imprisoned, subject to the random dynamics events around, aren't capable of human self-discovery. Eventually we will realize that the intelligence of ancient Athens, c.450 B.C.E., is still the wave of the future, not Mexico City, 2005 C.E.

The modernly educated who are capable of posing questions about human nature will be forced to establish the criteria for deciding what our model is to be. This is not possible for the billions who live below the ken of middle-class civilizational life. The pathology of intergenerational illiteracy, and social impoverishment must first disappear. How can we begin the process of cultural reconstruction that will reveal the civilizational character of human nature?

To begin, we have to agree about the problem. Then, two necessary, but not sufficient conditions will determine the enhanced consciousness about the *who* and *what* of humans. These challenges pivot on the creation of a global, secular, scientific, democratic, socially egalitarian post-twenty-first- second-century civilization?

1. We have to pull the human population of the Earth down to rational and sustainable levels amenable to attaining a decent quality of life for all. The absolute numbers as we go forward will and should be subject to analysis and debate. Some individuals and nations will refuse to have short-circuited their rights to reproduce at their own will. The world will have to let these folks and peoples face the consequences of their own behavioral freedoms, but also the impact of this freedom on their neighbors inhabiting this globe. Unlike today, no bail out except when global survival becomes at risk. Then, sharp international intervention. The caveat, freedom to fail is possible on the condition that the rest of humanity is not put in jeopardy.

2. A likewise necessary condition is the agreement by the world community to go forward in the conscious raising of intelligence, I.Q., levels. Once a consensus is reached as to how humans can begin to live lives of personal re-

sponsibility leading to economic security, social peace, democratic and humane political leadership, the pace of reform will rev up.

We must teach ourselves that human nature is not a given, either from the socio-biological clarities of lower animal behavior, nor from the theological mysticism of those who would force their own priorities of life down every one else's throat. Hopefully, we will not foreclose the future by banning biomedical research that might throw new light on the biosocial nature of humans. This means going forward in experimentation, possibly even leading to "asexual" reproduction, cloning. If it turns out to be a disaster, *then* ban it.

Some time in the future, we must be able to unlock more of the mysteries concerning human biosocial differences. We have before us a great frontier of knowledge to uncover that should make it easier to recreate the best that civilization has given us. Of course, over time we will have to agree as to the nature and extent of this high intelligence that we want shared among the citizenry of the world. Above all, we need to use what knowledge we have and can obtain to create the conditions so that high secularly educated intelligence can lead us once and for all beyond the random chaos of events that has before and is now leading us into international social paralysis.

The true difference between a "liberal" and a "reactionary"? The former does not fear the new, the rational challenge of lifting the curtain of knowledge. The "reactionary" finds ever new reasons to confront the experientially new by saying "*no*."

Demographic Rationality

The demographic history of our planet shows cycles of sharp increase in population, inevitably followed by social antinomies that drag societies and civilizations back into a less optimistic balance with nature.

Ancient Greece, late Christian Rome, and the twentieth-century shrinkage of population in the former Soviet states are examples. Without dollar-producing oil wells, the Islamic world might yet pull back from producing the 6 to 12 children-per-family now viewed as their divine right. The diminution of this wealth, even from afar, as in Egypt, Palestine, Jordan, could precipitate an awareness that nature's bounty won't be up to it. Here portends millennial impoverization. Could dimmed reason prevail?

Falling birth rates among the middle classes today in Europe and the U.S. reflect the reality that the frontier explosion of seventeenth- and eighteenth-century indigenous Americans and Europeans, the good old days of emptiness, no longer operates. As a result, individual family prudence argues for fewer children, more highly educated, the wealth less likely to be dissipated by filial division. No longer can we send one son to the monastery, another off on a crusade. In a world of the highly educated, where parents need not have many children to insure their security in old age, rationality and discipline should win out over profligacy.

Perhaps the most hopeful demonstration of the relationship of rational leadership planning for the future is exemplified in modern China. Mao and his cohorts, in their more conscious moments, sheared off northern Kashmir and then Tibet to insure the long-term water resources of China. They enforced an equally controversial one-child-per-woman policy, using police state methods to insure the discipline. Remember, in peasant societies, children are often the only guarantors that parents will survive into old age.

Recall the story of Chinese demography, so similar to the experience of the West. The population of China in the first century CE, the Augustan era, was in the Roman Imperial range of 50-60 million people, within a much smaller geographical swath than Imperial Rome, or even their contemporary continental reach. It was stable until about the middle of the seventeenth century, c.70 million. By 1750, the population is thought to have reached 140 million; 1850—342 million; 1930—somewhere between 342 and 478 million.[2] From 1930 to today, even amidst terrible political and economic chaos, Japanese invasion, internal civil war, the population has soared to 1.3+ billion people.

The communist leadership was well aware that even Mao's "Red Book" could not lift up this vast population of overwhelmingly impoverished people. This radical hope for population stabilization continued well after the death of Mao in 1976. As conditions improved, the forced abortions and sterilizations became less necessary and softer penalties were imposed on those Han ethnic Chinese without special permission for an extra child. No free education, health care, and other governmentally-sponsored privileges for such young. Second and third children were on their own.

Parents must have gotten the point. All women, educated or not, opted for this precious singleton. The educational demographics were in this way not skewed toward the lowest classes, as in the U.S. and Europe (welfare, poverty, and feminism). By 2004, China's population growth has dipped well below the 2.1-children-per-female necessary for population stabilization. The reproductive profile is now closer to the European norm, and population is beginning to decrease, to the great alarm of western liberal ideologues.

The message is clear even to the poorest of Chinese wanting sons to take care of them in old age. Ultrasound technology, sadly, would inexpensively help in such decision making. But also, parents can accept the fact that there is a greater good, both for the individual and society, in lowering this population burden on the land. Now, the nation itself will ensure the well-being of the old, especially so if their one child is educated and wealthy.

Japan also gives us a demonstration of the power of a high intelligence population, again under rational leadership, ready to take itself in hand and bring the demographic time bomb under control. The islands of Japan were already well filled with people in the latter part of the nineteenth century.[3] At the end of World War II, a defeated military staggered back into a ruined nation. Having lost many of its most able men in the war, cousins picked up the reproductive task, the population zoomed.

It was clear by the 1960s that Japan was going to recover, even prosper economically. But now, with 120 million people crammed into a group of volcanic islands the size of Montana, she would have to confront her population explosion. The teaser was the possibility of expanding living standards. The first solution was abortion on demand. There were no theological or ideological inhibitions to block the practical argument: first, the living must live decently. Life brought into our world should have the possibility of humane fulfillment. Else, what is the point of life? The introduction of the birth control pill in the late sixties allowed an odious, if necessary, medical procedure of national policy to fade into history.

Individual Choice Creates Human Nature

Since the early years of the twentieth century, we have had predictive scientific evidence about human intelligence variability *within* ethnic populations, as well as recorded differences in intelligent behaviors *between* ethnic, racial, and religious populations. There always has been a tacit recognition of the biological factor in human personality exemplified in the tradition of family elders choosing the spouses of their progeny. Elites have always attempted to marry within their own social class, else within their own ethnic group, clearly, to preserve their genetic interests.

The quickening fears of parents with regard to the abilities of their children, the efforts to give them every additional opportunity to rise within the educational and professional system reflect an awareness that if the genes aren't all that they could be, perhaps nurture and social influence might push them up one or two notches, and thus, success. Look at the Kennedys!

First, get them into Harvard, perhaps they will meet a nice Radcliffe girl. And if not Harvard, perhaps Amherst College, after all Smith and Mt. Holyoke are right down the road. The enormous dynamic of modern society has blurred these close controls over who marries whom, so, too, the feminist option not to marry, to have a career unburdened by diaper changing. In addition, the barrage of intimidating propaganda about the reality of environmental amelioration has blinded perceptions about the genetic sources for I.Q. differences. New ideological layers of confusion and disappointment, "why aren't my adopted children doing as well as they should, look at the advantages we are giving them?"

A story is told of a young Japanese-American college graduate, in the late 1940s, taking her egoistic Jewish fiancé (average, 115-118 I.Q.) to California to meet her parents. Unlike his future wife, he was not a scholarship student at the fine college they attended, but from a well off-family, and thus with excellent prospects. Her parents once had a fairly prosperous farm. But after being interned during the war, and a forced sale of the farm, they were reduced to a roadside vegetable stand. One day during the visit while the daughter was alone with her mother, the mother wistfully whispered to her daughter, "If you marry this Jewish man, how intelligent will your children be?"

The Northeast Asiatics have no hesitation in recognizing their own general superior intelligence, all the while not barring their women from marrying highly intelligent Caucasoid men. Personal observation argues that some of this preference is due to the more enlightened spousal treatment by educated men of European and American background. Despite deeply-rooted cultural traditions, the Asiatics are yet pragmatic. Since the downfall both of the Japanese nationalistic Samurai tradition, as well as the ideological communism of China, the Japanese opted for scientific and intellectual advance under the full cloak of the Western civilizational program. Egotistic about their own civilizational heritage and their conjoint national intelligence profiles, they expect to dominate the old West by the mid-twenty-first century.

The widespread use of ultrasound technology to determine the future sex of unborn children, the willingness to undergo abortion for family protection and advancement, argue for the adoption of any new technological advance that offers pragmatic possibilities for upward mobility and social security. If any new technology proves to predict the future post-natal intelligence of their children, they will most probably be the first to invoke its use.

Given the presently intimidated awareness of the reality of genetic intelligence by all educated populations around the world, there will still be a real possibility for individual initiative. The ideological leadership cadres will have to cede their suppressive constraints. Governmental power to mandate or prohibit in the intimate dimensions of life is always dependent on governmental power to deliver the goods. By the mid-twenty-first century, governmental pledges (welfare, Medicaid, Medicare, Social Security) will be radically diminished as compared with 2005. The social dynamics of constraint and individual responsibility among all economic classes may then enter into the demographic equation.

The cloning of humans could be a reality before the middle of the century. Even while opposed by the Western establishment on "ethical" grounds, the first cloned human baby could be delivered in a Chinese, Japanese, or Korean research hospital. Cloning a human being does involve a radical change from current forms of "artificial" insemination and birthing techniques, since it constitutes a form of vegetative reproduction. Vanity of the powerful may stimulate the funding of such research. The "leaders" love themselves too much for such experiments not to be undertaken. So, too, will be the legitimate challenge of expanding the horizons of science, medicine and technology.

The cloning of a human being may have implicit Constitutional protection under the First Amendment. Here, the right to research and experiment is likened to freedom of expression, unless there is a clear and present danger, public safety, national security. The attempt to ban such efforts in advance could hardly meet that standard of research preemption. As the legal profession has argued successfully before the courts, the banning of cloning would fall under the interdiction of such a governmental prohibition, unless there is a "compelling public interest."[4]

It is highly unlikely that the cloning of humans will turn out to be the universal or macro-response to a stirring human need for higher intelligence and behaviors. More likely, as the scientific study of the human genome continues to release its secrets about medical susceptibilities and wayward genetic outcomes in mental health, we will eventually unlock the metabolic tell-tale signs of intelligence variability. We are now able to predict in the fetus the sex of the neonate, Down's syndrome signals, cystic fibrosis, plus at least twelve other birth defects, both mental and physical. Given such indications, parents are almost uniformly choosing abortion, regardless of religious affiliation.[5]

Soon, the enzymatic signals of M1M1, M1M2, or M2M2 intelligent humans? So-called ethicist gurus are already horrified that this early fetal knowledge is being translated into such therapeutic abortions, soon choices among the Petri dishes. Sadly, too few ethicist tears being shed about medical experiments, involved in rescuing newborns, before the seventh month, these fetuses often weighing less than a pound, and almost always burdened with multiple and permanent disabilities.

When we begin to unlock the internal hormonal signals of human intellectual/neurological function, else gain this knowledge in the process of in vitro fertilization, a revolution is likely to occur. We may see the final transition from traditional sexual intercourse as the efficient cause of fertilization leading to birth of a human baby. Instead, we may find the reproductive process to begin outside the female body, in the scientific analysis of the entire post-natal biosocial profile of a future child. Soon future genetic intelligence potential, a large swath of knowledge about the medical and mental potential of this future human could be revealed. Sexual relations, both hetero- and homo-, could then make their formal transition to the world of entertainment pleasures.

If and when this occurs, there will surely be great indignation, attempts through the law to *a priori* (before the fact) prohibition of such procedures. Unfortunately, the genie is already out of the bottle. The only hope for the clergy of religious intractability is intervention by Deity itself.[6]

Something new is on the horizon *vis à vis* the cognitive abilities of future humans. We will no doubt be surprised by new genetic/cognitive intelligence models that differ from those set forth in Chapter 4. New knowledge equals new definitions as to what constitutes human nature. Here, the freely advancing core forms of knowledge will ever act to contravene given power structure arrangements. Given highly intelligent educated populations, decisions will be made by millions of independent free-thinking individuals. Here is democracy exemplified, where the rulers follow the lead of the ruled.

Just as with the Berlin Wall, which fell because people voted with their feet, so, too, the current egalitarian redistributionist myth will dissolve. As soon as ordinary people see positive results in pre-natal biochemical indicators for high intelligence, they will act. No power in the world can limit these kinds of free decisions.

The ongoing global network of information exchange will release such results and rapidly. News will spread like wildfire. Parents, traditionally hesitant about having their children out-span them in talent and energy, will soon realize the familial power that high intelligence progeny contribute. The excitement and portent for a life of security in all human *ethnes* will spread beyond the non-ideological nations, eventually penetrating the Third World, including Islam and Christendom. "Imagine, our fetus is going to have an I.Q. of c.130."

The blatant competitive implications for nations and peoples will cause new political decisions to be made by leadership and elite. How can national intellectual levels be increased, and rapidly? Perhaps a vial or two of Nobel laureate sperm or from the six-foot blond Danes of the Cryos International Sperm Bank at the University of Arhus in Denmark. Inseminated into volunteered populations, the educational outcomes of the progeny could be evaluated objectively.

Such choices are being made all over the world, even today. What matters is not the race of the donor, nor the ethnicity of the recipient. Who but a "racist" would oppose such internationally uplifting ventures? What matters only is that the nation or ethnicity prospers, producing generations of productive, law-evaluating and curious citizens.

Human Nature Is in the Making

We have certainly changed the "nature" of countless species of animal and plant life. Subject to the impact of humans on the ecology of plants and animals, most succumb; a few survive and prosper—starlings, rats. Else, through our conscious selection of certain geno/phenotypes, others are pressed into extinction. Our barnyards and fields are witness to the changing nature of life around us. Why not humans adapting to a world that can no longer operate randomly as heretofore? Too much suffering.

We have only historic models of human existence lived at the highest levels of what intelligent, educated, civilized peoples believed to be important for life itself. The actual concretia of life in the future has to be worked out day-by-day in the process of organizing the new, rationally throwing away some old patterns, integrating innovations that now seem possible for the enhancement of our intellectual and moral life.

There will be those who will say "no" before the fact. They, of course, have recourse to a higher authority, *Who* then transmits to these of the theological stamp this higher truth. The yet-powerful say we are enjoined to bow before such directives. The Scottish philosopher of the mid-eighteenth century, David Hume, friend of J.-J. Rousseau and master skeptic, long ago explained to us the fallaciousness of supernatural claims:

"No testimony is sufficient to establish a miracle, unless the testimony be of such a kind that its falsehood would be more miraculous than the fact which it endeavors to establish."[7]

Were the peoples of the world educated to the civilizational mark, they would, having ingested such arguments and, sharing Hume's eighteenth-century rationality in their twenty-first-century lives, have thrown off this social incubus.

We have two critical responsibilities with which we will struggle throughout our century and into the future: Our global asynchrony with civilizational history, 1: demography; 2. intellectual capital.

Once we gain control over these two concrete civilizational barriers, then we can truly face up to the challenges of carefully, experimentally, taking on the new that may remold our human nature. Face it, we have been molding human nature ever since humans burned down their houses in order to taste of a succulent boar.

In the meantime, there will be a struggle with the ideological naysayers who worry more about the possible creation of a few thousand cloned humans than they do about a century of environmental despoliation caused by a tidal wave of humans, the detritus of the internal combustion engine. Which of these has and could change human nature more?

Important intellectual and societal struggles are not won in a day. As long as individuals can maintain a modicum of personal autonomy (human nature?) from the long reach of the reactionary ideological institutions of the moment, they will determine their own human nature. That is how this battle will be won.

Endnotes, Chapter 5

[1] Klinkenborg, Verlyn. 2004. *The New York Times*, 9/4/2004.
[2] Latourette, K. S. 1934. *The Chinese, Their History and Culture*, Vol. II, N.Y.: Macmillan, pp. 6-9.
[3] Japan had an estimated population of 36 million in 1875 (geographic size of Montana); the United States, had a population of 50 million in 1880.
[4] Alexander, B. 2004. "Free to Clone," *The New York Times Magazine*, 9/26/2004.
[5] Harmon, Amy. *The New York Times*, 6/20/2004.
[6] Henig, R. M. 2004. *Pandora's Baby: How the First Test Tube Babies Sparked the Reproductive Revolution*, Boston: Houghton Mifflin.
[7] Hume, D. 1992 (1758). *Writings on Religion* Ed. by A. Flew. La Salle, IL.: Open Court.

Chapter 6

Democratic Polity

The Problem

It is not an abstract demand to argue that a futuristic, secular, scientific world community has to opt for a democratic system of governances in order to fulfill the cognitive demands of high intelligence. Democracy is ostensibly the freely-established, self-imposed right of citizens of a nation or nations to determine how they will live.

From time immemorial, humans have lived in a dangerous and dynamic physical and social environment. We are individually too weak to go it alone, as contrasted with certain lonely animal survivalists like bears or gorillas. We cling to our fellows both for physical and emotional sustenance. We form communities of deeply-rooted allegiances to protect ourselves and to meet a wide variety of critical challenges.

How to decide what to do in such challenging environments? In days of yore when the world of man and nature was simpler, groups of elders would meet with the younger warrior elite to make what were often life-or-death decisions. These decisions had to be met on a monthly, yearly basis, often, momentarily. The old veterans had the experience, their passions softened by age. Here, democracy functioned so that it harmonized with social necessity.

Today, it is more complicated because time-essential decisions come as a steady barrage. Also, a world having such vast numbers of citizens spread over extended geographies makes it impossible that national action will issue out of face-to-face small group decisions. Manipulating vested interests, political and economic, is a common theme. The mass media now have their own power agendas, the purpose often to warp sober reason.

Modern industrial, urban environments of the twentieth and twenty-first centuries have reshaped the original meanings of democratic urban life. It is a long stretch to compare the so-called twenty-first-century "democratic" formulas with those of the Sumerian towns, the Hellenic cities. We can no longer call the assembly of five hundred to the civic theatre in town center, and after a six-hour debate call for a vote by a simple majority of the citizen representatives to decide on the spot, on to Lagash, sail for Syracuse, or not.

The structure of modern urban life and communications has radically changed the focus of democratic decisionmaking. But more so are the humans who are presumed competent to be making these decisions by plebiscite. We have learned the hard way about the phony elections of tyrannical societies, coerced, fearful people giving their 99.5 percent okay, or else. So, if the vote is often a joke, so is the "constitution," along with the intimidated and corrupted judges who interpret the "law." Most often these situations occur in nations where the people are uneducated, or miseducated, living in hellish "urbs," their economies barely subsistence. How can they resist the phoniness and fear that yet persuades the United Nations.

It is difficult but necessary to distinguish between nations such as Germany under the Nazis, or Japan under its militarists, that, a generation after defeat in war, became learners of the democratic way. They had the educational and economic infrastructure to venture forth from their former mental cocoon. In the Third World: Africa, the Caribbean and Latin America, South Asia, it is difficult to foresee an informed citizenry in control of its destiny. In certain North African and other Muslim societies, if the people had the democratic right to choose, they would open the door to the most reactionary fundamentalist, intolerant groups. As with the ayatollahs of Iran, the Saudis would enthusiastically vote in Osama, and there never would be a free election again. Algeria was a recent example of the military nullifying a fundamentalist victory. Is Iraq next?

The problem of democratic life in the twenty-first century arises from the vast populations that need to be reached to make ever more important national and international decisions. Yet, the meat around the ancient structures of democratic life, as they were shaped into the American Constitution and the British Common Law—the Parliamentary structure formed to administer this law—was built on a world with no resemblance to our own. The world is now an international universe of races and ethnicities, living under the most diverse socioeconomic conditions conceivable.

The American and British founders were educated, middle-class Anglo-Saxons. Today these advanced economies are post-industrial, service, technological, with a heavy dollop of welfare, urban subsistence. In the eighteenth century they were agricultural, craft, and mercantile. Truthfully, much of today's Third World lives below the horizon of contemporary awareness.

The eighteenth-century Anglo-Saxon presumption was that the average farmer or workman could be educated to participate in the ongoing economic advances even then being precipitated by craft and science. Today, only redistributionist zealots truly believe that the majority of humans aboard lifeboat Earth can be educated to participate in the new economy. The political challenge created by this great mass of twenty-first-century humans now comes from the non-educable regions of the world. Some of these lie within the borders of ostensibly modern nations, the United States.

Democracy in the Industrial/Urban Society

This was the challenge that the American philosopher, John Dewey, 1859-1952, sought to solve. Born to a traditionalist Congregational family in Burlington, Vermont, Dewey was educated in the newly-minted state university in that city, went on to do graduate work at Johns Hopkins in Baltimore. Johns Hopkins also was brand new, a graduate-student-oriented university modeled on late-nineteenth-century German research institutions. Dewey's religious commitments were abandoned during his first teaching position, in philosophy, at the University of Michigan. Here he was exposed to the scientific revolution taking place in agriculture, impressed with the practicalities of the newly evolving mechanization of farm life, new seeds, fertilizers, pesticides, the beginnings of industrialism in the mid-west.

Now a scientifically-oriented humanist, he joined the so-called American pragmatist movement, represented by Charles Peirce, then teaching at Johns Hopkins, and William James of Harvard University. Offered a position at another newly-minted and progressive university, in Chicago (he taught here 1894-1904), he became deeply involved with the social and scientific/industrial dynamics of that rapidly expanding city. Dewey, highly motivated as thinker, teacher and writer, elicited an invitation to Columbia University in 1904. He remained, to retire in 1929. By 1904, he was one of the most influential social philosophers of a rising secularist/scientific orientation among Western intellectuals. At Columbia, in New York City, he continued his leadership of this progressivist tradition in American thought, even past his retirement years.

Many attribute the reforms of Franklin Roosevelt's New Deal to the writings of Dewey. Even more broadly, Dewey's writings impinged on the very nature of the democratic life in this new urban industrial America. His great theme: the necessity to accommodate democratic participation in our civic culture to the dynamic nature of our society; the need to harmonize within this context polyglot immigrant cities, rapid social and technological change, new forms of communication, media, transportation. The key to maintaining our democratic institutions in a time of enormous change, Dewey argued, was the need to go beyond theological rule-making to a more secular and experimental approach to life problems. This task was to be centered on public education. Many of his writings, exemplified in *Democracy and Education*, 1916, were devoted to this expanding institution and its role in creating rational, scientifically-oriented citizens.[1]

Democratic Polity

His model was essentially that of the original New England town meeting, where citizens came together to argue different points of view with regard to the critical issues of their community life, then to decide democratically by vote. This rational, instrumental, pattern of thinking could be extrapolated into larger urban contexts by a universal attempt to involve children in their schools. So-called progressive education was focused on practical problem-solving projects, rather than rote repetition of established views.

Dewey also realized that the enormous dynamics of modern industrial societies in which the rich could become inordinately powerful, politically and socially, could be tempered by the government taking a more active role in creating safety nets. By this he meant not merely through temporary welfare support, but by the support of counter institutions—labor unions, the National Education Association (NEA-1916), and the like—that could meet Big Capital and bigoted state government at the negotiating table or court room. Active associations representing all walks of life, varying economic, regional, ethnic interests, would now stimulate participatory democratic life by allowing for the flourish[...]gue.

[...] outlook, but frightened by the growing [...]ed in the inquiry into the Stalinist trials [...] Trotsky's heresy.[2] In 1940, one of Sta[...]exico. Most importantly, Dewey held [...]en, universal public education system, [...] a rational, open minded, progressive [...]ith the expanding massiveness of the

[...]mitment to equal rights for all minori[...]9. Dewey assumed, awed by the incor[...]grants into the dynamic American sys[...]y of a whole cloth and that all humans [...]e American public educational system, [...] His only caveat was a fear of the then-[...]. Here, the nub was the potential theo-[...]king of children as they arrived from their Catholic homelands in Europe, and entered Catholic parochial schools.

Dewey's great hypotheses: 1. The power of the public schools to show the young the way to rational, experimental modes of thought; to immunize them from reactionary ideology.[4]

2. The belief that all humans needed equal educational potentiality to learn and participate in a secular, scientific world. His implicit questions: Could the human mind be shaped to search for new knowledge, always able to withhold assent from established belief, stay with a problem-solving focus?[5] 3. Could

humans be educated, not to degenerate in thought and behavior, not to surrender to emotional, ideological or theological hysteria when having to face crises and danger?[6]

Looking down from above, it is questionable that events would have persuaded John Dewey that in the half century since his death there still was hope for an achieved universal educability. Given the ever-declining results of public education, could the twenty-first century sustain more than the most superficial institutional veneer of the democratic life?

When Populations Change

One of the great mysteries of human history is the rise and fall of civilizations. This is too large a problem to be undertaken in any one- or multi-volume tract. Leadership and dominance of a nation or an *ethne* have been ephemeral. The popular explanatory theme is the aging of institutions, the fixation on the political status quo, the waning energies of peoples who have stepped back from the ongoing struggle for dominance. This inability to adapt and meet the challenges of the ever-new in human social existence is the sociopolitically preferable explanation.

Another largely unexaminable explanation for the weakening of a people is the destruction of the manpower base as a consequence of war. The Hellenes were constantly at war with each other; the bravest young hoplites were destroyed in the constant internecine conflicts. It had to have lowered the possibility of finding a Pericles, a Sophocles, a Plato in each succeeding generation. The same applies to Renaissance Italy where the carnage among these talented townspeople, always at each other's throats, had to have destroyed the flower of manhood. The same testosteronic juices that produced a Benvenuto Cellini urged Siena to try to slaughter Florence. In turn, the pride of Milan, Venice, Padua, Pisa joyfully mounted their steeds. This explanation could hold true for the Amero-Indian peoples who lost so many of their most vigorous braves in futile struggle with their own and the "white man." World War I, for the English and French, has been cited for their respective falls from leadership. Germany will rue its own price for the wars that allowed for the committing of the *Holocaust*.

World War II was a central moment in human destructiveness on a wholly new level. Starting with the Armenians and climaxing with the Jews, the twentieth century itself may be seen as the self-inflicted dimming of European civilization. Interestingly, democracy did return to Europe, the bare bones remnants of a once intellectual civilization now held together in democratic procedures, and with a welfare economy.

For a while, America stepped into the breach. With relatively few war losses, even given the added wounds of a Korea and Viet Nam, the vigor of its institutions in a setting of great plenty and openness of opportunity, this egalitarian and philanthropic world power emerged to show the democratic way. America dreamed that a Muslim Iraq was deemed hospitable to the germ of rationality and democracy, here a great experiment coming at a time of waning wealth and power.

Another cause for the descent from leadership arises in the shifting demography of intellect within nations and regions. Ionia, once Greek, now Anatolia, western Turkey, was not intellectually inferior to the mainland Greeks. Thence came the Turkish peoples with their commitment to Islam and to concubinage, polygyny, slavery. It had to have had enormous deleterious impact on their internal vigor. Their conquest of the Orthodox Christian Greeks, the subsequent invasive imposition of non-democratic Turkish social and cultural patterns added new blood to Greece. Since that time, Greece and Turkey both have been backwaters of modern Europe.

Today, both Europe and North America are in the process of changing their demographic profiles. Extremely low birth rates among the indigenous Europeans, rightly adapting to the congestive environment, the slowing of economic opportunity and growth, signal an attempt to preserve the economic and social standard of living. Add to this stagnant balance large-scale non-European immigration. Muslim immigrant populations having extraordinarily high birth rates will soon challenge the existing democratic secular institutions on that continent. Is there any evidence that these newcomers will be able to compete intellectually and educationally with their patrons, or with the hungry East Asians beyond Europe's horizon?

The U.S. is a paradigmatic exemplar of the impact of a changing demographic intellectual profile on a dynamic two-century-old political revolution. Hundreds of millions of dollars are expended in political contests that are more manipulated popularity/defamatory contests hyped by the mass media than considered political debates over serious and complex issues. Increasingly, the social separation by education and intelligence hints deeply of incipient class warfare. Between 1950-2000, the results of the trillions of dollars of redistributionary wealth that had been directed back into the expanding minority populations, largely African-American and Hispanic, have been mainly illusory. These monies have barely sufficed to keep the seeds of class warfare from sprouting, As they recede, what kind of political dialogue can we expect between 2000-2050?

The political debates in the U.S., for example, center on the recapturing the halcyon days of middle-class expansion and hope, endless horizons of wealth and civilizational amenities. Who and what caused this dream to begin to recede, the people implore anxiously? They dare not be told. The truth: new centers of John Dewey's dream of education and modernization are coming into their own, India and China. These rising nations are vastly overpopulated. A large proportion of the citizenry, however, is being educated quickly and efficiently to do the tasks of American unionized wages of $15-per-hour with health and retirement benefits, for $1-per-hour, and without the heavy health, sanitation, safety/Sarbanes-Oxley corporate legal requirements. The addition of new labor-saving technology resulting in increased productivity-per-worker, fewer hands needed, will only hurt our own employment statistics. The newcomers' wages will remain low.

The population of the U.S., unlike South Korea, Japan, China is surging, primarily immigrants, legal and illegal from the poor nations of the world, eager not merely for paying work, but also for free education, Medicaid, health care, and a variety of welfare benefits. They live like kings and queens on these static benefits, as compared to life in their impoverished homelands. In 2005, close to 300 million Americans live on the same land mass that 150 million Americans inhabited only two generations previous. And, the American public educational system, so different from that required by John Dewey to achieve his vision of an enlightened participating polity produces some of the lowest achievement results of any developed nation in the world. These educational outcomes border on the educational never-never-land of the failed nations of the world.

> [A] study by Achieve, Inc., a non-profit organization created by state governors, business leaders, analyzed high school exit tests in mathematics and language arts from six states, and writing tests from four of the states. The states were Florida, Maryland, Massachusetts, New Jersey, Ohio, and Texas. The report found that the tests were "not pegged at a very demanding level"…The study also compared the material from the Third International Mathematical and Science Study, concluding that in math, the skills tested on high school exit exams {12th grade} in the United States…in Arizona 84% of the students failed…are taught in middle school {5-8 grade} in many other countries.[7]

More and more residents of the U.S. are supported by the wealth-producing skills of ever fewer Americans. The ideology of the day only produces class resentments, the demand for entitlements spawning the political opportunists who will go after these votes. Presidential candidates make their play for the votes of minorities (pro-illegal immigration lobbies), the elderly (drug benefits), extended jobless benefits, hoping for additional taxes from wealthy individuals and corporations.

Early in the twenty-first century, there is a vigorous, relatively diverse print, radio and television media. The judiciary is still largely unimpeachable, the middle class vocally protective of its hard-won standard of living. Raw class warfare, *e.g.,* Venezuela, Hugo Chavez, is still in the future as long as some wealth trickles down. But as the economic expansion of the corporations must take them far afield to China, India, Eastern Europe, Russia, nations for the moment in their expansive phases, it should be clear that productive wealth for an expanding ill-educated American demography is diminishing. The domestic economic pie will get smaller, the burgeoning needy of all ethnicities at the bottom, more restive. The necessary trillions for redistribution can only be taken out of the hides of an ever more pressed working middle class. A whole new form of political democracy is on the horizon for the United States. Forget the visions of Thomas Jefferson and John Dewey.

What constitutes the final chapter in the descent from the democratic ideals of a high egalitarian international civilization? What can interdict the global transformations of human freedom into the model of the spurious "democracies" of today? What will happen to the ever more media-manipulative democracy of the United States?

The myth is that all of our ethnic groups will equally produce the educated and the uneducated The requirements of the global scientific, literate culture of today will instead inevitably hurl a majority into the abyss of the unskilled, the socially dispossessed. Could the masses, demanding economically suicidal inflationary redistributionist programs, bring down the entire democratic edifice, a new pseudo-egalitarian revolution? We know it would fail to reap their desired results. Totalitarianism all over again? Could it happen?

Conditions of Democratic Polity

Thus far the political process in the free market democracies has been dynamic and fluid. It has moved through cycles of varying orientation. Focus for a time on a temporary welfare state solution for the capitalist depression. This move started with Roosevelt in the U.S. and Bevan in Great Britain. It was reversed, by popular decree, with Reagan in the U.S. and Thatcher in Britain. The democratic process feeds on historical change to allow shifts even in cultural style, if not in substantive policymaking, *e.g.*, from the presidency of a Jimmy Carter to that of a Bill Clinton, both Democrats. Is there that much difference between the policies of Thatcher (Conservative) or Blair (Labor)?

As we have noted above, unless the basic educational, social and economic life experiences conducive to democratic participation are strong, low intelligence, narrow education in the polity will allow those who seize power to manipulate a façade of democratic politics. Historians conjecture about when the Romans became aware that the Empire was no longer, or that it was no longer even largely Roman. Certainly in the days of Charlemagne and his sons, c.800 CE, the memory lived on. When did the substance of democratic political life leave us?

There was an assumed awareness among the writers of the U.S. Constitution that the size of the political unit was critical. Our Federal structure, for reasons of defense and economic intercourse, attempts to balance the needs of the larger geographic entity with the importance of localism and participatory fertilization from below. It is difficult to believe that a world of 9 or 10 billion people, massed in great urban heaps, disregarding for the moment the intelligence and educational issue, can long maintain any semblance of democratic participation, nor political functionality, getting things done.

The hypothesis presented here, a world population of around 1.5 billion people, a United States with 100-150 million citizens, especially given our modern communications and transportation technology, will easily keep people in touch. A world community of nations and ethnicities physically separated, with much pure air to breathe and mind space to think and create, could interact, trade, visit without the fear of breakdown, unobserved anarchy, terrorism, and war.

No dream of social equality has ever meant uniformity in income, profession, way of looking at life. It merely demands that given generally equal levels of high intelligence, inevitably there is going to be some economic differentiation, some people able to afford a 10,000-square-foot house or two, another a 1,500-square-foot cottage in the countryside. What political stability requires is that the lesser wealthy have the wherewithal to educate their children on a level equal to the wealthy, and that social differences not be intergenerational, not become castes.

> Our love of what is beautiful does not lead to extravagance; our love of things of the mind does not make us soft. We regard wealth as something to be properly used, rather than something to boast about. As for poverty, no one need be ashamed to admit it: the real shame is in not taking practical measures to escape from it. Here each individual is interested not only in his own affairs but in the affairs of state as well: even those who are mostly occupied with their own business are extremely well-informed on general politics-this is a peculiarity of ours: we do not say that a man who takes no interest in politics is a man who minds his own business; we say that he has no business here at all.[8]

The above quote is part of Thucydides' paraphrase of the funeral speech given by Pericles, the Athenian, at the beginning of the war against Sparta and her allies, 431 BCE. The speech was meant to buck up the Athenians for the sacrifices to come, but also to distinguish their democratic constitution from that of their more militaristic, traditionalist enemies.

The Athenians were an ethnically homogeneous people living in a modern industrialized, mercantile, economic setting. Their claim, Athens was the most modern state in Hellas. Sounds like America's boastings, c.2000 CE. There could be no question of multi-ethnic intellectual differences in a community of c.250,000 people. Thus, economic and social differences were viewed as outcomes of individual idiosyncrasy and personality. After all, a leading intellectual and military hero such as Socrates could not have arisen to such prominence from the *hoi polloi* (urban "dusty foot") without a fluid acceptance of the possibility of citizens both rising to wealth or prominence and concomitantly descending. The Athenians were all voting and thinking citizens, even if, sadly, moved by demagogues in times of stress.

It is quite likely that Athens and the other Greek city-states implicitly recognized the principle of regression toward the mean, in terms of I.Q. and the other impacting intellectual factors. One need only read Book One of Plato's *Republic* to note the Greek awareness of the ups and downs of family wealth and fate. This once was an American understanding, too.

By contrast, the awareness of the irremediable nature of the social fate of some of our ethnic minorities, the effort to change nature, has reached hysteric levels. Today, a sum in excess of $11,000-per-pupil per-year is spent on the almost 100 percent African-American student population of Washington, D.C. This sum is the highest of any large city public school system in the nation, higher than the tuition for most private day schools. The tragedy is that these mainly impoverished students achieve at very low levels, in no way commensurate with this expenditure of wealth by the middle-class taxpayers of the nation. This fact will largely be forgotten in the class warfare rhetoric that we will see down the road in the U.S.A. as we pass through the twenty-first century.

Democratic, free market societies that produce surplus wealth, as in the Western aristocratic tradition, engage in philanthropy. In the United States, it derives from the Protestant commitment to doing good works as a sign of approval from on high: hospitals, universities, research institutions, museums, high culture. Such institutions will be hard put to retain their intellectual *élan* as modern populist government tends to degenerate, in pursuit of the mollification of the lowest common denominator.[9]

Even our twentieth-century royalty, the Rockefeller, Ford, Kennedy wealth is eventually dissipated within the family, often living on in their good works. History produces new wealth in the guise of a Buffet, Gates. In the free dynamics of a democratic society, new centers of affluence and power will always be created. Their wealth and then their power will as always dissipate over a few generations, *viz* the Roosevelts. The exceptions are nations where the people are yet ideologically intimidated, weak in education, unable to rule themselves, Egypt, Jordan, Saudi Arabia, and elsewhere. The familial rule of the tyrant is maintained, the national *élan* grinds to a halt.

The beauty of high intelligence flowing forth freely in creative activity in a democratic, free market environment is that the pleasure centers are widely distributed. People have enough material resources to live a wide variety of independently and culturally diverse lives. The wealthy often live empty, wasteful, ultimately unhappy lives. Their children are destroyed. By contrast, the minister of a rural church will nurture a future computer tycoon next to his hearth. A real estate mogul will produce children dedicated to the Peace Corps or Green Peace.

The human mind is rich in variation of talents and interests. It is not merely I.Q. that directs the individual into pre-programmed money accumulations. High intelligence leads an individual into the arts, medical research, even monkish seclusion with a fishing rod. The result is a peaceful, productive, forward-looking political environment.

Governmental Labor

In February, 2004, a jobs statistic disheartened the body politic in the U.S.A. Only 21,000 new jobs had been created in that month, an augur of things to come. Productivity improvements and the competition of world corporations to employ the best and cheapest labor drew jobs away from West Europe and the U.S.A. Millions of new entrants into the U.S. labor market and enormous productivity advances, produced perhaps as much as a 17 percent disjunction between people and jobs over the last several years. So what if we have produced several hundred thousand new jobs over the year? More millions are peering into the newspaper and the internet help-wanted listings. The irony is that many of the new jobs are governmental, state education programs. These are surely to be cut in the first phase of slimming down the cost of government. That is, before the populists win out. Private employment adds to the tax base. Public employment takes from the tax base to drain investment monies for those potentially laboring in the non-governmental sectors of the economy.

Here, a clue for the democracy of the future. When everyone works for the government there can be no real democratic life. What a nation decides to enact into law then must allow for the retention of these governmental jobs. The great problem of Western European economic stagnation lies in the government and labor unions intrusively interjecting themselves into the free flow of the labor and productive markets. In effect, workers in the so-called private sector are working for the government, which sets the rules for their employment by the private sector. The Europeans are beginning to complain. As private sector employers go bankrupt, can't meet competition from cheaper more flexible labor market nations, the taxes begin to dry up, national deficits explode, and the dream of retiring at age 55 floats off into the wide blue.

It is one thing for government to level the playing field, for certain standards of humanity are required of the private sector, else we are back to the old sweatshop and coal mining eras of nineteenth-century labor conditions. Here lies the value in a rational, educated polity and its representatives. It can fine tune the political machine, keeping it flexible as the world moves in new directions. It is important to argue that a democratic society must ensure that no great political advantage is accumulated in momentary power, *e.g.*, Microsoft. Most important, fight every governmental monopoly that could extinguish the nurturing breath of innovation.

This pathway into government ownership of the means of production and consumption, the ostensible goals of socialist and communist societies, has to result in restrictions on the freedom of the citizenry in every other cultural area. A stable nation is an amalgam of different symbolic modalities of life and thought. Coerced impositions on the freedom of action, *laissez faire,* in one domain, economic free enterprise, will have implications in the arts, civic culture, in the deeper network of personal and family behavioral psychology. This is what happened in the Soviet Union. Repression in economics and politics led to repression in every area of human relations. Eventually, the system collapsed. This might not have happened peacefully had there not been another human model of political and social life beyond the walls and the barbed wire.

Another danger in the monopolization of power by government is the growth of the welfare state in the West, including the U.S.A. Those who work for the government do yet vote as citizens of the state. And you can bet your life that they will vote for those who promise them the retention of their soft perks, as members of the governmental bureaucracies. Added to this heavy load of government dependants, and controllers of the nation's destiny, are those vast millions who now lobby for aid from the state, whether Medicare, Medicaid, drug benefits, Social Security, food stamps, unemployment and welfare payments, driver's licenses for illegal immigrants. They will follow their class conflict demagogues into voting for ever-higher confiscatory taxes on the working middle classes who support them out of this public purse.

When Adam Smith, in the mid-eighteenth century, wrote about the "diminished state" as the basis not only for economic freedom, but political as well as intellectual openness, he was not merely aiming his pen at divine right monarchy. He was pointing to a perennial trend. Big government eventually and fatally will undercut democratic progress. That is why the writers of the Constitution added the ninth and tenth amendments as part of the Bill of Rights, *e.g.,* the retention of unexpressed rights of the states and the people, unless specifically limited in the designated powers assigned to the federal establishment.[10]

The Withering State

Karl Marx was right when he envisioned his communist utopia as coming into reality as a consequence of the withering of the state. His analysis saw class exploitation as the root of class power. Each cycle of history could be defined by those who, in the light of the reigning modes of economic production, had seized control of these institutions of material wealth. New class oppression is always initiated by those quick to seize the moment of historic change. Marx, as are we all, was present-minded about mid-nineteenth-century states of affairs. The then-great advance of industrialism and industrial capitalism seduced him into believing that this "new" form of economic domination heralded the end of history.[11]

The ultimate revolution was about to take place. Alienated urban factory workers, miners, the cumulative exploited of earlier regimes would rise to overthrow the existing oppressive power structure. Since industrial capitalism seemed to be the culmination of all earlier modes of production, this revolution would constitute the end of all revolutions.

Then, no longer heavy-handed class exploitations, political structures as instruments to squeeze life out of human flesh and blood. The modern industrial system was a product of human ingenuity. As it was co-opted by the capitalist class it displaced humans from their earlier small community self-subsistence lives. The now alienated industrial proletariat was thus subject to a new form of class oppression. Thus the failing post-revolutionary state would wave a new banner of freedom, "from each according to his ability, to each according to his needs." No class oppression—no state, the moral bedrock upon which all subsequent political life would be based. Industrialism and egalitarianism were both lure and challenge.

This is not a half bad idea. The main error in Marx' analysis and one on which he should have amplified, lay in the implications of the phrase, "from each according to his ability." Marx recognized the reality of natural inequalities in humans *vis à vis* intellectual aptitude. To be sure, in making the distinction between "ability" and "need," he realized the practical significance of the needs of the medical doctor or scholar from that of the industrial worker or farm laborer. Even the Soviets made this distinction as they desperately ensconced prized scientists in their Novosibirsk scientific cocoon.

Marx, through his knowledge of Darwin's writings and his vicarious explorations of the planet beyond Europe, was aware of the racial and ethnic differences in cultural accomplishment of the peoples of the world. He saw these differences as marking earlier historical modes of production. Thus he saw the West European social class distinctions as marking the modern point for revolutionary action and justice.

As we have learned by experience, war and genocide, time and further industrial/technological as well as educational advance were needed to bring about his vision of European/North American classlessness. It would be accomplished by contemporary free market capitalism, not by his delusional totalitarian followers. Interestingly, Russia and the rest of the world were either far behind the historical dialectic, else doomed never to create a classless society, economically and socially.

Politically, the classless society was and is achievable without blood in the streets. As noted above, Europe and North America almost attained it. Implicit in Marx' view of the withering away of the state through the achievement of classlessness was that the redistribution of wealth through the agency of government would diminish in time.

The people freed to create their natural institutions of restraint and giving, government would become but one of the political instrumentalities for legislating a common national or international direction through time and history. The judicial and executive branches of democratic government would strive to ensure a level social playing field.

Key to the attainment of a classless society underpinned by a substantive democratic ethos, as both Marx and Dewey intuited, is a uniform level of high intelligence and secular education in the citizenry. Democracy demands rationality because history presents change and the need for humans to decide. Here is postulated the inherent decency of humans.

Endnotes, Chapter 6

[1] Dewey, J. 1916. *Democracy and Education*, N.Y.: Macmillan.
[2] Dewey, J, Chairman. 1937. *Commission of Inquiry: The Case of Leon Trotsky at the Moscow Trials*, N.Y.: Harper.
[3] Dewey, J. 1927. *The Public and its Problems*, N.Y.: Henry Holt; Dewey, J. 1935. *Liberalism and Social Actions*, N.Y.: Capricorn; Dewey, J. 1939. *Freedom and Culture*, N.Y.: Capricorn.
[4] Dewey, J. 1900. *School and Society*, Chicago: Univ. of Chicago Press; Dewey, J. 1902. *The Child and the Curriculum*, Chicago: Univ. of Chicago Press.
[5] Dewey, J. 1922. *Human Nature and Conduct*, N.Y.: Random House.
[6] Dykhuzen, G. 1973. *The Life and Mind of John Dewey*, Carbondale Ill.: Southern Illinois Univ. Press.
[7] Schemo, D. J., *The New York Times*, 6/10/2004.
[8] Thucydides, c.411 BCE. *The History of the Peloponnesian War*, Book 2, tr. Rex Warner, London: Penguin Classic, 1954.
[9] Zakaria, F. 2003. *The Future of Freedom: Illiberal Democracy at Home and Abroad*, N.Y.: W. W. Norton; Caruthers, T. 2003. "Zakaria's Complaint," *The National Interest*, #72, Summer, 137-243.
[10] Smith, A. 1776. *An Inquiry Into the Nature and Causes of the Wealth of Nations*, Dublin: Whitestone; Smith, A. 1808 (1759). *The Theory of Moral Sentiments*, 2 vols., Edinburgh: Bell and Bradford.
[11] Marx, K., and Engels, F.. 1992 (1849). *The Communist Manifesto*, Oxford, Eng.: Oxford Univ. Press; Marx, K. 1977 (1859-1867). *Capital, A Critique of Political Economy*, London: Lawrence and Wishart; Marx, K. 1989. *Basic Writings on Politics and Philosophy*, ed., L. Feuer, N.Y.: Anchor Books.

Chapter 7

Twenty-Second-Century Economics: Beyond Mass Production

New Modes

We are on the cusp of a new revolution in the material and social relationships between the peoples of our world. The West is now in the intermediate phase of this revolution away from mass industrial production toward the service/technology economy. Toward the end of the twentieth century as technology advanced, the more prescient economists, technologists, politicians realized that the magic word *productivity* semantically veiled the beginning of a new economic era.

This dawning realization has occurred as a result of the lessening requirements for human muscle in the production of valued material things. Heaps of humans producing, then consuming mounds of things and energy are no longer needed to insure the fulfillment of the basics of life, the food, clothing, shelter, nor the lifestyle requirements of modernity. At the same time, these masses contribute mightily to the pollution of our physical environment. Living ant-like in our enveloping urbs, they require ever more emergency resuscitation, which adds increasingly to the tragedy of twenty-first-century life on this earth.

In the U.S., the sharpness of this perception is evidenced first in the gradual displacement of the great wealth-producing industries to cheaper labor climes that offer competitive educational skills. There is as yet a vast mountain of accumulated wealth in the United States and the West to buffer the sharpness of this radical homeland change. The service jobs remain, but at gradually ebbing wage levels given the demographic outpouring of new American bodies, homegrown and immigrant, onto the job market. In early 2005, Bear Stearns, the New York-based brokerage company estimated that 20 million illegal aliens in the United States were competing for low-paying jobs in a growing one trillion dollar untaxed underground economy.[1]

We speak of the pittance loss of a few thousands of these service jobs to a rising Indian educational elite. Around the modern technology campuses in Bangalore, India, a center of the *new*, the streets are rutted with the *old*, the stench of sewage wafts over the city, the impoverished millions outside the golden gates barely touched by the economic opportunities of the global information age. Productivity change: first, the family farmers were sidelined from their scrub farms. Then the small-time poultry, pig, and cattle ranchers were bypassed by industrial farming, Big Ag. If now, shrimp are being dumped on the market from farms in Brazil, soon Beluga sturgeon caviar will be harvested in ponds along the lower Danube and off the Pacific coast of the state of Washington. The millions of desperate hands that once passed buckets of soil to build Chinese dams are replaced by a few hundred Caterpillar earth-moving machines.

The internet is changing the process of searching for information, communicating by mail, researching in dusty libraries, doing so many things that people and shops did for us in years past. We need many fewer people to do the work of the world, at least that for which the educated middle class will pay. The political demagoguery about jobs being off-shored to cheap labor sources is echoed in the ongoing plight of the least-skilled Americans. But it can't be stopped. In the corporate world, it is forever the survival of the most efficient.

Germans are being pitched from their lush welfare smugness, an ever increasing 12.6 percent unemployment rate that won't move downward, budget deficits plummeting deeper into the red. Too many people are searching for good work, as the job base of such middle-class productivity shrinks. The poorest of the educable are hungry to get a piece of the action. The prediction, the uneducated of the developed world are on their way to becoming a new governmentally-supported class. Once they were the pride of the American public high school, the *lycée*, the *gymnasium*.

Jobs involved in the production of things are fungible today. The poorest Chinese and Indians can now produce equal quality technology at a tenth of the cost of German and American workers. The only hope for the present king of the mountain nations is being more able than ambitious Chinese, Koreans, or Indians, creating desirable new technologies or crafts that these rising nations cannot yet produce. The global genie is out of the box, the Intels and Mercedes are producing all over the world, searching for the cheapest and best labor. Most American and German production workers will soon be superfluous. The winners? The smartest German optical craftsmen, the cleverest French cognac producers. Not too long ago, this exportable manufacturing muscle reaped wealth that funded the complacent welfare state.

However, before there can be a new economic beginning, the current system must implode. It will. The political mythology of the ruling classes is a fantasy: a world going from c.3 billion (out of a total of 6 billion residents) to 10 billion middle-class consumers, naturally of the products of the West. To purchase these goodies, the newcomers on the planet will have the wherewithal to pay for the products of this specialized labor, intense capital expenditure.

The real questions are for how long and how far can the World Bank subsidize such modernities. To survive, these poor nations must therefore export what the world wants to buy. At this point it is only oil. Aside from oil—a gift of nature—the Saudis produce practically nothing for export that the world wants to buy. Even now the Saudi population is too large for oil exports to support the current lifestyle for much longer. American big agriculture sells vast amounts of soy beans produced in Brazil by slave labor. This wealth doesn't touch the São Palo slum. It does, however, serve to put the Minnesota farmer out of business.

A new economy must come to terms with the perennial human desire for the materiality of middle-class life. The powers of science, technology, medicine, the enormous global productive capacity for the basics will not disappear, even as social paralysis spreads to vast portions of the planet. Eventually, the intelligent minorities in the West will protest as they see the optimism of their grandparents disappear courtesy of the present class structure, *i.e.*, ideological "liberalism." The more homogeneous intellectual potential in present-day Eastern Europe and Northeast Asia will likely provide the I.Q. and educational seeds for future civilizational renewal.

Economic Meaning

What has happened to our intellectual perspective-of-the-possible is the above-noted political/economic mythology. We are gearing up for a world of 10 billion humans. We are told that this underclass tide of humans can be educated to a level equal to the old West, here including the new Northeast Asiatics. True, few expect that this process of gentrification can be wholly achieved by 2050, our target year. The consensus view is that if the population surge can be slowed by this date, all things being equal, we could see stability and the gradual homogenization of this mass of humans. A slow diminution of the population will occur as the centuries slip by. All will be well with the middle-class world.

The present crisis within the world community: intercontinental terrorism; pandemics; global environmental deterioration and *tsunami* events. The plight of the masses in the urban hell-holes of our planet does not seem to hint to the powers-that-be that the ideological dream is beyond our grasp.

It sounds insanely utopian to suggest this reality to the ruling classes, Kofi Anan, *et al.*, at the United Nations, the World Bank, International Monetary Fund, Congress of the United States: that together we make a concerted effort to plan for a world of c.1.5 billion scientifically-educated and internet-connected communities of association around the world. This can be done over a realistic timeframe of several centuries.

Our human nature is a product of the symbolic outpourings of our brain. Throughout history, great civilizations have been created by relatively small populations as compared with those of today. The economic achievements of such civilizations have been defined by the skills of the craftsmen who produced the economic basis for a life lived cognitively, and produced beauty as well. True, the computer, the internet, the cell phone, are works of economic grandeur, as is the jet airplane, the fine automobile. Much in our material civilization can compete with the best of the past. But to continue such efforts, we must have the leisure, the creative breath of openness, economic and cultural opportunity.

Struggling to stifle the despairing cries for help from billions of people sinking below minimum levels of human dignity will efface any hope for a global economy of fineness. In our attempts to subsidize these masses, minister to their infinite needs, we fool ourselves into thinking that the material detritus of current mass production and communication will pull us through. We cannot gate ourselves off from this suffering. A world three-fourths enveloped by hell will exhaust whatever surplus of mind and value that a civilization requires.

It is important to understand that the underlying *raison d'être* of our current free enterprise system, capitalism, is not money, acquisition, or materiality. Material things are part of a system of cultural ideals, symbols of value. It is the chase, the creative ideal that counts, not the acquisition.

The earliest Upper Paleolithic (35,000 B.P.) blades, knives, scrapers were useful, but they were also always items of beauty and delicacy. These cave dwellers were middle class consumers *in nutrio*. Just as they corrected the wall drawings of their young, they perceived the beauty that lay in skill, the power of high intelligence. This critical middle-class discriminatory *élan* defines the material culture of any historical era.

These Cro-Magnons, living in caves for over 30,000 years, prospered by dint of the surpluses of a high-protein hunting economy. We don't necessarily need homes in Palm Beach, Aspen, on Park Avenue or in Monaco for our human material fulfillment. Nor do we need yachts or private planes. Sometimes it is enough to climb the distant peak and look beyond.

Clearly, the *élan* of hunting and gathering that economically and socially bound together the Cro-Magnon communities, so similar to the North American Indian lifestyle, was the product of corporate effort. But this corporate working together released artistic skills, the hunting tools, clothing, ornaments that were the personal achievements of individuals within a family.

So, too, with the Uruk Sumerian civilization, 4000-3000 BCE. All indications are that the surplus of economic wealth that eventually expanded the community larder, that funded the great architecture (ziggurat-temples), the art, music, and dance, was an organizational achievement of an *ethne*. Small cities, deriving energy from their civic and linguistic/religious identity, centered in the temple of the god who protected the city, arranged for this productivity and distributed the wealth equally. But there was room for the private plot of irrigated land, the individual craftsmen employed by the city or temple, as well as for trade and the independent internal economy.

Out of our interaction with matter, we produce foods clothing, housing. In a civilized community such productivity has no meaning without an accompanying esthetic dimension. Greek pottery, with its artistic decoration, was valued highly by the ancient Hellenes, much as they now decorate our museums. But these *amphorae* were utilitarian holders of olive oil or wines, to be traded throughout the Mediterranean. In those days the artistry was ubiquitous, the wine and oil necessary, though expensive commodities. With that added esthetic dimension, they were especially negotiable. Much like the chrome wheels on the Buick, but only if the basic body did not rust out or the motor explode.

The Northwest Canadian Kwakiutl Indians burnt their accumulative wealth to show their power (the "potlatch"). Status was won through indifference to the loss of valuable, beautiful "things." By contrast Westerners exult in the power represented by the construction of the pyramids, the Acropolis, essentially holy endeavors. The point of putting paintbrush to canvas is not merely the lure of the gallery or the museum, but more in realizing a vision latent in the paint, brush, and canvas. We cannot realize the esthetic ends of these acts without interacting with the material as challenge. Do you really believe that the motivations of a Bill Gates, Michael Dell, billionaire creators, were solely the money and power that came at the end of the long road? It was the excitement and the challenge of creating something new and of value to the world.

The explosions of craft, engineering, mercantile, industrial, and technological progress have come from the spirit of adventure, the symbolic possibilities of the new in the human mind's interaction with the physical world. We entered this world as naïve explorers, our gift of cognitive intelligence only gradually becoming self-conscious of the power of high intellect in its interaction with this world. That is why the late-twentieth and twenty-first centuries have exploded. They are products of an accumulating scientific dynamic, computers, the internet, soon wireless communication around the world, the falling away of nature's barriers of time and space. Here, the accumulation of bits and pieces of theory, explained cause and effect, and then the breakthrough into a new conception of economy. The so-called material drives of the capitalist entrepreneur are the same as those that lead us toward the Moon and Mars.

Attempts to stifle this free flowing of modern mental adventurism, disdainfully called bourgeoisie capitalism by the communists in the Soviet hegemony, China, Viet Nam, Cambodia, ultimately failed, and will always fail, as long as high cognitive intelligence exists to propel curiosity and tangible works. In attempting to smother this energy, the reifying of mentally mediocre bureaucrats into power dividers of the existing pie, the communists and socialists attempted to bring all human creativity to a halt.

Social progress requires the sympathetic interaction of all of our accompanying cultural institutions, our human psychological rainbow, arts, politics, science, knowledge itself. Shut down one important human domain of behavior, and you will suffocate the entire mental system.

Innovation, in the human material or mental sphere, economics or entertainment, without its social reward, cannot long go on. The new must elicit recognized value. Inevitably in our kind of dynamic material world, some humans will become richer than others, some obscenely wealthy such as a Ford, Rockefeller, or Gates, yes, financial opportunists, too, (J. P. Morgan, Buffet, Khodorkovsky, Milkin). Most societies erect defenses against the extreme accumulation of wealth, the danger of caste formation, given equally intelligent competitors.

After all, it is the community that itself establishes the protective lawful setting for this pyramiding. We have anti-monopoly and anti-trust laws, progressive tax rates, moral and tax inducements for philanthropy so that the wealth will pour into socially valuable institutions. In effect philanthropy serves to limit the reach of the state into the heart of individual and small community life, *e.g.*, into hospitals, universities, nature preserves, philanthropic foundations, museums, cognitive music.

The documented scientific observation of intergenerational intellectual regression toward the mean argues for the gradual smoothing out of the time spike of wealth accumulation in powerful families. Regression toward the mean is explained as taking place, for example, when a couple with I.Q.s that average 140, rare intellects in potential, give birth to c. four children. Odds are that one may have an I.Q. of 150, two may have I.Q.s of 130, one an I.Q. of 120 or less, the old mean of the Caucasoids being 100. Examples such as the Kennedys and Rockefellers reflect this gradual dissipation of wealth and intellectual energy over several generations. So long as the playing field of innovation and free enterprise allows other genetic profiles to appear, capitalism itself will exemplify in real terms the democratic system that values fluid social classes, equality of opportunity, and secular decisionmaking.

Also critical in a free society is the lesser economic role of the state. Here the use of tax monies to fund public enterprises, whether electric grids or postal service, can degenerate, without external private competition, into a corrupt and incompetent state capitalism. On the other hand, no one denies the proper role of the people's government, through the legislative and judicial system, to police the behavior of the private sector.

Modern nations have constitutions to establish the rules of the social game. The flaw most often lies in the corruptibility of the judicial system. Highly intelligent and alert citizens, a free and aggressive media will help to ensure the relative honesty of the entire economic system, private and public. As Thomas Jefferson famously noted, if the structure of supposedly democratic government takes a turn toward tyranny, then, the right to violently revolt is never finally revocable.

Economic Justice and Morality

Jason, the Greek, to Medea, the foreigner, mother of his children: "A good Greek land has been your lasting home, not barbary. You have experienced our ordered life, and justice, the long still grasp of the law, not changing with the strong Man's pleasure," Euripides, *Medea.*

This is our ideal, the temporarily strong, in this case, the rich, have to face the same "music" as the little person. In our own moment, the Enron crew, Martha Stewart, Tyco's Kozlowski, Adelphia's Rigas family, Ebbers of bankrupt World Com. It is one thing to put the rascals away for lawbreaking; it is another to label the class of the rich as evil, deserving of the ultimate penalty, as often happened, sadly, in revolutionary and class-sensitive classical Greece.

In a balanced society, demographics, natural resources, humane ecology, and, above all, a people of similar intellectuality and education, differences in achieved material wealth should not burn. There is much more to life than the playland of the sportive rich. The caveat is that the universal middle classes by definition should have enough material wherewithal to do their own things, to empower their children with the skills necessary to supplant the present-day rich and powerful. The law should make it clear that if the power brokers toy with the rules of the game, they will be rigorously punished and their political toadies turned out of office.

Welfare Morality. In our own time, reality is turned on its head. The words "justice," "morality," often have odd configurations. Consider the well-worn slogan of the left, "government and the institutions of power must live up to their social responsibilities." What this means is that we must provide the poor with their basic needs, needs that they cannot satisfy on their own. Since it is most often the non-European, non-East Asiatic minorities who are the supplicants, the shibboleth of racism is raised, here to ideologically taint the middle-class institutions of individual achievement and merit.

The dream of the moral Stalinists among us: to create an egalitarian society, gray ants in the hill. Naturally, these moral adjudicators will then assume their "responsibilities" as the queen commissars.

One presumed indicator of such injustice is the fact of the incarceration of a disproportionate number of minorities in prison. The ideological assumption is that all human groups are of equal intelligence and personal responsibility. The logical conclusion must be that this justice system result constitutes *prima facie* evidence for racial and ethnic injustice. With regard to the specific adjudication of the crimes themselves? Don't look at the concrete facts; draw your conclusions only from the consequences. Accept this assumption on the face of our given ideological truths.

It is never mentioned in these theological redoubts that the rising proportion of the poor might be a consequence of the yet-existing rich platter of redistributionary offerings—medical, educational, police, food and housing subsidies. These poor pay no taxes. Yet, the dominant ethos as to cause is the supposed racism of the very middle classes whose tax dollars support the growth of these tragic populations. Embarrassing evidence, the fall-off in welfare supplicants when the Democratic Clinton administration oversaw a reform of federal welfare regulations.

The post-twenty-first-century civilization rebuilding phase will not suddenly diminish the need for help by portions of the population. The historical genetic residue from our uneven human heritage will not suddenly disappear. There will be the I.Q. needy, plus plenty of legitimate orphans, widows, flood and drought victims, society's perennial social responsibility. As populations are reduced, middle-class secularly educated voluntary citizen groups should begin to take control of this human agenda.

Every society from time immemorial has had to take care of the innocent needy. Given the built-in welfare protections that all human societies have ever required of themselves, stemming from a world that is often cruel without human cause, we must create institutions of care: retirement homes, hospitals, shelters for the homeless. Also, complex societies, freewheeling in their open market experiments, will create the need for temporary public assistance programs such as those that the New Deal instituted as a result of the speculative excesses of the 20s and the depression of the '30s.

Here, there is real meaning to the term "social responsibility." Indeed, the ideal is that at some advanced civilizational stage in our evolution, deeper communities of affiliation, our families, else, our religious institutions, fraternal organizations, ethnic brotherhoods and sisterhoods would come to the rescue. This presupposes a level of richer social connectivity in our populations, not the current alienation of the vast rootless urbs, with only big-brother bureaucracies to minister to the chaos that they themselves might have wrought.

The old philanthropies, religious or ethnic, always exercise a critiquing role in adjudicating responsibility for supposed bad events. Here, individuals were judged as to their own role in their descent, and their responsibilities to their fellow citizens. Today, ideology demands that the needy are always pure unscathed recipients, as in "don't blame the victim," no questions asked, always the consequence of inhumane institutions. The basic question unasked: Why? You can't read beyond the fourth grade level, dropped out of school, you became a sperm donor or pregnant at 15, had six children before you were twenty-five, can't find work, need to be supported along with your progeny. Your parents never educated you, themselves suffused in a household of drugs, alcohol ,sexual casualness. What is society's responsibility here? How does a society deal with individual irresponsibility?

These issues will always confront us, even in the most progressive societies of the educated. In yesteryear, in subsistence societies, the dysfunctional were dealt a primeval form of cruel justice that balanced the survival of the community with tolerance and forbearance for the individual. Today, we attempt to rehabilitate. By the end of the twenty-first century, as need becomes Himalayan, how will ideological liberals balance the two responsibilities?

Just Principal: To those who cannot rise to social and economic competence in the highly abstract world of tomorrow, we will have to continue to say "yes we will help you." One suspects an additional phrase will be added, "not to the extent, however, of allowing you to send your disabilities into the next generation."

Obligations of the Privileged. As for economic morality, the responsibilities of the rich must find a balance with the responsibilities of the less wealthy. Our obligation lies in the judicial harmonization of the economic interests of the most productive with the least, in order to buttress the viability of the nation, even the world community. The freedoms provided by a twenty-second century middle-class economy are made possible in the breath of air given to us by a government that keeps its distance from our personal lives. As stated in Chapter Six, the founding fathers of the United States understood the need for freedom from governmental power. The diminished state is implied in the 9th and 10th Amendments to our Constitution, part of the Bill of Rights. All powers not explicitly delegated to the federal government are reserved to the people and the states (local government). On the other hand, great wealth and power should command from the community a responsibility to give back to the community in the form of philanthropic good.

As argued in Chapter Three, American corporate executives are significantly overpaid relative to the average line-worker, as compared to other developed nations, *e.g.*, Germany and Japan. It can be argued that higher intelligence levels in Germany and Japan produce a larger pool of executives waiting their turn to show what they can do, thus restraining top executive pay as the others pant for the opportunity in the hallway. Another explanation for such a discrepancy would stress the slower growth of Germany and Japan, as compared to the United States. Here the prima donnas at the top are well-rewarded for gunning the torrid growth rate of the U.S. economy. It is amazing that with such a strong middle-class ethos of justice, and an ambitious and irreverent press, corporate boards should have allowed such abuse. One would expect that the highly-stratified cultures of Brazil or Mexico would reveal a higher ratio of remuneration differentials than the United States, considering that Latin American executives are far more *sui generic*. The truism must be that, if the middle class is still getting "theirs," they will tolerate such abuse.[2]

Timothy O'Brien catalogued a recent exemplification of this capitalist moral disease. He listing the retirement perks that corporate boards have granted their CEOs. Robert Nardelli, Home Depot $100 million plus; Charles Gifford, Bank of America, $100 million; Richard Grasso, New York Stock Exchange, $140 Million; Franklin Raines, Fannie May, forced into retirement, under possible indictment for manipulating the books, $ 60-70 million.[3]

The 2002-2005 CEO scandals in the U.S., the failure of the governing boards of corporations, accounting firms, mutual fund regulators to oversee their responsibilities judiciously and impartially underscores such moral and legal failures of the powerful insider. It will require impartial scrutiny, if not control of that human minority who would always abuse and steal.

This does not necessarily mandate heavy governmental controls or stifling bureaucratic regulations. It does require of a free, educated people, independent institutions, the media, academe, to scrutinize these power centers carefully, subjecting them and the governmental agencies themselves for abuses of their responsibilities. Government equals power; civil servants equal corruptible wealth. They are symbiotic. In most autocratic societies where the masses are ignorant and thus weak, this gangster class creates tyranny.

High punitive taxes against the wealthy and the corporations ostensibly to redistribute to the needy have never worked. First, in a free society the wealthy first generations are usually the most hard-working, productive, and creative. But, they need to be educated to behave well. The *hoi polloi*, swept into power can attempt to soak them. The Democrats in 2004 claimed to be able to raise taxes on the top one percent to the tune of $250 billion over ten years. This is a dream, the tax codes are a sieve, the investor classes will buy non-taxable municipal bonds, live in the Bahamas, accountants and lawyers would become busy and rich.

A truly egalitarian civilization shines a spotlight to find ways to persuade the *nouveau riche* to use the wealth for good, not glorifying behavior, as does the excrescence that represents the mass media. Nor should we require the existence of large government bureaucracies to slice their icing from the cake. The people require of government that it exist to insure that the law is obeyed and justice prevail. For how long will a modern civilization need big government: civil servants, teachers, the police, military, public works, highways, health care, social security, all on the public tax payroll? In a society of the equally competent, we may surprise ourselves as to how cheaply government efficiency and justice can be purchased, and, how much thinking people can do for themselves. Look at New England town government.

End of the Great Corporation?

This issue will become one of the great battlegrounds of ideas and practices of the post-twenty-first century. It is not in the interest of the basic structure of modern corporate organization even to think of any reduction to more efficient and profitable mass production. The predictive caution here is that, as we proceed into the twenty-first century, the geometric growth in quantity of items produced and sold for a profit will run into the antinomies of modern technology and demography. Even the modern technology corporation demands productivity. Cisco Systems laid off 8500 workers in 2001 when the productivity (sales) of each worker in the corporation fell from $710,000 to $470,000.[4]

This has to led to a stable or shrinking work force in order to increase the stream of income. Naturally there have to be an increase in customers who will buy, corporate or individual. On the other hand, every day a flood of hands is coming into the world. How do we balance out the smart people who are devising ever more efficient ways of eliminating jobs and the not so smart people who are flooding out of our philanthropic medical facilities? What do we do with this mass of humans with time on their hands? How de we support them, keep them entertained? Who will then pay for the products of high-tech efficiency?

In this scenario, the long-term maintenance of the entire system of high technology and mass entertainments is fragile, generating its own inner contradictions. The shrinking paying customer base must eventually put an end to this "business plan." Its premise is based on the expanding global system of trade and prosperity that floats all boats. Without this vision of economic growth, not alone a prosperity based on World Bank philanthropy from the current *haves*, the system has nowhere to go. It becomes moribund.

In a demographically stable world economy of middle-class thinkers and producers (the highly intelligent), the only alternative is a long-term transition toward a more intense capital and productive system of craft technology. Here, we would promote a long-term demographic balance that would harmonize with the humane maintenance of our physical and biological environment. In contrast with the present vision of the future, we here conjure up an infinitely expansive, creative, innovative system that would require more skilled makers and entrepreneurs, and a more discerning customer, within a balanced demographic profile.

In a world of 1.5 billion souls, we might be surprised to see the flourishing, of a wholly new economy of small-scale business operations, with much international trade. The ancient Sumerian and Hellenic states buzzed with unique tools, crafts, value-added raw materials (olive oil in hand-decorated jars), eagerly traded far from home, distant and discerning markets better known to them than we dare think. Growth was then defined in terms of newly-styled creations, the growth of the new, not in the vast numbers of sameness that belch from our factories today. This economy functioned in the still restrained demographies of the European Renaissance and the early modern period, the seventeenth and eighteenth century. It is quite likely that similar cases could be made for the economies of China and India before the great population bloat of the late-eighteenth to twentieth centuries.

Mass production and consumption came at a time when the exploding populations of the world were still in balance with the capacity of the earth to provide raw materials, along with its expansionary move into less dense population ecologies. Also, the stimulation for growth by the high intelligence, educable populations of Europe, North America, Northeast Asia in the twentieth, early-twenty-first century created a blizzard of scientific and technological products.

Modern medical research also issuing from these Western civilizational redoubts created a new philanthropic One-World outlook toward the somnolent "third world" peoples heretofore subject to colonial supervision, else slavery. It is this barely century-old uncontrolled explosion of the dependent of the world that will ultimately collapse the present economic system. The natural reduction of fecundity in the developed world, its sensitivity to the need for ecological balance, is contrasted with impoverished Muslim farmers or unskilled laborers barely able to read or write, many still practicing polygyny, their women brutalized and coerced into having ten or more children.

When we argue for localized and specialized crafts, technology, products of distinct individual minds in their contextual nationalities and ethnicities, we do not foreclose the long reach of a Microsoft, even a Coca Cola. There will likely always be transnational corporate entities that have patent rights over their discoveries and developed technologies, medicines. These products will be traded, the wealth transmitted back to the home nationality in return for value-added items from the recipient nation. The smartest, most productive ethnicities will live somewhat better than the less innovative. But not much, as the buyer will still have to have the wherewithal to buy. It is quite possible that such global brands will have their local subsidiaries producing in the setting of consumption. This is what Coca Cola does today.

Still, it is likely, as with a variety of products including automobiles, that consumer cultures will desire somewhat different stylistic or functional versions of these international symbols of modernity. Thus it will make sense for the holders of the intellectual rights to products of such international import to localize their production. Here, a variety of taxation issues, the redirecting of profits to the home company, would become subject to international law, a useful function in which the IMF, WTO, and UN could be involved.

We will always require an international system of law to manage issues of technology, communications, transportation, as we do now. But clearly, it will be from the standpoint of our material prosperity, trade involving a far more interesting array and choice of products that contrast with today's dreary stereotyped production by the modern multi-national corporations. Today, the struggle is for international dominance of similar products in the market place. This type of fierce competition will wither as the possible returns from further expansion dry up.

After the present systems freezes into dysfunctionality, and we become more rational about the need for demographic balance and intellectual potential, localism will begin to shape the dynamic of economic relations. What we should buy or sell will be determined by a more discerning and disciplined consumer. Perhaps there will be less wealth per individual than today for the purchase of things. But things will be bought, determined more by what delights and seduces the senses as they are directed through the aegis of the cortex.

We will lose the armies of factory workers. But we have already lost armies of farmers to the machines, great rows of accountants, typists, secretaries in the great insurance and financial organizations of the 1940s. The productivity of labor goes up, the jobs shrink, and the labor force with the greatest skills at the lowest possible productive cost will win out.

In classic pre-industrial settings, free, innovative enterprise has underpinned the prosperity of cities and nations. The freedom to make something new, provide a new service, allows the most creative humans to stimulate their fellows into more imaginative envisionments of the present. Here will reside the great economic theme in a world beyond this century, when reason finally takes hold in our halls of power. A practical human dream: the international explosion of mind power and talent, in harmony with the diverse richness of human intelligence; a search for new knowledge through science.

The Classless Society

Marx envisioned a world in which material differences between individuals and families would be conditioned by functional reality. Humans need different material accoutrements in order to pursue their livelihoods and lifestyles. The engineer, a personal shop within which to "fiddle around." The doctor, offices and lab facilities to do his work. The musician, a place to practice so that neighbors do not pound the ceilings demanding surcease. The scholar, a quiet library space, today the internet. No place in this world for the squalor of the garbage dump, shanty, or the streets of the homeless, the multi-homes of the super-rich. Marx accepted the reality of differences in humans, but these not to be contaminated by power enforcements.

Perhaps Marx would have tolerated a world of "equal ignorance," where the relatively well-off trucker would choose cultural preferences at high variance to the minister of the local Presbyterian Church or the classics scholar at Yale. If the raw intellectual skills of the individual, the jack-of-all-trades workman suffice to gain him/her a place in the economic scheme of things in an environment of free competition for such a place in the sun, then we are all wiser for the lesson learned.

Classlessness was realized in the period 1950-2000 in both Western Europe and Japan, as born out by the statistics given above with regard to comparisons of compensation between CEO and average employee. This was achieved through the dissemination of educational opportunity for all, resulting in skill levels even enough to provide for real competition for positions of responsibility and power. Underlying this attainment of educational and relative economic parity was a heritage of ethnic/national inbreeding, the mating of cousins. The result, the intellectual uniformity of these peoples.

Indeed, there were French esthetes, and English traditionalists, Dutch burghers, but all were part of that basic European-descended Cro-Magnon heritage. No question that the Europeans are greatly diminished in brain power from their nineteenth-century potential. Here, the horrors of two world wars and the *Holocaust*. What remained of the old intellectual creative potential was still equal to the upwardly moving line of techno-economic learning required by the advance of scientific knowledge. The same can be said of the Japanese, who also suffered serious losses of some of their most intellectually talented men during the wars. Yet the Japanese rose to the challenge of the times: to create a society unriven by class tensions. The remaining cousins reproduced; they were all Japanese.

We thus have a model of a world without the terrible differences in material and educational conditions that we see today in most of the Third World and in the underclass minority ethnic populations, the non-European Hispanics, Africans, Muslims of the developed nations. The great obstacle to achieving the classless, egalitarian society of the future is one of mind. The blockade lies in the recalcitrance, the raw intransigence of our own educated classes to understand the factual basis for the oncoming failure of our global culture, and thus, its ultimate corrective. It may seem ironic to blame our mental quicksand on these most "bright and beautiful" but it has always been thus.

The ordinary bloke on the street, or as the reactionary, William Buckley, once said (here paraphrased), pick at random any hundred names from the Boston telephone book, and you will find more common sense than in one hundred randomly-chosen names from the Harvard faculty.

Marx himself perceived these mental barriers in the world of the nineteenth-century power brokers. His perspective, true, was from the reading room at the British Museum. But also, he had a good street view from his decrepit flat in Soho. His followers, intoxicated with reading room intellectualism, gained their power over the twentieth-century mind. They were remiss in not looking down the avenues of reality.

Endnotes, Chapter 7

[1] Justich, R. 2005. "The Underground Labor Force Is Rising to the Surface," *Bear Stearns Asset Management,* New York.

[2] Morgenson, G. 2004. *The* New *York Times*, 1/25/2004.

[3] O'Brien, T. L. 2005. "Mayday? Payday? Hit the Silk: Golden Parachutes Glow Again," *The New York Times*, 1/11 2005.

[4] Mendy, K. D. 2002. "What's That Floating in the Punch Bowl?" *The Net Economy*, May.

Chapter 8

Religion Digs Deep

Obdurate Pulsations
How many times have modern intellectuals tried to bury religion, and failed?

During the French Revolution the hatred against the Church was so great that the Enlightenment vision of a radical emancipation of humans from the mental imprisonment of the priesthood became uppermost. Confiscate its property, institute a new culture of free thought. How quickly this Enlightenment ideal was reshaped into the thump of the guillotine. Then, under Napoleon, came the *Marseillaise* of international conquest.

In the new United States, a more sober and egalitarian agrarian society sought to harmonize its political freedom with the rationalism of the Enlightenment and its scientific ethos of knowledge and mastery of nature. Under the Constitution and its Bill of Rights, religion was separated from the political supervision of the state. Here, a rebirth of the old two-fold truths of high medieval philosophy, the private truths and worship of the citizens, now separated from the public, secular truths engendered in our civic political life. A high wall of separation, Jefferson suggested.

In the nineteenth century, Marx and the socialist movement once more railed against the superstitious hold that the churches and synagogues of the West still maintained over the people. Marx peered behind this blur of presumed irrationality, concluding that religion was imposed on the proletarian masses, themselves excluded from real educational enlightenment. In this way, the economically dominant classes might exploit the workers themselves as they were enthralled by the mystery, the pomp of religious ritual. Religion was the opium of the people, according to Marx, the means by which these masses could assist in their own abject subjugation.

The twentieth-century communist political incarnation of this atheistic theme ultimately failed in the heartlands of East Europe. Poland and now Russia led the way to the gradual re-establishment of Roman Catholicism and the Russian Orthodox Church as new state religions. Israel is an officially Jewish state, even if this definition is more ethnic and historical than strictly theological. And, of course, the Islamic world knows of few secular freedoms, in process, spinning off a worldwide terrorist movement dedicated to "jihad," the Islamicization of the globe.

Wherever one goes, except for the advanced states of the West, organized religion enters the twenty-first century far more powerful in influencing the shape of international culture, the politics, the general intellectual outlook of the people than it did a century earlier.

There are complexities to this picture. The United States in its multicultural, multi-religious commitments still holds valiantly to the constitutional injunction of separation of church and state. In Western Europe religious participation drops "alarmingly," the churches are empty, the moral birth control/abortion interdicts from the hoary centers of Roman Catholicism, Spain and Italy, are ignored. The high intelligence of the Northeast Asiatics, their recent submergence under totalitarian forms of belief, may hold off a revival of their own ancient traditions, even the new infatuation with Christianity.

Religion's Search for Meaning

Nature did not present to humans a brain and a nervous system with a well-detailed handbook of operation, in good English, of course. We had to learn what this powerful instrument could do for us. In the beginning it was an inchoate power machine for the survival of the species, anticipating and smoking out causal relations, integrated memory associations. The brain with pulsating nervous energies vibrated in expressions from that of the animal and human killer, to sexual passion, then love and compassion. Little by little, humans learned about the usefulness of this brain. Above all this radiation of mental energy throbbed with that unexpressed word, *WHY*?

To find meaning and significance in the interactions of the individual, with his group, and an unforgiving outside world, we reify symbols into realities. Such meanings and acts are commonly associated with primitive religious practices, human and animal sacrifice; totems of value; sacred objects, sacred animals, sacred places on high. The negation, too, taboos and prohibitions, human actions, places, animals, and objects, all sacral objectifications of signification that seem practically irrelevant to our own sophisticated eyes. Yet, a lightning bolt, a split tree, drinkable water discovered coming from a hillside, a bird hovering over a dying animal, all symbols of meaning to life and survival, could precipitate wonder, and that question, *why*, what does it mean for our destiny?

A hilltop, the ziggurat or pyramid rising from the plain, an artificial mountain close to the sun, stars, moon. These were special places in the human search for meaning. No longer casual celebrations of the seasons, of the crops, or even sexuality on high. The sense of wonder and the weakness of humans in the face of remorseless nature conjure fears of personal weakness, the breaking of unstated moral laws, and thus the iniquity of the act, which requires expiation. There comes a need to appease the anger of the gods. In primitive annals of tribal survival, it leads to the sacrifice of the eldest male. "Take your son, your only son, Isaac, whom you {Abraham} love, and go to the land of Moriah {temple mount in Jerusalem}, and offer him there as a burnt offering on one of the mountains that I shall show you." {Genesis 22: 2}

The religious emotions of awe, humility, reverence express themselves in painted images of animals, hunting scenes, Madonnas, mosaics, magical rugs, ritual dances around the fire, tribal fife and drum orchestras, all exploding the many sensual powers of mind intertwined with an infinity of appeasing religious acts. Think of a Baroque cathedral, the roar of the great-lunged pipe organ soaring forth the counterpointal linearity of a Bach cantata. Chorus and soloists, setting aside their measured Puritan phrases, utter transcending guttural exhalations of esthetic and religious commitment to these unseen powers. Don't look askance at this human force.

Evidence from the primitive tribal world of subsistence hunting and gathering hints at an emotional world of religious feeling that is pervasive and overpowering. There is hardly any dimension of life that does not pulsate with the emotional rhythms of the religious sensibility. Most involve the moral directive of right and wrong, the proper ministrations of ritual in every minor dimension of life. Naturally, the punishments for violations of these rigid regulations and ceremonial obligations are severe. The religious Jew or Muslim must worship in the proper manner so many times during the day, keep the Sabbath, observe rigid food restrictions, certainly conform to rules for sexual behavior.

What is right or wrong, if not a guidance system for survival in a world no longer known by instinct, but by choice?

One need only read the Old Testament to see the intellectual articulation of these primeval tribal patterns. It is rare to find any raw behavior that is not under sacramental control. The religious web of obligations to the group knows of no exit for individual freedom to experiment with the new, the possible unknown.

This is why for both tribal groups as well as ancient semi-literate societies, religion ultimately can become a dead weight. The ancient Egyptian priesthood had the insurance of the Nile to save it from change. But even after three thousand years of ceding change for ritual and the clergy, the Egyptians would be subject to three thousands more years under the heel of the outsider.

It is hard to say whether the Cro-Magnons, c.25K BP were under the thrall of such mystical experience. There is little evidence for clear religiously significant evocation in their art or technology. Perhaps it was absorbed into the mystery of sexual energy, the reproductive pulsations of animal and man, the significance of fecundity and survival. Certainly the extent to which the female vulva is ubiquitous in the carvings and paintings of male artists reveals their objectification of the allure and power of this magnet. But whether such evocations were more than male ribaldry bordering on the pornographic, we can only wonder.[1]

When we consider Sumerian city life, c.3000 BCE, it is clear that the secular world has carved out an independent inertia for itself. The religious symbols, civic temples, as in Greece, were separated from the mundane secular, both as ritual memory, often with bloody sacrificial festivals, and also as a communal Fort Knox of storehouses and supplies. The Biblical warning of the seven hard years was an ancient holdover of the search for cause and effect over life and death. This sober acquiescence we have cavalierly ignored. Priests, then, as with the later Dominican and other friars of the medieval monasteries, specialized in cultivating and managing agricultural gardens, but also in the literary accounting skills necessary to keeping track of this community wealth. In Sumeria, the "lugal" (big man) the powerful family leader, was transformed from tribal autocrat into diplomatic, spiritual, and military leader. He negotiated irrigation agreements with other towns, adjudicated family disputes, coordinated the wealth of the community, organized the military force. He eventually assumed an independent non-religious function.[2] Thus went the democratic practices of the placid Sumerian towns.

Egypt was insulated and infused with the ancient rhythmic rewards and punishments of the Nile. The powerful religious symbolic structures, including the pharaohs' great mausoleums, gradually took on an institutional life of their own. Withal, the privileges of the ancient animal gods and their priestly protectors, the more conservative Egyptian culture took care that the worship of deities, the role of priests and shamans would yet not interfere with the practical requirements of farm and craft. The Egyptians, as well as the Mesopotamians, attempted to separate the psychic worlds of religion and natural causation. Especially in the case of the Mesopotamians, the gods themselves took on qualities of the economic and civic struggle with uncompromising nature. The kings could only proclaim their nearness or alliance with the gods, rarely King as god.

The mythological world of gods and goddesses created by the Greeks and the Romans symbolized the mysteries of human nature and behavior, the lusts for power, treachery, faithlessness. The special gods were community protectors symbolizing the heritage, power, and secular glory of the people. The Acropolis in Athens, like the ziggurats at ancient Uruk and Kish, became a center for their festive observances—architectural beauty and grandeur on the high place. Below, no less articulated, the special civic reverences for the ordinary citizens, the *theseum*, for workers of the *agora*, the theatres and the drama.[3]

The Greeks united their religious sense with the esthetic, the centripetal civic allegiances symbolized in the Pnyx, the site of the democratically elected assembly, the nod to the historicity of the city. Building on ancient achievements, they opened themselves up to the cortex, in science, philosophy, conscious political discourse, saying to the ceremonial priestesses, this far no further, often too far. Colloquial religious beliefs separated Socrates, Euripides, Protagoras from tradition-wise Athens. To the Oracle of Delphi, priestesses of Dodona and elsewhere, a nod to the mysterious world of life outside the powers of the secular human body and mind. For the religious *hoi polloi*, a consultation about unknown fate, if only for a few drachma.[4]

It has been a slow process of cortical clarification that has advanced this separation of the powerful call of religious feeling and identification from the secular realm of knowledge-seeking and then political decisionmaking. The priests, rabbis, mullahs, monks, whose clericalism has served as guide through these always venerable institutions of worship and signification, give up their claims over human secular behavior, only with great resistance. Both Ahkenaton, c.1360 BCE in Egypt, and Nabonidus, c.540 BCE in Babylon, failed to master the power of the ensconced institutionalized priesthood.

It has been only with great difficulty that the Roman Catholic Church has stepped back from its magisterial claims for secular power, not only political control over kings, but over economic estates and banking wealth, most especially over the mind of humankind. The glory and the weakness of Catholicism lie in their established theology, and the philosophical/intellectual world view that the monks derived from these values. Confronting modern science, issues such as birth control, abortion, cloning, alone remain on the battleground of public policy for the Church.[5]

In the Muslim world, no overriding theological claims bar the human mind from the secular scientific world, and, in turn, applying this knowledge to political and economic matters. Rather, it is the weak intellectual profiles of Muslim populations in general that hinder the adoption of modern scientific technology, as both program and guidance system. This could have revolutionized their material and social lives and transformed Islam into an eastern Protestantism.

Rather, rote incantation of the catechisms of ancient religious devotions now constitutes the core Muslin educational program. In northern Nigeria, Province of Kano, 2003, radical Islamic mullahs persuaded the local population to refuse anti-polio vaccines (to be distributed by the United Nations), claiming that Americans had laced the vaccine with anti-fertility chemicals in order to degrade the Islamic population of Nigeria. This has led to the rapid spread of polio in the region. Such superstition and religious obeisance explain much about the decline of this once-powerful historical force.

In the twenty-first century, Western religious leaders will search for new and "relevant" ideals from increasingly alienated congregations. Momentary flirtations with seemingly fashionable social issues, exuding a veneer of moral urgency: redistributionist social programs, homosexual rights in and out of the church, wars against out-of-style tyrannies. Are these the issues that have traditionally drawn humans into holy temples and led congregations to pray, think, renew one's religious identity?

A need will always exist to reflect on the sacred and the profane, the weakness of self, the unfairness of events, the complexities and tragedies induced by inexorable nature, the need to bond together with others of like commitment and heritage in wonder of this eternally hostile universe. Humans will always ask the unanswerable *why* about birth, life, individuality and mortality. The logic of scientific analysis is helpless before such concerns.

The Role of Religion and Science

The rise of Protestantism in the sixteenth century brought with it the great transition in the emancipation of the instrumental mentality to deal with the world in terms of secular cause and effect. By turning away from the political controls of the Roman Church, the Protestant communities of northern Europe could proceed to a reanalysis of their Christian roots. This opened the door for capitalism and science. Going back to the original Biblical texts, interpretation and understanding now undergirded by the injunction to the congregation to become literate, to learn to read and communicate, Protestantism freed the critical mind. To be sure independent Catholic thinkers Giordano Bruno, Nicolas Copernicus, Galileo Galilei made their impact on the Renaissance world of inquiry. The burning of Bruno, 1600, the judgment by the Inquisition in 1632 of Galileo's guilt, had their inhibiting aspect.[6]

It was not easy in the north. Calvinism attempted a strict community-centered and puritanical interpretation of scripture. Michael Servetus earned disciplinary condemnations from both Catholic and Protestant theologians, being finally burnt to death in Calvinist Geneva, 1553. The overriding vision of an omnipotent God who willed the inevitable destination of the soul, heaven or hell, could give scant comfort to the uneasy individual in an increasingly dynamic world. Choosing to live was ever more dangerous. Thus good works marked by worldly success, contributing to the philanthropic efforts of the Protestant churches, run by the voluntary communities of assent, became essential signs of an individual's immortal destiny.

Knowledge coming out of navigation, the industrial crafts, astronomy and trade began to take on a super-ordinate religious value. But the rational, practical mind, as Max Weber (1864-1920) chronicled this evolution in *The Protestant Ethic and the Spirit of Capitalism*, gave ever more significance to the power of natural philosophy and the sciences to improve life and thereby to serve God.[7] These Protestant northerners while maintaining deeply devout households and community disciplines through their freely chosen denominational commitments, entered onto the road of a new philosophical exploration of nature, to secure the bounty that the human brain could reveal by its study.

The explosive power transmitted by this new method of thinking about the external world as an object of human experience led to the expansion of Europe beyond its geographical confines. Concomitantly the awareness that this mind could choose to rule itself democratically, emancipated from divine injunction as represented in a Church and its monarchical overseers, expanded into a broader philosophical understanding of the significance of this powerful knowledge. The world of nature external to humans was now viewed by the intelligentsia not as a product of a divine being, but as a set of evolving laws given in nature, to be discovered by man.

Immanuel Kant, 1724-1804, writing in the pivotal century of the Enlightenment, c.1770, could separate religion and the other modalities of human thought and experience from reason and science. In his *Critique of Pure Reason* (1781), an encomium to Newton's scientific theories, and in his subsequent *Critique of Practical Reason* (1788), a setting forth of the rational principles underlying religious, ethical, and esthetic thinking, Kant logically separated the two realms. He believed that the human mind was so structured as to impose the laws of Newtonian science—and by implication other scientific laws—on external experience. That is all we can know. About God and the religious, other mental emotions and principles apply. But these are separate from secular knowing.[8]

We must reiterate that the existence of certain cultural universals among the ethnicities of our world indicates a basic similarity of brain structure in the human species. For, it is our bio-neurological structure that spews out these cultural symbols upon the world. And it is this similarity of psychological make-up, a product of our biology, that allows us to create the institutional forms of religion, art, politics, war, family structure, even rational philosophy.[9]

The evolution of culture into civilization can be described as a process of gradual self-conscious awareness through which humans exhibit a great variety of different psychological vectors (interests). We have discovered that, in addition to hunting deer and picking berries, we were interested in fabricating beautiful stone tools, gemstones, in shaping clays and the images and forms that our minds envision to be contained within these natural objects. The same goes for the natural language. Our minds have spontaneously moved us to use language in discourse, song, poetry, narratives, the curses of hatred, the murmur of love. Myths, ritual incantation are there, too, in potential. We discover these possibilities as we develop this rainbow of symbolic articulations that lie within our deeper intellect.

The ability of humans to encapsulate these different modalities of thought and behavior into their most appropriate functions in the pantheon of civilization reflects a higher superordinate type of philosophical understanding. If religion only symbolized miracles, belief in immortality, a tangible judgmental deity, as the radical ideologues of the eighteenth to twentieth century believed, the successful creative scientist would never subsidize his church or synagogue, the business executive would avoid religious and ethnically-oriented philanthropies. Parliaments and legislatures of democratic secular states would enforce the literality of church and state separation. Instead, Parliament, Congress open their terms of office with religious invocations, government buildings are yet decorated with biblical, talmudic, or koranic homilies. True, the Ten Commandments etched in marble is still barred from courthouses.

This higher philosophical capacity of *Homo sapiens sapiens* can objectify these psychologically separable vectors of thought. Then are constructed the various symbolic forms of meaning, along with their civilizational institutions, museums, court houses, universities, churches. Our cultural interests and involvements, arising as they do from this complex of human ways of looking at experience, can serve to reinforce each other. They can build an integrated civilizational approach to human existence. But to do so they have to be recognized for what they are, different thought dimensions of a total human being.

So philosophized Immanuel Kant in his great treatises analyzing the nature of scientific and religio-esthetic, even biological thought. So, too, his twentieth-century neo-Kantian follower, Ernst Cassirer, 1874-1945, who developed his "Philosophy of Symbolic Forms" to save these other, non-scientific, secular modalities of behavior from being labeled *irrational*, as many twentieth-century intellectuals, socialist and democratic saw them, including our own American, John Dewey, 1859-1952.

Their rationality, agreed Cassirer, as with Kant, was not in their scientific logical structure. Rather, it lay in their different map of thinking and its social rules.[10] One cannot thus degrade the thought of the great theologians of our own time and before. It fell to them to explain the inner principles of a different way at looking at human experience. Here, the philosophical religions showed the way in transforming the ancient practices of magic, sacrifice, totem, and taboo into conceptual moral and community values.

Where the Protestants of the Enlightenment succeeded was not in disdaining religious expression, rather in keeping it at arms length from secular thought and social relations, thus promoting the independent and integral evolution of each. In doing so, Protestantism opened the lanes for our explosive and generative scientific civilization.

As we enter the twenty-first century, we are experiencing the consequences of this emancipation of mind, this venturing forth into the shadowy borderlands of scientific, artistic, economic, technological exploration and achievement. New perspectives from our international civilization have now entered this dynamic equation of intellectual, economic, and social exploration. The Chinese, Koreans, Indians, and Japanese have widely different traditions and outlooks on the religious dimension of life and thought. They will thus seriously challenge the old European and the newer North American civilizational mix.

In contrast with the newly modernizing nations of India and Northeast Asia lies a new challenge to the rational integration of the religious modality with the other institutions civilizational life. This antinomy of cultural life rises from the nether world of the failed nations and regions of our world.

For example, in the Philippines, 2004, where contraceptives and birth control pills are readily available, Catholic priests have railed against their use among the poor. The population growth here of 2.4 percent-per-year is one of the highest in the world, 2005 population, c.80 million. At current levels of increase, the population of the Philippines is slated to reach at least 160 million by 2035, the vast majority slated to live at levels of impoverishment that make their present condition utopian.[11]

Even in the U.S., the hold over the minds of a large proportion of the population, controlled by both the Catholic hierarchy as well as fundamentalist and evangelical Protestants, is powerful. Issues such as abortion, stem cell research, cloning—"intelligent design"—are now pondered in the halls of government, often ruling in harmony with theological claims. Much of the involvement of local clerics is based on the rulings of the leaders of the faith. With regard to the nature of life's beginnings and abortion, lay Catholics and priestly scholars have questioned the legitimacy of the 1930 pontifical encyclical, "Casti Conubi," of Pope Pius XI, based on God's killing of Onan {Genesis 38:9} as a patently incorrect interpretation of this passage {see Deuteronomy 25: 5-10}.[12]

When the Pope, speaking *ex cathedra,* revealing the word of God; is later found to be in error by his own clerical, intellectual community, these are signs of liberality. When the laity falls away from the Church because of the pedophilic and homosexual indulgence of a once celibate priesthood; the European and American Catholics inevitably become alienated from their Church and its hierarchy. Already, in practice, they have rejected the Church's birth control prohibitions. There is then, hope for a more rationally directed Catholicism, and in turn a more functional place for institutional religion in the cultural pantheon.

Where Religion Dominates

The Islamic world is the contemporary paradigm of the ancient domination of theism over the secular mind. But, in general, we can say that in the nondeveloping parts of the world, Africa, Latin America, except for a thin minority at the top of the social ladder, the masses are still steeped in superstition, subject to the domination of their churches, and mosques and the exploiting cliques that rule these nations and pay off the "priests." There are calls by the leadership of the West to introduce the institutions of modernity, democracy, free markets, secular schools, emancipation of women from their slavery. And there is much hope that a cleansing war in Afghanistan or Iraq will serve as the model.

But this will not happen. Why?

The reason is the changing nature of social, economic, and technological forces that the modern world has released. There is no longer a developing market for "hands" in the industrial, productive sectors. Indeed, for a decade or two more, a few. But they will be decreasing, perhaps geometrically as ingenious Ph.Ds find more inventive uses for computers, robots, the internet, modern means of producing things that employ fewer people. What jobs will remain will require persons of high educational abilities, persons who will operate where no smart machine can go. This is an information economy, they tell us. Here abstraction, conceptual learning will be required, more than the mumbling of a few rote phrases of repetition extracted from a holy book.

The Northeast Asiatics who have entered the economic race course recognize this. No sooner had Mao died than his eventual successor, Deng, determined to substitute empirical reality for Mao's "little red book" of ideological aphorisms. And China is off to the technological races, graduating in 2003 over 200,000 engineers as compared to the leading technological light of the West, the U.S., its paltry 60,000 engineers, many of them foreign students who will return home. Admitted, Chinese education is often rote. Beyond the school, however, the Chinese learn quickly. Chinese, Japanese, Korean I.Q.s are high, the role of religious and ideological obscurantism fading. This is not to say that the search for a deeper human glue will be not found within some religious home.

But what of the peoples where priest, minister, rabbi, and mullah dominate? Can they ever be guided from without or within to proceed down the same road as India or China? The answer, not now. The evidence for the high intelligence required to proceed upward on the curve of abstract scientific education, except for the few, does not exist. The sad facts are given in the recent historical behaviors of these populations.

They are as much exposed to modern information about social reality as other modernizing nations. No Berlin Wall can withstand television, the internet, the cinema. The reason for the descent into the religious modalities of thought, the subordinate humiliation embodied in truly fantastic views of reality, lies in the facts of a general cultural and educational failure. Simply, abstract intellectual, scientific, mathematical learning cannot here be mastered on the level of the West at its best and now-confident Northeast Asia.

What can an individual do when faced with learning failure, the inability to comprehend abstract texts, to understand complex principles and their dynamic application? What can an individual do with barely basic skill levels? Merely receiving a diploma or degree from an educational institution with rudimentary standards will not suffice. Physical labor supervised from above, perhaps to drive a truck, but be unable to repair it, to hoe a small plot of land, all for subsistence remuneration. Billions of humans throughout the planet are and will be so consigned life to at the periphery.

Their only recourse against this implicit subjugation at the hands of the great technological powers is religious abjectness and terrorism. They know there is no future for them in the information economy. Even the state-owned oil industry of the well-endowed Arab nations is managed by the western oil conglomerates and their surrogates. Without these outsiders there would be constant breakdown and chaos.

To find meaning in an unfriendly climate, those defeated in the competitions of a cognitive world turn to simple, even primitive explanations of their personal fate. They view the successful, often wealthy nations and their cultural emancipations as evil. They fall back on either ideological or theological explanations for their own state of affairs. They view themselves as exploited underclass victims of prejudice and ruthlessness. The modern dominators are religiously tainted, morally despicable groups of non-believers who must be eradicated.

Is it any wonder that in this setting of defeat and non-comprehension, suicide terrorism is born? Back home these rejected will worship charismatic clerics who teach them to hate a world beyond their comprehension. These religious dominators rule the hapless by their supposed closeness to God. The abject defeated have no other source of meaning.

Bear in mind, the hopeful do not kill themselves merely to carry off with them those that they envy. There is a millennial self-denial in this act.

We humans all crave understanding of our lives in this befuddling world. When one is unable to rise up to the educational bar that admits one to the world of science and complexity, there is no other choice but to obey, follow, abnegate oneself before those self-appointed representatives of supernatural power. For many billions throughout our world, and of a variety of faiths, there lies the sole option for finding meaning. The world will remain a place of dizzying change, one that has far outdistanced the skills that their minds can grasp.

Perennial Religious Motivations

Ministers, mullahs, priests, and rabbis are only humans. They intervene to establish an institutional presence in what is a deeply emotional and valued-laden outlook of humans on their own experience and the mysterious outer world. Humans trust them because of their fidelity to those values. We feel the need to have humans who are better, purer than ourselves, who are closer to that universal and higher physical, intellectual, moral presence to which we are all sensitive. Lose that trust, as with the twenty-first-century Catholic priesthood, and the religion itself is shaken to its roots. Yet not all were culpable. Scandal has from time to time rocked this Church, and others. The institution will perdure. Humans need it. This repetitive tale merely testifies to the power of the clerisy to endure and survive, with mediators between this higher mystery and fragile humanity below.

There is a biosocial, indeed an evolutionary explanation to this powerful symbolic form in the pantheon of cultural expression. Realize first that *Homo sapiens sapiens* is an evolutionary "sport." Not beyond the grasp of the Darwinian conceptual trinity: variation, adaptation, natural selection, our extrusion from nature lies at the very edge of tradition.

It starts with the early ontogenetic explosion of the brain in size (*paedomorphism*). The process of variation and "selection in a straight line" that precipitated the growth of the human brain is not rare. Called *orthoselection*, it signifies the successive expression in the phenotype of one trait in a line of animals. This means that the variation, here, brain size and thinking, was extraordinarily successful. Natural selection does not deny positive encores.

This hypertrophic cortex enabled *Homo* to go beyond the selective reach of competitor animals, perhaps to the limit of the more slowly evolving primate pelvis of human females. Because of the historic genetic linkages in the human brain, the cortex dragged with it much of the mammalian underpinnings of affect, the limbic system and the allo-cortex. In the process, this new human brain neutralized much of the ancient mammal and primate instinctual triggers. Emanating from the iso-cortex, cause and effect thinking became a supremely powerful survivalist tool for *Homo*.

A Rubicon was crossed some time in the past 500,000 years, after which the instinctual system faded in its usefulness as a selective behavioral attribute. Perhaps this came about when the dynamics of competition turned *Homo* against *Homo*, thinker against thinker. The lethargy of traditional mutational rhythms, awaiting the right mutations to be fixed in the line, then to move to a new static adaptive relationship with nature, no longer applied. Learning and reacting now had to take place within the generations. New challenges were often human.

Without a libretto of instinctual behaviors, a set of unthinking triggers to action, humans were on their own. Nature and evolutionary history could no longer provide automatic scenarios, time-tested responsive behaviors. The so-called environment of the redistributionist egalitarians no longer existed outside of culture. *Homo* created culture, an environment requiring recreation, momentarily.

This awareness of the concept, thinking about things, was probably reflected in the markings on the decorative plaques, else stone scrapers of Cro-Magnon, 35,000 B.P. These markings are highly reminiscent of the hunter's carvings on his shaft to represent kills, the slash through the four lines to indicate five. Alexander Marshack, who first interpreted these marking for the anthropological community, saw them as chronometric incisions, as attempts to represent abstractly mysterious but regularly occurring phenomena—the menstrual period of the female, the phases of the moon, the days between the break-up of an ice-clogged river, and the return of the salmon.[13]

In the same way, the more general awareness of the seemingly eternal stars and planets, migrating birds, could be countered by the sudden catastrophe. Perhaps it could be the sudden disappearance of the herds, a cave collapse that destroyed a band's comfortable, protective home. Why us? Why not the stupid Neanderthalers hugging the shallow cliffs across the river? The need for explanatory gods relates fundamentally to the fact that we must now create our own *raison d'être* for being and experiencing.

Our gods symbolize our dependence on ourselves for survival, now reified into explanatory forces beyond our ken that will bless us with victory or condemn us to disaster for some incomprehensible free-will behavior. They help us to explain and protect our fragility, to succor the group—in ritual prayer, war dance, the building of a temple on high, even the burnt offering sacrifice of a first-born child.

Science can never satisfy such questions. It is almost comical to see the hypotheses fly forth from the astronomers and cosmologists as to the origin and meaning of the greater universe, the galaxies, dark matter, red shift, nebulae at the edge of perception. They are merely hypothetical shots in the dark, speculations that are formed from these percepts of things distant. We will never be able to understand them, or bring them under the cloak of scientific predictability. Immanuel Kant long ago explained it. Humans cannot jump over their own shadows. The perceptions they receive through these great telescopes are mirrors in which we see ourselves.

We will always feel the need to express this ontological humility. Out of an awareness of our smallness and vulnerability arises the central element of the religious experience. In church, humans often hold the hand of the stranger.

How Far the Need for Religion?

In our mass democratic society, one of the burning issues is the relationship of national policies and the deeper religious values of the various sects. It was one thing for the fathers of our constitutional system to set apart these two great institutions, political and religious, hoping that each would flourish without interference from the other. The Catholics seceded from the tainted King James

Biblical recitations of the Common (Protestant) School in the 1840s.[14] Today we fight over abortion funding, the Pledge of Allegiance, subsidization of private and voucher schools having religious affiliations. The Supreme Court has a long list of critical decisions, made to adjudicate between the common good of the child, the indigent, the fetus, economic exclusion. The all-encompassing state yet has the public tax revenues to be parceled out.

Is it possible for us to achieve the rule of scientific secular rationality and still preserve the rights of those who yet wish to practice ancient or innovative religious, moral, or theological values? It is difficult not to believe that a high I.Q., a modernly educated population will normally reject the literal claims of a God on high, transcendent, an unseen being transmitting dogmatic truths through His or Her mortal agents on earth. These agents, naturally conceived and born of ordinary women, constitute the caretakers of the dogmas and institutions of organized religion. Surely, the legislatures and judiciary of the relatively intimate communities of the post-industrial mass production world will gently strive to protect even such recidivistic deviants from the dominant ethos of the day.

It will be difficult to restructure the traditions and rituals now practiced by the established religions in the practice of those sacral moments of life. Once, a Bible or a Koran reading by a "holy" person could soothe troubled but educated souls. Today, there is a ubiquitous substitute for such traditional sacral commemorations. Millions if not billions of souls, in Europe, America, and Northeast Asia have turned to the secular state to satisfy these deep yearnings for remembrance or celebration. Eventually we could see national cultural, ethnic, civic ritual satisfy such needs. Recall the many million married by a justice-of-the-peace, a representative of the state, all with flowers, wine, family kisses.

The inner personal discipline, the respect for others, many questions of value are ultimately resolved by a person nurtured in the family, reinforced by the ongoing life of the intimate community of value in which we live. These public values are extended further by the rule of law, written and enforced by the larger national or international community.

The slippage in the influence of the clerisy is symbolized in the emergence today of a new professional, the "ethicist," he or she who speaks gravely on questions of contemporary behavior and value for those who have no religious affiliation. Even the thousand year old adjudications in the Talmud cannot tell us what to choose to do *vis à vis* the fast moving social changes of our day. These dynamics will not change in the twenty-first or twenty-second century.

In short, the forms of religious thinking and valuing surely will be altered. Gone will be theological questions as to why God killed so many innocents in the *tsunami*. "Man is the measure," Protagoras intoned in the days of Socrates, in Athens, c.425 BCE.[15] Even for the sophisticated Athenians, this was one secular step too far. They were in the midst of a bloody, unforgiving fratricidal war, so often the bitterest of wars, and in no mood to loosen the bindings of mythological tradition. The peaceful, productive modernism that Pericles had offered to them was hidden by these war clouds. So they deported Protagoras, the visiting foreign *sophist* (teacher of wisdom). Later they would sentence Socrates to drink the hemlock. Socrates surprised them. He stayed and drank.[16]

Modern philosophy was born from these experiences. Questions of ethics, truth, virtue, and the boundaries of moral civic life were thus raised on high, a theme of every future's debate. Today, much of the secular assertion of liberation from the religious hinges on the refutation of the primitive fundamentalisms of contemporary religious practice. We should not discard this primeval psychological vector for its current degradations. Perhaps a culture of reason will be born out of the monstrous horrors of twentieth- and twenty-first-century life. The French revolutionists hoped for such an emancipation evolving from their own bloody date with history.

The key to our external material future lies in the capacity of the human species to think abstractly, carefully and logically, balancing, as the Greeks endeavored to do, the passionate impetuosity of the young with the timorous restraints of the old, perhaps *vice versa*. Ernst Cassirer saw religion as a primal form of human thought and behavior, gradually evolving from it nightmarish emotionalism of the holy versus the tainted. In the highest expression of religion, the writings of a St. Thomas Aquinas (1225-1274), an Averroes (1126-1198), a Maimonides (1135-1204) united the emotional and the rational, giving birth to the two-fold truths of the latter two holy men and their English Christian successors, William of Occam (1285-1349), John Henry Newman (1801-1890). Gradually, out of the weight of such enunciations, the independence of the rational grew into natural philosophy, scientific experimentation, American Pragmatism's "instrumentalism." The supernatural and thus the metaphysical underpinnings of religion may have been carved away. But the pull of tradition, of communality and ethnicity, remains.

It is because of the core perplexities over mankind's place in the world; the mysteries and fragilities of our nature and existence; a species of life, now without nature's close genetic supervision, that the religious dimension will remain a force. Its formal cloaking will change. Recall that for an historical moment the Communist Party served that purpose.

In the medium future new and deeper mysteries will be incubated from the learning gained as a result of the twenty-first-century collapse of our civilizational heritage. By understanding the nature of the powerful psychological intentionalities involved in the symbolism of the religious and its institutions, we may be better prepared for their return. But, it is to be hoped, never at the price of sacrificing science and reason.

Endnotes, Chapter 8

[1] Campbell, B. 1985. *Human Evolution*, 3rd ed., N.Y.: De Gruyter, Fig. 10.3, p. 296; Itzkoff, S. W. 2000. *The Inevitable Domination by Man,* Ashfield, MA: Paideia, pp. 278, 281.

[2] Postgate, J. N. 1992. *Early Mesopotamia.* London: Routledge, Chs. 6, 14; Bottero, J. 1992. *Mesopotamia,* Chicago: Univ. of Chicago, Part IV.

[3] Bowra, M. 1971. *Periclean Athens,* N.Y.: Dial.

[4] Jaeger, W. 1947. *The Theology of the Early Greek Philosophers,* Oxford: Oxford Univ.

[5] (Ahkenaton): Freud, S. 1939. *Moses and Monotheism,* N.Y.: Knopf; Darlington, C. D. 1969. *The Evolution of Man and Society,* London: George Allen and Unwin, pp. 119-121; Thomas, H. 1979. *A History of the World,* N.Y.: Harper and Row, pp. 132-133. (Nabonidus): Sayce, A. H. 1911. "Belshazzar," *Encyclop. Britann.*, 11th ed., N.Y.: Cambridge Univ., Vol. 3, pp. 711-712; Saggs, H. W. 2000. *Babylonians,* Berkeley: Univ. of California, pp. 167-172. (Roman Catholic Church): Pattison, R. 1991. *John Henry Newman and the Liberal Heresy,* N.Y.: Oxford Univ.; Medeley, J. T. S., *et al.* 2003. *Special Issue on Church and State in Contemporary Europe,* London: Portland.

[6] Singer, G. 1968. *Giordano Bruno, His Life and Thought,* N.Y.: Greenwood.

[7] London: Fitzroy Dearborn.

[8] Cassirer, E. 1918. *Kant's Leben und Lehre,* Berlin: Bruno Cassirer.

[9] Boas, F. 1911. *The Mind of Primitive Man,* N.Y.; Macmillan; Eliade, M. 1961. *The Sacred and the Profane,* N.Y.: Harper and Row; Levi-Strauss, C. 1962. *The Savage Mind,* Chicago: Univ. of Chicago.

[10] Cassirer, E. (1935) 1955. *The Philosophy of Symbolic Forms,* II: *Mythical Thought,* New Haven: Yale; Cassirer, E. 1946. *The Myth of the State,* New Haven: Yale; Dewey, J. 1934. *A Common Faith,* New Haven: Yale; Langer, S. 1957. *Philosophy in a New Key.* Cambridge: Harvard Univ. Press.

[11] United States Library of Congress, 2002.

[12] Wills, Gary; Turner, F. M. 2002. *John Henry Newman and the Challenge to Evangelical Religion,* New Haven: Yale Univ. Press.

[13] Marshack, A. 1972. *The Roots of Civilization,* London: Weidenfield and Nicolson.

[14] Kliebard, H., ed. 1969. *Religion and Education in America,* Scranton: Intex; Pope Pius XI, 1931, *Encyclical, Christian Education of Youth.*

[15] Plato (c.390 BCE). *Dialogue, Protagoras*; Zeller, E. 1931. *Outlines of the History of Greek Philosophy,* N.Y.: Humanities Press, pp. 98-101.

[16] Plato (c. 385 BCE). *Dialogue, Crito.*

Chapter 9

Art: Civilization's Center

Criteria

The arts are different from other cultural forms, religion, politics, economics, for example. In religion we can attribute the perdurance of churches, synagogues, mosques, to stagnant tradition, clerics transmitting the transcendental words of a God unseen except by themselves, as transmitted through the holy books. As modern intellectuals, we can deride these verbal and institutional fictions. We attribute their longevity, their hold over the masses to a lack of sophistication, or lack of emotional control of the lower brain over the cortex. In politics we are on strong ground in viewing democratic institutions of decisionmaking as the political form critical to the enhancement of human dignity. In economics, we know that the free enterprise system, a market economy, produces more for the common good than controlled, state supervised, socialist forms. There are here solid criteria for judgments.

We can identify failed states and failed cultures. When Russian airplanes fly, or Chinese space vehicles zoom into space, we can compare such achievements with American efforts in design and articulation. When the Muslim world fails socially, economically, militarily, as compared to the West, we can point to its illiteracy, their ignorance of Western knowledge and science.

Art doesn't conform to such criteria. On Newbury Street in Boston the paintings of a Haitian folk painter can vie for value with a Barbizon landscape. Lulu, the chimp in the Chicago Zoo, in glorious delight, splatters a canvas with paint. We compare it with the considered splotches of a Jackson Pollock, and wonder who's who.

In *The New York Times* Sunday arts section, a concert of the works of Edgar Varèse is reviewed with great gravity. Across the page in the same music section is an analytical consideration of the latest rap CDs for 2005. It's all music isn't it, democracy at work? In all seriousness, it is a tough controversial job to evaluate the late work of Renoir or the landscape paintings of Monet. We argue about the depth of Shostakovich as compared with his contemporary, Prokofiev. Can we engage in an exercise of comparative architectural esthetics, the Roman aqueduct at Nîmes as against the Pantheon, English *vs*. French gothic cathedrals?

Why is it so difficult here to judge, evaluate? Perhaps it is because the arts are pure value. A pile of rubble could constitute a good and solid engineering accomplishment for safe living. But we want to live in something that is "beautiful." In that one word, we come to the heart of the significance of the arts. What we value there is something intangible, a love created by the mind that immediately transcends the materiality of that which is in question. Add it all up, a smell, a sound, a visual image, even a black and white etching or photograph. We smile at Peter Paul Rubens nudes, all avoirdupois, gaze in disbelief at tribal women, lower lips vastly stretched. Even here, female beauty, who is to say?

Meaning

From the time of their first discovery, the so-called Acheulean scrapers and pounders from the very earliest phases in the evolution of *Homo* were viewed with awe. These scrapers were large rocks whose edges had been fluted by chipping to give them symmetrical shapes. To us, they have great esthetic quality. Some scholars have reinterpreted these various utilitarian but esthetically-shaped tools as merely the residue of the chipping process itself, produced to obtain blades to cut, puncture, pound, to kill animals, perhaps humans. Beautiful Acheulean tools the mere residue of a more practical endeavor? Whatever the case, it is difficult to believe that the apparent shapings of these tools, 400-200K B.P., did not have an element of esthetic appreciation-in-the-making.[1]

The awesome specializations in the seemingly practical tool kit of the Cro-Magnons, their inherently conscious beauty, sometimes including tiny blades of puzzling size and shape that could not have had any utilitarian use, add a dimension to the already much discussed cave art of these people, c.35,000 BP. Their dances and songs will remain permanently beyond our ken.[2] Ancient hollowed-out bone tubes with incisions, as if for a flute, and of apparently great age, have been discovered. They hint at a conscious fabrication of musical instruments, c.100,000 BP.[3] In our own time we have reproduced the simple use of natural objects, leaves, human hands, shells, to create interesting sounds. Early pathfinders on the road toward civilized behavior, such as the Cro-Magnons in Europe, indubitably cultivated a rich esthetic life, deeply hidden today beyond their visual residue.

Since we find decoration, art objects, dance, music, in even the most "primitive" peoples of our nineteenth- and twentieth-century worlds, it is clear that the esthetic area of life, while tied closely to religious ritual, aggression and war, sexuality, still can be recognized as an independent dimension of our core

Art: Civilization's Center

psychological make-up. What does it signify for human nature, and for civilization?

We have to consider the special evolutionary conditions of the human advance into sapiency. As the brain grew in size, churning nervous energies poured forth. Evolution witnessed a cortex that expanded beyond the boundaries of natural selection for the ever more useful practical exigencies of life survival. *Homo sapiens* also has a limbic system, an allo-cortex, the ancient primate assemblage, which was enlarged in genetic linkages with the new thinking brain. The result is a highly intelligent anticipatory, relational (cause and effect) thinking creature, within a frenetically emotional primate, both dimensions sharing in the flood of perceptions that enter the nervous system through a sharply discriminatory sensory system.[4]

Clearly much of this sensory input was channeled into the more practical dimensions of earning a living. So, too, were these percepts absorbed and tied emotionally and cognitively to the religious, social, sexual rituals, the creation of myths, magic, the sacral, the feared and tabooed. There are thus many ways in which the emotions of our mammalian heritage and the cognitive hominid ordering of these symbolic cores of meaning are finally expressed in overt social institutions. The interaction between what our senses absorb from the outside world, those energies that well up from below, and the final cortical interpretation and shaping of these perceptions, is also what creates the esthetic product.[5]

Critical to the process of producing a beautiful textile, a lovely tool, a song of haunting feeling, is cortical organization. Certainly, a people threatened, with their survival in question, will have neither the time nor the energy to entertain the new in their art forms. Ossified traditions, fixed in place by religious or political forces will also dampen the creative effort. Yet the Jews, in prosperous "captivity" in Babylon, sang their laments for the memory of Jerusalem to the accompaniment of lyre or harp. And the Chaldeans came to listen, and ask for more.

In traditional art, skill is central to beauty. There is a fine line between the craftsmen symbolized in the medieval guild and the artists who soar beyond the merely fine. Antonio Stradivari, 1644-1737, a great violin maker, was recognized in his own time and became wealthy. Joseph Guarneri (del Jesu), 1698-1744, an extraordinary artist, was unrecognized and died in obscurity.[6] Many other fine violin-making craftsmen of the seventeenth and eighteenth centuries were truly masters. A few rose above this line of recognition to create instruments that were unrivaled in construction and beauty, never hence to be matched.

The fact that we differentiate in this way from the ordinary journeyman and the craftsman, skills shading into artistry, has to do with special talent. We recognize unique talent and genius in a variety of primeval human attributes: the religious shaman, the military or political leader, intimidating and charismatic, the poet or singer who surprises and enchants. The artist contains in special intensity that which we all share. We rise up in appreciation of these talents. Here is something universal before which we can bow.

There is logic to these talents. It is the same logic that allows great thinkers, physicists, or military strategists to cut through the present to perceive new possibilities, relationships. It is argued that the invention of written language was critical to the remembering and ordering of information. How else to achieve some control over nature's irreverence, to secure the hearth and refrigerator? The transition from the aurally-remembered word to the written was critical for the expansion of civilization in time and space, materially and politically.

The written word, in all of its diverse forms, uncovers the congruency of the structure of nature with the form of our minds. Mathematics and geometry, which exploded on the wings of writing, transitioned slowly, from an experimental and heuristic set of guild techniques to become a profession in itself. The world and our mental explorations through language and mathematics are indeed circular; we can never break out. However, within this world of human experience, with so many different dimensions to explore, we seek for the causes and effects of things, relationships, a mental structure as to how things work, and thus how we can live.[7]

So, too, the artist discovers in this perceptual and human world a logic of presentation, whether poetic qualities in language or a new musical form advancing upon the old. Humans built on the forms of existing engineering and architectural knowledge to construct the Giza pyramids, the ziggurats at Nippur and Uruk, the Parthenon in Athens. There is a primeval human interest that creates holiness out of the high place, spanning the prosaic world below. In a tychistic universe, the high represents our closeness to unknown powers.[8]

The esthetic vision while it builds on the different sensory entry points of experience, this outside world, reshapes these images into a logic of perception. Thus we are fascinated to observe today in our museums, the unending creativity of the ancient jewelers. Seemingly prosaic rock viewed with intuited beauty, is fabricated in endless variation. Jewelry, created to enhance mysterious natural beauty, the female form.[9]

This logic of perception is different from the logic of experience expressed in writing. Poetry translates the spoken language into expressive rhythms, a music of words, but not into instructions or directions. Esthetic forms build on an inner logic of appreciation that we find to be inherent in the perceptual materials themselves. Thus the spoken language itself hints at this verbal emotionality, now written down in suggestive form.[10]

The redolence of flowers, interesting food transmits different sensory meanings. We need to objectify such perceptions into perfumes, a gourmet feast.

Art: Civilization's Center

149

See the style sections of newspapers and magazines in their efforts to communicate the esthetics of ordinary daily experience, the wine analyses and tastings, the flower arrangements having both visual and olfactory impact. Words, to attempt to describe the indescribable.

How do we understand the "ugly": smells, visuals, sounds, tastes? Are they culturally relative? Olfaction? Out of curiosity, we might ask what we can do esthetically with the smell of gasoline, burning garbage, sewage, chemical effusions, the visual horrors of urban slums, the cacophony of the city, notwithstanding Gershwin's *An American in Paris*. Cognition will strive to create art forms from what strikes us positively, but will usually reject any esthetic considerations for the culturally repellant.

Touch is also difficult to objectify discursively. How do we objectively symbolize the experience of soft infant skin, cool smooth marble, delicate rose petals? Compare touch to the jottings of notes on paper as prelude to the composing of music to be played; the preparatory drawings of a painter; the architectural and engineering plans for a great skyscraper.

This difficulty is true of the esthetics of taste. A cookbook is a poor hint of the great things to come on the table. Perhaps that is why these three sensory modalities, touch, taste, smell, create the most private, effete, kinds of esthetic involvement. And thus they are more closely bound to culture and community, and relative in appreciation. Conclusion: esthetics that evolve from diverse sensory inputs have varying cognitive public communicability.[11]

Many have wondered why Asiatic students and publics have embraced, and with a vengeance, Western music and art forms. Part of it comes from the same power that Hellenic Greek culture and art exerted over the subsequent international Hellenistic, 300 BCE-300 CE. A powerful culture militarily and economically comes armed not merely with guns and butter, but also the cultural institutions that increase their significance alongside secular material creativity and power.

Drama, music, art have largely become public forms. They enjoy powerful cognitive as well as dynamic innovative qualities. The home-grown, though intellectually rich historical arts of Northeast Asia no longer resonate for their own populace. The Asiatic students and citizens have been able to take this public cognitive quality inherent in the Western visual, dramatic, musical arts, and to move themselves rapidly into those modalities of thought. So, too, armed with the intellectual wherewithal to appreciate the cognitive powers inherent in Western arts, they have also turned the tables on the West in the more discursive areas of technology and business.[12]

Sound and sight require distant receptors for animal adaptation. They have evolved over evolutionary time as the major "time to think, attack, or run" information-giving senses. These sense receptors were increasingly coordinated with the cortex in its integration of information, giving the bearers of these sensing/thinking structures that breath of time for momentary behavioral adjustments. Here adaptation for survival surmounted the transgenerational processing of seemingly random genetic mutations, aiming for adaptation and fitness. The brain was a paradigmatic "within-the-generations" means for survival. These distance senses integrated into information for brain and behavior allowed for successful procreation, another day in the sun. As passed on to *Homo sapiens sapiens*, these two perceptual modalities are highly amenable to intellectual and thus universal human judgments.

Touch, taste, and especially smell, as noted, are culturally sensitive. Smells deemed normal or even enhancing can be repugnant to persons of other cultures. One can love the architectural beauty of the ruins of ancient Cambodia, Angkor Wat, but be revolted by ordinary village aromas of the local towns nearby. The residents themselves would normally think nothing of these scents. Chinese aristocrats once derided the intense body odors of visiting Caucasoid Europeans. So, too, the first Europeans explorers visiting Africa below the Sahara felt free to comment negatively about the body odor of Africans.[13]

The highly personal, non-objective, non-discursive world of smell in humans contrasts sharply with our ancient mammalian heritage in which olfaction was a principle source of information about the outside world. The visual and auditory were secondary. Far back in evolutionary history, the ability to separate out the different significances of smell could automatically trigger life or death behaviors. Even today our Fifth Avenue poodles articulate their world, without words, by sniffing and burrowing their way around our cities.

Musical Form and the Cognitive

Of all the perceptual receptors, sound that seeks to make music is perhaps the most paradigmatic searchlight into the relationship between our biological energies and their transformation into symbolic meaning. The visual is the most conducive to abstraction and subject to cognitive control. The three perceptual realms, taste, touch, and smell, can be refined and cultivated as art forms, but with the modest exception of smell, they evoke few powerful throbbings from the limbic system.

Music has this connection. Instrumental music, linked to song and dance, digs deep into the basic rhythms of the heart, the soul, and the libido. But at the same time, music is capable of being organized intellectually, when written in musical notation, whether as a piano sonata in the diatonic form, expressed according to the geometrical plans of the Joseph Schillinger system or Arnold Schönberg's twelve-tone modernities.[14]

Probably since the beginnings of civilization and the development of writing, civic leaders have been tempted to organize and control music. On the one hand, individuals remember songs for their emotional connotations. They want constant recall. Wild Woodstock events threaten to bring down the walls. Civic events have included children's choruses probably before the Greeks institutionalized such celebrations. In this vicinity of participation, memory and repetition do not suffice. The chorus masters will devise some kind of mnemonic notation.

Voice and dance are combined in the body. In all cultures, they are already amplified in their expressive power by technology, the fabrication of instruments, even if only percussive, rhythmic articulation. Dance requires costume. Europe celebrated the ballerina. The Sumerians thought dancing to be essential to womanhood.

In the first moments of cultural development, music required more than the voice. It is probably true that modern rock, rap, even the revival of ersatz folk music that we hear at the various festivals would not be what they are—mass popular cultural entertainments—were it not for the electronic microphone and amplification systems and all the glittery lighting effects that go with such entertainments. Only if it is loud, outrageous, and heavy with thundering beat will the roaring throngs pay the tab.

Technological and craft inventions are critical to the advancement of all the arts. The Gutenberg printing press created a religious revolution (Protestantism and the vernacular Bible). But it also made possible universal literacy and the broadest dissemination of literature and drama. Would we know of a Shakespeare, beyond the Globe, were not his thought soon put to print? The perfection of the techniques for making oil paint allowed a budding art to flourish up to our own time.

Architecture presents an interesting example of the limits of pure material enhanced esthetics. There has always been much controversy over the trade-off between esthetics, commercialism, and engineering. The Twin Towers of 9/11 tragedy exemplifies such problems. An old example: It is now hypothesized that the supervising masons of Beauvais Cathedral in France, 1571, once the tallest in France, had a plan of engineering plausibility to remedy the earlier collapse of the great apse, and would support the even higher tower. Advice ignored, the new tower collapsed in 1573; no longer would this great monument reach for heaven. The Uruk civilization of the Sumerians, c.3500 BCE, 5000 years earlier, had attempted to fabricate concrete for use on their temple platforms. They failed, and they went back to using baked and dried mud brick.[15]

In music, the rich but muted sounds of gambas and medieval organs, the golden-voiced church choirs were superceded by ever more powerful pipe organs. Papa Bach, invited to give critical judgment of new church organs around Leipzig in the 1740s, blessed those with "good lungs." The pianoforte supplanted the plucking clavichord and the tinkling harpsichord. Eventually the steel innards of the modern nine-foot Steinway or Baldwin grand allowed for the Rachmaninoff Second Piano Concerto.

The model of the violin was the tiny German peasant *fiedle*, shrill and penetrating. The gamba, soft, rich, aristocratic, gave way to this newly-evolving esthetic which paralleled the great bourgeoisie craft, commercial economic revolution in the making. With this new social phenomenon rose up a middle class attuned to this overt artistic form, a form emerging from both the church and the landed aristocracy. What resulted in music was one of the great mechanical inventions of all times, the violin family. Here, from this complex of woods, constructed in classic proportions of spruce, pine, ebony, maple, poplar, and covered with a mysterious transparent varnish of varied colors, emanated a brilliant range of expressive music. Here, this little wood box, its cat gut strings set in motion by a pernambuco wood bow fitted with horse-hair, would produce sound qualities equaled only by the human voice.

Together with the creation of the diatonic scale, the ability to modulate into a variety of keys, which was not possible in the ancient Greek and medieval modes, the invention of new esthetically varied choirs of musical instruments, a great new expressive form was born. This explosive exploitation of musical form was accompanied by concomitant advances in Western science, militarism, and economic power, the cognitive discursive areas of thought.

Study has shown that the medieval polyphonic music of the Gothic cathedral, with its parallel vocal linearity, may have been as powerful intellectually and emotionally as our own recent classical musical forms. Certainly, over a several-hundred-year period, the polyphonic Mass went through a steady development, an evolution of structure and esthetic characterized by increasingly cerebralized compositional techniques.

The timeline between Machaut and Palestrina (fourteenth to sixteenth centuries) reflected a mysterious unity of the Gothic cathedral, Catholic intellectualism, theology and philosophy, and the mystical, if sublimated expressive passions of powerful musical and cognitive minds. We know the names of these artists, the modern transliterations of their compositions, and the resultant stylistic progressions. Sadly, this world, too, is now beyond our auditory and esthetic appreciation. The form of medieval polyphony did not exhaust itself or become barren. It was overtaken by modernity, supplanted by a wholly new set of esthetic, intellectual, and structural possibilities.[16]

One might compare this transition to what is happening today. The old forms have reached or passed their culminating possibilities. New musical grammars are being born. Attendance at symphony orchestras has dwindled; "pops" concerts magnetize audiences far more than the well-repeated classical repertoire. It is old stuff, too, often mimicked by the media as background music. At the grassroots level, symphony orchestras are falling by the wayside.

Art: Civilization's Center 153

Public support for the arts shrinks; schools budgets ignore them. Special education, police, drug enforcement absorb too much of the budget to be spared to enhance for the young a model of meaning espoused by an elite white-haired culture. The great difference between the seventeenth century and the twenty-first century in terms of this transition of musical sensibilities is that the seventeenth century tradition was an intellectually worthy supplanter of the medieval polyphonic forms that had had their own three-hundred-year run.

The classical tradition in music since the seventeenth century represents the discovery of one of the most important creative forms in the history of civilization. It touches us most powerfully, in our emotional biological framework, in its resonance for our abstract intellectual nature. One selects, Monteverdi's *Orpheo*, Bach's *St. Matthew Passion*, Mozart's *Marriage of Figaro* or 40th Symphony, Beethoven's final quartets, Berlioz' *Symphony Fantastique*, Brahms' First Piano Concerto, Wagner's *Parsifal*, Debussy's *La Mer*, Stravinsky's *Firebird*, Bartok's Six Quartets, and so many other composition that take us through a range of styles, from the seventeenth century on. This creativity of mind and body lay implicit in the opportunities for creation by this formal structure.[17]

Students of composition may learn the ins and outs of sonata form, the different developments reflected in the ongoing compositional use of this structure, from the Rococo to the Romantic, for example. But the form as studied in the classroom cannot release a Schubert, nor even a Gilbert and Sullivan, no less a Mahler. Here is the power of the human mind, an ability to see abstract relationships not in numbers or words, but in sounds. Here developed a semantic of knowledge and feeling that could not be transcribed into other symbolic forms. To understand music, it had to be listened to, perhaps followed in score. The logic lay in its capabilities of moving and coordinating both the cortical neuronic structure of our minds as well as the ancient and powerful lower brain, the source of those energies that make us *Homo sapiens sapiens*.

We respect the physicist, molecular biologist, the mathematician who finds beauty and harmony in the equations and structures that they study, in the abstract. In music, it is different. For, in the living performance of a work, a Charles Ives Symphony, iconoclastic and uniquely American, the cognitive takes on a public biology that echoes millions of years of surging vertebrate evolution.

What fascinates the connoisseur of classical music are the many different interpreted (again intellectual as well sensory) versions there will be of the same composition. There are many possibilities for bringing the written notes back to life. That is why lovers of this art return again and again for more. Even in Beethoven's First Symphony, his simple take on the form, a Furtwängler, Toscanini, Beecham will find much that is new and significant.

Exhausted Forms

The Greek temple, the concept of an Acropolis, the variation between Doric, Ionian, later Corinthian capitals and styles, all constitute one of the great esthetic breakthroughs in human history. We copy these models today in our public buildings, to signify majesty, officialdom, and justice. But this is dead architecture, used for want of any other alternative to impute the symbolic civilizational values of a purportedly great people.

Even the Romans, however, attempted to modernize the vision. For, after half a millennium of dominance, these forms had begun to age. The Pantheon in Rome represents an attempt to go beyond. Fortunate we are that it became a church in the Christian era, and thereby survived.

Architecture subsequently went through a series of formal developments, the Romanesque of late Roman Imperial times, the churches extending these pagan engineering techniques and esthetics into the early Christian era. Then came a breakthrough, a new architectural sense of possibility in the Gothic cathedral. Certainly, the engineering advances, the flying vault and other innovations of the unknown geniuses who envisioned these soaring and richly decorated buildings of faith, contributed to this distancing from the past. We can today observe this evolution in the form and substance of an art. Buildings endure. The Roman wall frescoes have faded, the Greek children's choirs, the flute-playing damsels are beyond memory.[18]

> In one of the earliest descriptions of the Pythian games given at Delphi in the fifth (or sixth) century B.C., a certain Myron is recorded as having received a special victory citation for his performance on the aulos, a double-reed oboe-like instrument, an instrument used both in Dionysiac festivals and military celebrations and combat. His was a long series of variations on the mythological theme of Apollo and the Minotaur. (One can guess that this musical tradition was not too far from the Hindu virtuoso improvisations made famous by Ravi Shankar and his company in the mid-twentieth century.)[19]

And so it has come to be with the modern artistic forms—in painting with its own half-a-millennial exploration of both the outer and inner visual world, classical musical forms with their four-hundred-year hold over the civilized European and, more recently, Northeast Asiatic mind. Great social, demographic, and techno-economic changes have now come over the world of the twenty-first century. Vast new populations with neither the heritage nor the interest in these forms of expression reshape our perceptions of the artistic.

For the moment, these transitions flood the fearful perceptions of the well-ensconced, -educated European and North American middle classes. What is happening to our cultural heritage? To be fair, there are also internal formal and esthetic causes for the loss of creative verve in the arts. One candidate, symbolic of esthetic decline, is the increasing academicization of this Western tradition.

Art: Civilization's Center

The art forms retreat from the "public street" to the museum of academia; always a hint of the gradual arteriosclerosis of both the visual and the musical arts.

In the case of the visual arts, the invention of photography in the mid-nineteenth century, followed by its own internal development as an art form, certainly challenged painters and draftsmen to seek inspiration in other interpretive pictorial traditions. The development of cinema added another technological enhancement to the visual as well as dramatic experience. Both inventions added to the palette of the esthetic.

Their popularity lies in their modest intellectual potential, overpowered by the sheer virtuosity of the medium, and their inherent and tremendous mass commercial possibilities. Modern art competes with its own high-flying commercialism, now under the umbrella tutelage of the ensconced critics. They alone can sit in judgment. Private and corporate wealth pours in. After all, given Matisse and Picasso, why not other $40 million paintings by any one of our current favorites? All we need is to persuade the esthetic arbiters to reify the chosen into classical eminence. Lulu, the chimpanzee at the Chicago Zoo, as well as her students, would salivate at the bananas here to be won.[20]

In music, more than in modern art forms, a similar set of circumstances intrudes on the esthetic scene. But here, the controlling "critical" establishment must meet the test of audiences/listeners as well as the critics. Musical scores garner few kudos hanging on the walls of the S and P 500. And while the smears of color that decorate great homes gather "oohs" and "ahs," the raw limbic needs of the music-hungry are unevenly met by the tone rows of Arnold Schönberg's modernist system or the clunks and scratches of John Cage's prepared pianos.

As with photography, cinema, for the visual and dramatic arts, modern materials and engineering technology in the case of architecture, music too has been impacted by an explosive set of influences from the expanding international culture, and modern electronics. African-American jazz, Latin American motifs, the music of the "big band," Broadway musicals, all have exponentially expanded our aural repertoire.

The response of the classical tradition to this new opportunity to shift from contra-limbic system academicism to a more balanced equating of the deeper rhythmic and emotional power of the new popular semantic has been weak. Except for a few compositions—George Gershwin's *Porgy and Bess*, *Rhapsody in Blue* are examples—the two worlds have not met. With the introduction of synthesizers, which produce the virtual sounds of real orchestras for the ballet and Broadway, listeners of CDs in one's home, the supplantation of the classical traditions in the twenty-first century may well be paradoxical. Our destiny, limbic system cacophony, a cortical whimper.

Elitism and the Arts

Much is made in the contemporary view of the arts that the classical, the paintings for Renaissance princes, or merchants, the classical music of the aristocratic and bourgeoisie wealthy in the eighteenth and nineteenth centuries was inimical to a truly populist view of art. Such art would ostensibly grow from working and middle-class modernistic social conditions. In our own time, the populist argument reads that the cultural *élan* of the West is not descending in intellectual and esthetic standards. Rather the new popular arts are readying the masses for a truly universal egalitarian culture.

This was the rationale for the Stalinist critique of Russian high cultural productivity, which after the revolution, 1917-1929, still stimulated painting, music, literature, dance. It was still Slavic in nature, continuing the Czarist heritage of the nineteenth century, itself a noble esthetic tradition flourishing parallel with autocracy. Stalin, after he gained power, c.1930, substituted paintings whose subjects were noble factory drivers for abstract art, censored Shostakovich and Prokofiev for their *avant garde* dissonances, preferring the Gayne Dance Suite of Khatchaturian, exiled numbers of poets and novelists to the Gulag, killed others in a final 1950s orgy, and in general destroyed the East European Slavic esthetic tradition while coercing his satellite partners east and west.[21]

The truth is that great intellectual art has been for the people, for all people with an educable intelligence capable of appreciating its inner meaning. The aristocracies were, indeed, intellectually sensitive opportunists who gained power first. The rush of sculptors, architects, painters, from every village in Italy during the fifteenth and sixteenth centuries, the most successful becoming extremely wealthy by the completion of their careers, is evidence of the depth of intelligence and talent in Renaissance Italy, and throughout modernizing Europe during these centuries and beyond. The subsequent lunge into music by talents all over Europe as it was itself transformed in form and technological performance gives the lie to the pretensions of our populist critics as they rationalize contemporary "esthetic" drivel.

The Globe in London saw the performance in the late-sixteenth to early-seventeenth century, not merely of Shakespeare's creations, but also of Christopher Marlowe, Ben Jonson, Sir William Sidney. The audiences, some 2,000 every day in London at the various theatres, were largely plebian workers. They understood and loved the language, the poetry, the show. They delivered their hard-earned pence for more of the same.[22]

The Hellenes built their theatres to accommodate 15,000-20,000 patrons at one time, (see the extant theater at Epidaurus), a large portion of the city's population. The works of Athenian poets, Aeschylus and Aristophanes, were not written for an elite. They were the Broadway of the average Greek citizen. Even the Olympiads were not merely athletic competitions. They included drama, musical performances, the entire panoply of high Greek cultural aspirations.[23]

The claim that the great art forms are really for an elite social class besmirches these achievements. The criticisms fall into the same class of rationalizations as those of the Leninist, Stalinist, Maoist, Pol Pot stamp, excuses for pseudo-egalitarian tyrannical enforcement over artists, writers, and musicians. The intention of these "socialist" monsters was to destroy community independence, to reduce the inner creativity of all their citizen/prison inmates to one controllable level of public debasement. In a sense, the cheapness of the modern media entertainments, the overwhelming downward push in sensibility is the subtly coercive equivalent of the political totalitarians of the twentieth century.

There is a kernel of truth in the search for a "people's" art. We understand that intellectual art has historical roots, often rustic, in our poetry, music and dance. Folk music represents the spontaneous flow of the passions of the cortex and limbic system in its social embodiment. Folk art is always culturally unique, pluralistic. The music of ordinary people—that of the Irish bard, Black plantation spirituals, Slavic *tsardas*—finds its response to this spontaneity of esthetic form that pours out in all self-contained communities.

The political left abstracted this fact so as to apply it to the modern industrial world, the ostensible war between capitalism and socialism. Keep it basic, said the radicals, not understanding that even peasants and slaves desire to rise beyond the passionate soul music of the fields. Listen to the rich intellectual possibilities of Bach, Ellington, Charles Ives, or George Gershwin. Listen to a Tschaikovsky or Vaughn Williams symphony and you will still hear and feel the folk creativity that shaped the national medium. But now it is raised through intellectual form into a universal expression.

Intelligence and the Fine Arts

What should be fundamental to our understanding is that the arts define a civilization. In the population of a true civilization will be found a mixture of extremely high on-average intelligence united with a homogeneous ethnic mix of limbic juices, sexual drives. The former makes possible the cognitive element, the latter gives color and definition to every great civilization. In all ages of Eur-Asian civilization, the sense organs have sought to find a formal receptacle within which to channel these energies. There is no art unless there is brain-power and the social means to express this brain power in artistic transformations of both emotional and intellectual experience.

What made Greek art so powerful is that it took on many neighborly influences, especially from the Near Eastern civilizations, and transmuted these historic ways of looking at the world into their own community synthesis. This stimulation of more ancient cultures percolated and evolved within the Hellenes over many hundreds of years. Greek art was remarkable in that it reflected, as both Edith Hamilton and Johan Huizinga have noted, the freedom to play. Civic athletics and the arts, later the life of the mind, philosophy were their media.[24]

We ought not be too critical of the early Near Eastern peoples, especially the roughneck Assyrians. (We describe the origins of literate civilization by the mysterious Sumerians in the Appendix). The Assyrians were tough and war-like, originally from the north of Mesopotamia. But still, they stimulated the rich artistic creativity of the craftspeople in their home cities of Assur, Kalah, and their later capital, Nineveh. They built libraries to preserve the ancient Mesopotamian writings, which went back to the Sumerian civilization. Were they not so defined by their ferocity in war and peace, we would be impressed with their sensitivity to the arts and literature of that region. They were true preservers, in the great library at Nineveh of their then-two-thousand-year-old heritage.[25]

When high art withers, as it did in late Rome, it could signify an internal political/military decadence. It could symbolize the gradual transformation of a people's direction, in this case searching for a religious, moral, and community road that would lead to the preservation of a dying way of life. Now in obeisance to a Church that despised the old esthetic, they had neither the time nor the wherewithal to build the new at a rapid pace. Eventually, the Church itself would sponsor new and intellectual art forms.

If the arts are to regain any measure of intellectual creativity in the twenty-first century or, more probably, much later, they will need to find communities that are re-energized to search for the best in terms of their own person-to-person interactions. It will never happen in the ersatz mass media world of today. It is no longer clear what music is: Ludwig van Beethoven, Bob Dylan, or Rap-a-Dap.

Of course, some pop stuff is exciting, sensuous, innovative. The human mind has always found room for the ecstatic and depraved, below Mt. Sinai, on the Ziggurat in Ur, in the Temple of Dionysius at Eleusis, at a good burlesque show on Lower Broadway. We are creatures with a powerful lower brain. However, the explosion of pornography in every area of modern culture epitomizes this disintegration of *sophrosne*, the mean, self-discipline, that defined Greek education, *paideia*. It signifies a world in which human culture is out of kilter. What else can it mean but that the sensuous passions that once drove this intellectualization of human perception and libido no longer have the communal brain power to give it form and depth of meaning?

The potential is represented by the active desires of a few of our educated young to express deep and passionate *interest*. At Columbia University's Miller Theatre there is today a series of *avant garde* concerts of newly-composed music that is attended by crowds of involved young people from all over metropolitan New York. No matter that they represent a minuscule proportion of the city-wide population.[26] It is this passionate search for an experience that joins mind and heart that will signify the germ of renewal of the arts in living communities. Unfortunately, at concerts of classical ballet, opera, chamber music, one now sees a homogeneous carpet of gray heads.

Sadly, for the vast preponderance of the masses of the world, even those brought up in the U.S., true inheritors of the great musical and artistic traditions of the West, these arts no longer resonate. For the masses, the mentality is not there. We are swayed and inundated by the primitive in culture and entertainment; it is thus that the twenty-first century is being defined for us. And yet, because the new, the computers, skyscrapers, Boeing 757s, do not now crash, the consensus is that all is well. After all, all art is relative!

Endnotes, Chapter 9

[1] Dibble, H. F., and Bar-Yosef, O., eds. 1995. *The Definition and Interpretation of Levallois Technology,* Madison, WI.: Prehistory Press.
[2] Clottes, J. 2003. *Chauvet Cave: The Art of Earliest Times,* Salt Lake City: Univ. of Utah Press; Abrams; Clottes, J., and Courtin, J. 1996. *The Cave Beneath the Sea,* N.Y.: Abrams.
[3] Conard, N. J. 2003. "Early Figurative Art," *Nature,* Dec.18. Describes one-inch-long ivory carvings that date to 30K, B.P.
[4] Dimasio, A. R. 1994. *Descartes' Error,* N.Y.: Avon; MacLean, P. 1990. *The Triune Brain in Evolution.* N.Y.: Plenum.
[5] Langer, S. 1942 *Philosophy in a New Key* Cambridge, Mass: Harvard Univ. Press.
[6] Hill, W. H., *et al.* 1902. *Antonio Stradivari, His Life and Work,* London: W. E. Hill and Sons; Hill, W. H., *et al.* 1931. *The Violin Makers of the Guarneri Family,* London: W. E. Hill and Sons.
[7] Lakshumikanthan, V., and Leela, S. 2000. *The Origin of Mathematics,* Lanham, Md.: Univ. Press of America; Cuomo, S. *Ancient Mathematics,* London: Routledge; Chiera, E. 1938. *They Wrote on Clay,* Chicago: Univ. of Chicago Press; Thomson, M. I. 1987. *The Sumerian Language,* Copenhagen: Akademisk Forlag.
[8] Moffett, M., *et al.* 2004. *A World History of Architecture,* Boston: McGraw Hill, Chs. 2, 3; Seton, L. 2004. *Ancient Architecture,* Milan: Electa; Tzonis, A. 2001. *Classical Greek Architecture,* London: Thames and Hudson.
[9] Munn, G. 1993. *The Triumph of Love: Jewelry, 1530-1930,* N.Y.: Thames and Hudson.
[10] Goodman, P. 1973. *Speaking and Language: Defence of Poetry,* London: Wildwood House; Cooper, G. B. 1998. *Mysterious Music: Rhythm and Free Verse.*
[11] Langer, S. 1953. *Feeling and Form,* N.Y.: Scribners.
[12] Lai, D. 2004. "The Rise of Asians in Classical Music," in *La Scena Musical,* 9:5, Feb. 9.
[13] Stoddard, D. M. 1990. *The Scented Age: The Biology and Culture of Human Odor,* N.Y.: Cambridge Univ. Press.
[14] Brand, J., and Hailey, C. 1997. *Constructive Dissonance: Arnold Schoenberg and the Transformation of 20th Century Culture,* Berkeley: Univ. of California Press; Frisch, W., ed.

1999. *Schoenberg and his World*, Princeton, N.J.: Princeton Univ. Press; Schillinger, J. 1976. *The Mathematical Basis of the Arts*, N.Y.: Da Capo.

[15] Heyman, J. 1967. Why Beauvais Cathedral Collapsed," Transactions of the Newcomen Society," Vol. 40; Charvat, P. 2002. *Mesopotamia before History*, N.Y. Routledge.

[16] Hausmann, H. 1962. *Medieval Polyphony*, N.Y.: Leeds Music Co.; Sanders, E. H. 1998. *French and English Polyphony of the 13th and 14th Centuries*, Brookfield, Vt.: Asugate.

[17] Rosen, C. 1976. *The Classical Style: Haydn, Mozart, Beethoven*, London: Faber.

[18] *Op. cit.*, endnote 8.

[19] Quoted in Itzkoff, S. W. 1990. *The Making of the Civilized Mind*, N.Y.: Peter Lang International Publishers, p. 213.

[20] see Wolfe, Tom. 1975. *The Painted Word*, N.Y.: Farrar, Straus, and Giroux.

[21] Gunther, H., ed. 1990. *The Culture of the Stalin Period*, N.Y.: St. Martin's Press; Taylor, B. 1991. *Art and Literature under the Bolsheviks*, Concord, Mass.: Pluto Press.

[22] Riggs, D. 2004. *The World of Christopher Marlowe*, N.Y.: Henry Holt; Singman, J. L. 1995. *Daily Life in Elizabethan England*, Westport, CT: Greenwood Press.

[23] Bieber, M. 1961. *The History of the Greek and Roman Theatre*, Princeton, N.J.: Princeton Univ. Press; Bowra, C. .M. 1971. *Periclean Athens*, N.Y.: Dial Press.

[24] Hamilton, E. 1942. *The Greek Way*, N.Y.: W. W. Norton; Huizinga, J. 1950. *Homo Ludens: A Study of the Play Element in Culture*, Boston: Beacon Press.

[25] Oded, B. 1979. *Mass Deportations and Deportees in the Neo-Assyrian Empire*, Wiesbaden: Reichert Verlag; Laessoe, J. 1963. *People of Ancient Assyria*, trans. F. S. Leigh-Browne, London: Routledge Kegan Paul.

[26] Columbia Univ., Modern Music Series at Miller Theater, 2004.

Chapter 10

Universality and Nationality

The Primal Dialectic

The great debate today is over the dominance of internationalism *versus* the supposed atavism of nationalism. Which shall perdure? The European Union is the current classic example of the pull between the needs of economic efficiency to dissolve borders between nations and their recalcitrant historic linguistic, ethnic, and religious traditions. Efficiency and seeming equality of competitive skills *versus* the pull of the local heart. Elsewhere in the world the tensions of nationalism revolve around bitter terrorist struggles for dignity and self-affirmation amidst the defeat of their religious and ethnic heritages in the international race for economic wealth and power. The global community demands *entrée* even here, not merely to calm the internal dissolutive trends, but to maintain access to the oil.

If a people chooses to enter the internationalist/universalist world of science and technology, free trade, open communication, and borders, how long before the traditional cultural/moral heritage erodes? Given this petrification of the old, will we not have to welcome the economic hegemony of mass media controlled from Hollywood or New York?

No way, say the romantic nationalists. This trend will signal a final obituary for the diverse cultural heritage of all glorious traditions. Dissolved in an evolutionary rush, for what? The lure of technological trinkets, foreign tourists? Yet, say the smiling skeptics of internationalism, watch a soccer match, or the Olympics, the ethnic glue is still there with a vengeance. The struggle will continue.

The philosophical question: can't we live with a world internationally inclusive, unified in premise? At the same time, can't we still nurture our religious commitments, the mother language of our poetry, our neighborly dialects, the intimacy of family and clan? And what about ethnic cuisine, style, the arts that seem to flourish in face-to-face interactions of creator and connoisseur? Is great art possible in the context of an internationally mandated world of compatibly bland beliefs and assembly line behaviors mandated from Hollywood, New York, or Brussels?

We shudder at the idea of unification if it requires the flatland of cultural conformity. There must be a way to conceptualize and harmonize this tension between the plurality that grows from intimate community life and the unity and equality that we desire in the material apportionment of value, the need to live with our fellows in peace under international law. It is inconceivable that the human species in 2005 and beyond can tolerate the vast differences in our intellectual assessment of the nature of the world. Scientific method as the criterion for rational policymaking must be obligatory for all members of the international community. Otherwise, are we not headed down the slippery slope of eternal conflict and civilizational dissolution?

More than the diversities of cuisine, language, and religion, the arts strike us as most vulnerable to the principle of universality, the international uniformity of culture. Always, given a modicum of human freedom for association, the arts carve out independent pathways. In Roman times: one official language, one law, a unified political culture, seemingly. Yet from Palmyra to Londinium, shades of esthetic differentiation were evident. At the same time, Roman art, at the center itself, evolved. Cultural change seems unstoppable; it seems to respond to some deeper psychic movement, defying the enveloping, enervating international cultural system.

The potential resistance of art to internationalism in the constellation of civilizational forms lies in its role as a symbolic activity of human beings. When the work of life is completed, the mind seeks to play, in this case to play perceptually. No question, even the search for philosophical or scientific knowledge, what the Greeks called *theoria,* is closely associated with the soaring imagination, poking beyond the given. Human curiosity creatively engages perception and mind in the cognitive search for new formal causal relationships, laws saying "always, everywhere."

The inner drive to know, the energic thrust to look beyond the moment, continuously leads to new theoretical understandings, then ongoing mastery of the material world. This thrust of mind is akin to those other deeply creative perceptual/cognitive modalities of play, impulses that reveal themselves ubiquitously in art.

The universalism that we see before us in economic, political, scientific and technological efforts only seemingly contrasts with the arts. It is constructed from the same flow of mental energies. Our critical super-ego directs this mental flow into different logical as well as emotional *loci*. A fundamental palette of human interests leads to this primal divergence.

How do these mental vectors toward universality and/or pluralism fit together in our understanding of the human mind? Probing this richness of human thought, in the creation of high culture, civilization, then, becomes the key to directing the human future. By understanding these fundamental drives of human nature, we can avoid the historic disasters, the horrific pain that we have inflicted upon ourselves.

Unity and Diversity in Symbolic Thought

Aristotle, 384-322 BCE, perhaps our greatest philosophical mind, was practical in his evaluation of the possibilities of human thought. Unlike Plato, his teacher, who wanted to unify human knowledge in a rich system of metaphysical/ethical relationships, Aristotle was more a disentangler. Through his scientific, analytical, medical heritage, he sought for distinctions.

He believed that the fulfillment of man lay in the service of the body to facilitate the activities of the mind. Aristotle was deeply sensitive to the intellect's search to understand. Knowledge may start with perception, but it was not here fulfilled. From astronomical observations to the empirical study of plants and animals, the highest human striving was to be found in pure relational thought, to discover the laws of cause and consequence.

These views are applicable today. The philosophical attitude, as guide, is essential to our survival as humans. However, it is agreed today that too much of Greek intellectualism was absorbed (as with Plato) in the esthetics of such logical and metaphysical thinking. The lure of language in describing experience/reality was itself such an esthetic seduction.

Aristotle did recognize that we humans, a complex of elements divided roughly into the functional needs of body and mind, needed the entertainments. These cathartic experiences served to reify those emotions that were rooted more closely in the needs of our bodies. And he also recognized human frailty. His own Hellenes needed to be initiated into the mysteries, those sensuous and secret sexual rites, religiously and socially disciplined, but never repressed. They were holy Dionysian emanations that erupted from the depths of human nature.[1]

Aristotle was the son of a north Aegean country doctor to the Macedonian royal family. He taught in Athens, the Cambridge, Massachusetts, of his day. He was the teacher of Alexander, the Macedonian. Aristotle's school was financed by this impassioned *nouveau*-Hellene. His teachings were intended solely for the Greeks; beyond were the *barbaroi*. Perhaps his spontaneous absorption of the ethos of Greek *paideia* (culture-education) allowed him to take largely for granted the profound Hellenic involvement with the arts. It was so deeply rooted in their beings as part of their unselfconscious leisure/playfulness. Plato feared the "poets," not appreciating their distinctive social role. Aristotle's great passion was to know intellectually how the world worked, to fit it all together.

We must recognize, from the example of the Greeks, perhaps the paradigm for all the civilizational ideals humanity has yet experienced, that such civilizations do fail. This exemplar of the civilizational possibilities of humanity (we do not know enough about the far more ancient Sumerian civilization) was spontaneously created 2,500 years ago, and with much less scientific knowledge about the workings of the world. It should inspire us to believe that it can be done again.

The challenge, of course, is first to recreate the high levels of intelligence in the ordinary *hoi polloi,* peasants/workers. Thence, it is required to create disciplined material conditions of life (enough, but not too much) similar to those that forced the brilliant Greeks to mine their inner souls, to create democracy and community, then their great works of mind, philosophy, science, and art.

Koenigsberg (now Kaliningrad) philosopher Immanuel Kant (1724-1804), perhaps the most influential thinker of the Enlightenment, was struck by the power of the Newtonian system to predict events in our physical world, to unify our understanding of these relationships to the planets as well as to terrestrial objects. To save religion and the other softer dimensions of human thought and culture, Kant made a distinction through his analyses as to the knowledge differences between the two realms. The *Critique of Pure Reason* (1781), (science and discursive knowledge), he contrasted with the *Critique of Practical Reason* (1788) (moral and religious concerns) issues. (See Chapter 8.)

Religion could no longer speak to the world of material things; the universal and absolute laws of Newtonian physics were definitive. Another realm of knowledge did lie in religion, esthetics, perhaps even in biological processes. These two contrasting systems of thought seem to issue from the demands of human thought itself, as external expression of internal knowings. In a sense, Kant argued, we could never penetrate ultimate reality, limited as we were by the laws of our own mind. These inner laws of knowledge in the material or physical sense were seen as congruent with Newton's discoveries.

This perspective on human knowing, and the products of knowledge in the pantheon of culture was developed by the twentieth-century neo-Kantian, Ernst Cassirer (1874-1945), and his follower, Susanne Langer (1895-1985). Both took a more biological view of the process of knowledge building, searching into the symbolic structure of our cultural creations and the biology that produced it. Kant, living in the pre-Darwinian era, did not have the knowledge available to him to make this next leap.[2]

This was similar to Aristotle's conjecture in the pre-Copernican era as he hypothesized thirty or more *unmoved movers* (gods), which would determine the movements of the plants and stars, as then based upon the empirical research into such movements by the Hellenic astronomer, Eudoxes. The important issue is that, even at a remove of several thousand years, these philosophers used the available scientific knowledge of the time to attempt to universalize their perspectives into a larger system of knowledge.

Cassirer and Langer explained that there are different vectors of thought that create the cultural symbols by which we live. Their terminology contrasted "discursive" symbol systems with the "non-discursive." In this distinction, they attempted to reflect the universal scientific vectors of one way of looking at experience, the discursive, and the non-discursive, the personal, emotional, pluralistic flow of human symbol making into the arts, religion, language as drama or poetry, cuisine, style.

The point here is that human thought never penetrates something called "reality, the true and the absolute." Here, Cassirer and Langer disagree with Aristotle and Kant. Rather, these symbols direct our minds to create patterns of symbols (meanings), either in the universal (discursive) or plural (non-discursive) format. The discursive symbols can be subjected to universal confirmation or disconfirmation by the hard evidence of experience or experiment. In a real sense, truth here is what works. The non-discursive symbols are more difficult, extremely culture laden, *e.g.,* evaluating the merits and value of poetry, perfume, painting, cuisine.

Aristotle himself implicitly recognized this distinction. He was firm on the possibility of obtaining objective and universal knowledge of the material world, physical, biological, and psychological. He was more hesitant in the realms of ethics, politics, and esthetics. While it was important to subject these realms of thought and life to critical human reasoning and analysis, philosophy, he was hesitant, *unlike* his teacher Plato, to attempt to integrate such knowledge in a universal, absolute system of knowledge.

"Probable knowing" was the way Aristotle viewed human social behavior, ethics, politics, esthetics. That is why he required that his students at the Lyceum collect and analyze the various constitutions of the Greek cities. He wanted to come as close as he could to a "probably" good model of political life. His preference was a limited constitutional monarchy as the practical, most serviceable model of stable, just, political life. But he would never claim universal truth in any approach to human behavior.

The wisest philosophers of science concur that our theories are all constructs.[3] As we have learned even with regard to the laws propounded by Newton, we must discipline ourselves to see the conditionality of all of our beliefs and behaviors, wherein new ideas can displace older principles of our so-called physical "reality." We, as intelligent, thinking human beings, must rise up to take a more super-ordinate critical perspective, to rein in non-functional, non-workable ideas. In this way we may be able to push aside ideas that don't fulfill our predictions, set off on a new course of thought and practice. In so doing, we could create more instrumentally functional concepts around which to frame our existence.

The flow of ideas and images from our brain interacts with a world outside of ourselves. This interaction tends first to direct symbolic thought toward the universal, to discover the unifying predictable experiences found in human existence. All humans live under the same basic conditions of materiality, physics, engineering, computers, aerodynamics. This is why science has replaced divination as an explanatory tool. It predicts in a more consistent and universal manner what will come next. As we direct our thinking toward the problems facing our fellow humans, in politics, economics, war and peace, our symbolic perceptions become more suffused with non-discursive symbolic expressions of emotion and sensuality, the inner power of our mammalian heritage. Secular thinking involving prediction and causation become far more difficult to maintain.

The key is to look over our own shoulders as best we can, and say, "...no, no, you are being too *mechanical* here..." (else) "... too *emotional* there." Our symbolic effusions are rich and diverse. We need to be able to sort out our passions and apply our inner expression (psychology) to the most appropriate external experiences. We ought not, as the Arabs did in early 2005, conjure up vengeful gods to explain horrific "tsunamis."

By contrast, what has happened in recent historical experience is that through the power of the universal, science has so transformed the material conditions of life that those deeper and personal realms of symbolic expression have been torn from their traditional national and cultural roots. The world of things has radically altered the inner way we live and think.

The result is, for example, what has occurred in the serious arts. Once nurtured, then created in semi-independent communities, as scholars from Marx to Nisbet have emphasized, they are now detached from their nurturing soil, frozen into artificial performing arts centers or as mega-museum shows that travel around the world, from one international architectural "wonder" to the next.[4]

The universalizing implications of the internet, television, rapid air transportation have virtually destroyed the possibility for community cultural innovation. At the same time, the lowering of the intellectual levels of all populations, a consequence of the demographic explosion from the lower reaches of the I.Q. probability curve has had an even more percussive impact on esthetic interest. The low intellectual content of modern entertainments has melted any semblance of general public seriousness toward the arts.

This twenty-first-century internationalist culture borders on becoming a sea of crude pornography. It is not the sexual that frightens. Rather, it is the fact that counter to civilizational tradition, such underground passion is no longer ordered and remanded to a disciplined cultural domain—red light districts, sacred temples, under the counter art. Contemporary entertainments draw no attention from the masses unless they are suffused with the pornographic leer.

Evolutionary Meaning of Cultural Change

It is the modern human brain of *Homo sapiens sapiens* that creates high cultures, cognitive civilizations. The food of human existence is created from humankind's symbolic activity. This food is formed from the raw materials of human perception. It is then absorbed, digested, finally energetically and spontaneously projected into symbolic/mind activity. Symbolic meaning forms our outer world. This outer world of experiencing and organizing leads us eventually, after many thousands of years of learning, to the hard sciences, scholarship.

But there is more to human symbolic experience than that which Aristotle called *theoria*, the almost esthetic study of intellectual teasers. If Aristotle and the other classic thinkers, especially Plato, in his fear of the "poets" (really, the political mythmakers), tended to slight the arts, it was because they viewed the esthetics of conceptual thinking as that which most transcended the animal limitations of the body. The involvement of Greek ethnicity in the arts was ubiquitous; it came naturally to them, and with great passion, as their recurring festivals demonstrate. Because they were Hellenes, and their art was indigenous, they absorbed these enthusiasms as part of their spontaneous civilizational heritage, that which could not be lived without, and at a profoundly basic level of life.

Recall that the evolutionary process of *orthoselection* created a brain that exploded inertially far beyond the boundaries of biological need, natural selection. As a consequence, we have all these excess neurons spontaneously firing away in mental activity. There are thirty billion neurons in the human brain, at least one million billion connections between them. In the various areas of the suddenly complex *Homo sapiens sapiens* brain, our evolutionary inheritance of ancient and more recent structures, there are approximately 200 types of neurons interacting with each other.

Art is one of the paradigmatic human activities that spontaneously arises from this non-practical mental/bodily need of humans. Aristotle understood this. Thus art becomes the purest reflection of our sensuous self, now transformed by the neo-cortex, creating meaning by forming structures of perceptual (oil paint, marble, perfume, velvet, sound) and intellectual (formal) significance.

Into every creative effort, whether in computer design, political transformations, laws regulating the manufacture of drugs, there is always an imaginative element, by which new ideas and pulsations form to allow for new solutions. The creative process, the esthetics of the new and the elegant, carries with it an underlying psychological and formal logical force such that all work has the potentiality for being impregnated with human ingenuity. Certainly, some types of human physical or political activities have institutional or physical demarcations that are harder to alter, their realm of innovative freedom, narrower.

The great forms of civilizational creativity have their own inner laws of progress, most often having little to do with events in the political, economic, and social worlds around them. In post-Marxist communist ideology, the incubus on the creative mind was political ideology. Understand that in today's Western cultural ethos, the books, the music for the masses, the cinema, are also politically and economically influenced, now mandated by the economic and political elites for the lowest common denominator. No elitism in the content of our cultural food, except for a tiny group of esthetic outliers, else the cuckolded speculators into so-called "modern art."

Interestingly, our mass market arts demand constant change. Even on a low intellectual level, humans search for novelty, unfortunately too often, downward. How do we understand such changes in style, and, in general, in the arts? It is not, as in engineering, where new materials make new constructions and architectural styles possible. Thus we see advance. Many gurus associate esthetic evolution with dominating religious, political, or economic commands.

It is fair, for example, to distinguish between the independent evolution of the secular folk songs of the medieval and the post-classical-era Gregorian chant as sponsored by the established Church. We accept the gradual transformation of the latter in the context of Catholic institutionalism into the rich and complex polyphony of the medieval.

But it is hard to identify the external causal stimuli that created the unique art of a Dufay, that which distinguishes him from his contemporaries, or the changes that led to the creativity of Palestrina. Were there causal religious stimuli, the commands of the Pope or a conclave of bishops, that so determined these changes? Similarly, do we hear in the Seventh Symphony of Prokofiev the influence of Stalinist censorship. This work is almost classically romantic as compared with his earlier mechanistic dissonance. But then, Beethoven's final string quartet, Opus 135, was a relative let-down as compared with the earlier, almost abstract complex Opus 130 and 131 string quartets.

The Gothic cathedral is generically different from the Muslim mosque of the period. Yet Constantine's great church, Santa Sophia, was transformed into a mosque without redesigning the great edifice. So, too, with Hadrian's final redesign of the Pantheon, saved when it was transformed into a church. With the exception of David and Delacroix, try to find a political explanation for the evolution of French painting in the nineteenth century, or in the classical music of the period, from Berlioz to Debussy.

The mystery, of course, lies in the creative input of the great artists which moved painting and the classical sonata form through all their rich and varied transformations during this period. The creative possibilities that gave dynamic change to these arts lay within the formal structure that both disciplined and liberated artists from outside powers and events.

If we argue for the exclusion of dominating external institutions, but not the diffused financial or national stimulations that made such work possible in civilized climes, we are left with the mysteriously innovative mind. In denoting individual creativity as the force of civilizational change, rather than the great institutions that are often sponsors of such innovation, we have to acknowledge the role of uniquely intelligent individuals. The disappearance of their genetic talents, else their twenty-first-century corruptibility into the commercial world of pap augurs a decline in civilizational *élan*.

What happened to Athens after so many young geniuses were extinguished in the Peloponnesian War? Answer, decline. These young could have saved Greece from Macedonian hegemony. Allowed to mature, this annihilated talent could also have stimulated a reinvigoration of the drama, architecture, philosophy, even the full articulation of scientific method?

We value the externals, the institutions of our material lives, corporations, military uniforms and ribbons, the power in the White House because they are more easily perceived and experienced,. And in the dynamic changes induced by science and technology, this is completely understandable. Yet, the Acropolis was constantly in the making, undergoing an independent creative evolution, all while the deadly military campaigns raged. Greek intelligence was yet largely undiminished by heroism and *hybris*.

In the arts and the esthetic, more generally, we experience the silent nondiscursive free flow of symbolic innovation. Note the distinction we make between spoken and written language. Try to listen to an expert in the eighth or ninth-century English linguistic tradition as he/she reads an excerpt from Beowulf in "most probable" authentic dialect. Try again with fifteenth-century Chaucer. In the former, a reading will give only a faint hint of meaning to the modern listener. The oral version recited as it would have usually been communicated is probably unintelligible to modern ear and brain. Chaucer in the oral mode transmits greater meaning. The written versions have retained enough discursive elements of vocabulary, grammar, and semantics to allow serious college students to enjoy them.

This is the reason that some skeptics of so-called Baroque authenticity in the playing of Bach, Scarlatti and other composers on supposedly close-to-the-original instruments and sounds of the day, might well chuckle. "Prove it." The conceptual notation has survived, but the realization in sound? At least, say the skeptics, let us hear the power of the forms, even if we have to use modern instruments, rather than the modern grunts, scowls, and whines of the supposedly authentic.

The reason for the discrepancy is due to the fact that in the written version of any ancient text, fiction or non-fiction, attempts are made to convey some discursive, logical meaning. It is rooted in the basic practical uses that, for example, the Sumerians early on devised for writing, to calculate, legislate, contract, *i.e.*, to order the external world.

The spoken language is different. It serves poetic, romantic, sensuous purposes in addition to the didactic. Thus it is much more sensitive to the non-discursive esthetic re-creation that sound allows for human expression. The freedom involved in not being held close to tangible reality gives the esthetic dimension of spoken language, especially its close personal colloquial nuances constant opportunity to shape and be reshaped. As long as people speak or sing to each other, the spoken language will assume the essence of an art, even in contrasting use in the courthouse, the church, mosque or synagogue.

Gerald Edelman, a neurobiologist with a violinistic musical background, has attempted to confront this mystery of the fertility of the new in human creative expression. And with this attempt to penetrate the mystery of consciousness, and thus human self-awareness and expression, he is attempting to develop a theory of mind. A paraphrase of a recent article describing his writings on the brain does not radically deviate from the point of view argued above:

"Connections among groups of neurons that are most effective in their reactions to certain stimulations become strengthened and succeed in affecting behavior and perception...the brain will have more going on than seems necessary, more randomness variation than any humanly designed system...the brain has enormous redundancy in its functioning...no brain event happens the same way twice...memory is always a variant, a recreation, never a repetition. Neurons become elements of ever more intricate patternings and mappings. These stimulations and recurrent experiences create enduring object patterning which become the elements of recognition—objects. Patterns evolve and interact in a dizzying dynamic. The brain is not a logically structured organ. The processes of making connections between things and ideas resemble the processes of metaphor more than those of logic—consciousness is a consequence of these neural mappings—consciousness can be born out of diversity and accident—*there is no supervising soul or self, nobody is standing behind the curtain*" (emphasis added).[5]

Of course, these are verbal musings about neuronic events well beyond the symbolic simulations and envisionments of brain mapping and wave interpretation technologies. All that we can argue for is that the innovative capacities of the human brain to alter in every generation the entire cultural fabric of life, through new meanings, is exemplified in the freest and most ineffable manner, in the arts.

To so achieve the richest esthetic forms, as recognized by those who themselves strive to cultivate the arts, a high level of cortical intelligence is necessary. When humans of high Cro-Magnon heritage intelligence have disappeared from the earth, no one will miss the great arts. On the other, hand when intelligence once more reasserts itself, trying to figure how to produce fire from dry kindling, these intelligent souls may indeed be able to conjure up dim understandings about the workings of relic stoves, old-fashioned wood and micro-wave versions. Give them the score of a Beethoven symphony, and they will long scratch their heads.

The Power of Ethnicity

Great art needs the reciprocity of creator and audience—yes the purchaser of the art or the foundation commissioning the music. The deepest creations arise out of the context of people living in close proximity to each other. Citizens in relatively small social centers, of similar biological heritage, share with each other the contemporary dynamics and the historical meaning of these neuronic innovations. In ethnically homogeneous settings, there can be a give and take between persons in their mutual love of beauty as they develop and share ideas to create new material instrumentalities of meaning. Art serves to shape a way of life that identifies the particular group as a community, an interbreeding and evolving ethnicity.

Mature artistic forms, reflective of the Acropolis at then-modestly wealthy Athens, was still to be built out of local marble. Construction began decades after the triumphs of the Greeks over Persians. This holy site represents a fusion of many long-evolving Greek cultural traditions. Even as other Greek cities had spread throughout the Mediterranean, the ancient ethnic Hellenic heritage held these people together in peace and war. This architectural stylistic tradition was now recognized as distinctive by Hellene and barbarian alike,

Athens was relatively late in seeing itself as a powerful defender of Hellenic ethnicity. The Acropolis, when it was burnt to the ground by the Persian, Xerxes, consisted only of painted wooden temples. The new Acropolis, of marble, stimulated by their leader, Pericles, was built to glorify and possibly unify the Greek cities, under Athenian leadership.

It was in this unifying spirit of Athenian leadership, inspired in great part by the victories over the vast Persian Imperium, that the Boeotian (Thebes) poet, Pindar, this neighboring city often a bloody foe (ally of the Persians), of Athens, extolled Athens. Pindar died in 443 BCE, before the Parthenon had been erected. Yet his poetry commemorating the burnt wooden temples on high of the Athenian Acropolis was prescient and universally reciprocated:

"Fairest of preludes is the renown of Athens for the mighty race of the Alcmaeonidae {the founding aristocratic families}. What home, or house, could

I call by a name that should sound more glorious for Hellas to hear...sons of Athens, stay of Hellas...laid the shining foundations of freedom." Or "O glittering violet-crowned, chanted in song, Bulwark of Hellas, renowned Athens, Citadel of gods."

So it was meet that the Athenian architects and sculptors who designed the Acropolis incorporated all the artistic traditions of Greece—the Doric of ancient Corinth in the great Parthenon, the delicate Attic/Ionian in the small but exquisite temple to Apollo that overlooks the Saronic Gulf beyond, and the many-leveled Erechtheum with its unique porch of caryatids. What this religious, ethnic, civic architectural, and sculptural achievement tells us about the relation of great communities surrounded by associated ethnically-related towns, though sometimes enemies, is how significant the reciprocity of creative inputs can be that independent if associated peoples have on each other. Athens would never have searched for greatness had it not competed with Thebes, Corinth, Sparta, Megara, even distant Miletus, Lesbos, Akagra, and Syracuse.

So, too, the artistic renaissance of Florence in the fifteenth century, which arose from its competition first with Siena for commercial and military domination, then with a variety of rivals, Pavia, Venice, Milan. In all these cities, the glory of their communities lay not merely in manufactures, trade, and artisan wealth that had pushed their prosperity, but in the fine artists that it attracted to its courts to glorify this wealth with even greater creativity. These were small cities, as were the towns of northern Europe in the late Renaissance and early modern period. Universities—free organizations of scholars, philosophers, scientists—were part of this sweeping attraction to the new knowledge, the commercialism, and artistic invention created semi-independently in the various cities of Switzerland, the German principalities, Holland, Flanders. Here, a unity in diversity of richly indigenous artistic traditions.[6]

We know of the competition of the Sumerian cities, not merely for water sources from the great rivers to amplify their agricultural and then their craft and mercantile ambitions, but to build institutions that united civic patriotism and its concomitant religious embodiments, their communities as a home for the gods. With this aspiration came the effort to make the city significant, to bedeck their women with beauty, to exploit that inchoate realization of civilized life as art. The Sumerians built their ziggurats as local symbolic homes of significance, to reflect the ancient mountain domiciles of the gods.

So, too, Egypt, seemingly unified as one political entity since the early dynasties with their great architectural projects—pyramids, the sphinx, the many beautiful temples up and down the Nile, the rich art of the tombs, even the hieroglyphics that adorned the walls—had many competing political as well as esthetic centers. Pharaoh Akhenaton felt the need to transfer his capital from Memphis to Tel-Amarna in order to break the stagnant power of the priesthood

Universality and Nationality

and give Egypt a more philosophical monotheism and thus renewed historical vigor. Shortly after, another pharaoh, Rameses II, attempted to re-center the Delta region as capital of his realm, perhaps in deference to his Asiatic origins. His endeavors were memorialized in the Old Testament. Both attempts to break with the ancient dependence on the culture of the Nile failed.

There can be no question but that history testifies to the critical importance of a humane demographic/community relationship between creativity in the arts as well as openness in all intellectual endeavors. Even today the need for communities of the intellectual, is reflected in the loci of Cambridge/Boston, Massachusetts; Silicon Valley, California. These communities gather together like minds and their enterprises including the universities, the museums, musical institutions. All of these serve to cross fertilize the community search for the new, here in the universal modes of logic, science, and technology. This contemporary reality reemphasizes the fact that people of talent need to talk to each other, see each others work.

Why is New York City the center for finance, communications, the arts? Huge and indigestible as New York is, these institutions will not move out to suburban Perth Amboy or White Plains. Modest Cremona, Italy (1600-1750) had the Amati, Ruggieri, Stradivari, Guarneri, Bergonzi clans all making their violins within a stone's throw of each other. Is it possible that they did not have almost daily contact with the work of their rivals down the street, the founding members as well as generations of descendants?

Then there is ancient Rome. Great poets, historians, rhetoricians, artists, and architects were projected forward by the power and conquests, wealth and self-consciousness of this new absorptively universal Latin culture. Its century of explosive creativity took place in the last century of tumultuous Republican rule, until 27 BCE. Mainly in the West, the new empire attracted many of non-Latin blood, to create a universal civilization that spoke to the need for law and stability. Names such as Catullus, Cicero, Lucretius, Sallust, stand high in this Republican era, representing the optimism and expectations that accompanied expansive energy, wealth, even turmoil.

The end of the last century BCE, the triumph of Augustus as "primus inter pares," his long, relatively peaceful rule, forty one years, (27 BCE-14 CE) continued to ignite the potential of this Latin civilization. As the wealth of the now conquered Hellenistic world poured into Rome, figures such as Livy, Horace, Virgil, Ovid, Seneca, stood out as contributors to the first truly universal civilization which claimed to rule by virtue of the need for peace, rationality, and the law, to turn a new page in the evolving fecundity of the Greco-Roman/Indo-European mind.

The implicit claim for legitimacy of this civilization, again its universality of order, as well as the toleration of community life at the perimeter, not the least the allowance for the flourishing of Greek language and traditions in the eastern portions of the Empire, argue for the productive stimulation of an all encompassing global culture.

It should be remembered, that two hundred years into the empire, after the era of Hadrian (d. 138 CE), and Marcus Aurelius (d. 181 CE), Rome's universal civilization began its decline into a moribund traditionalism (legalism) held together by a variety of military tyrannies, eventually allowing for the triumph of Christian supernaturalism.

The question: how large the political, economic, demographic contexts of social life have to get before cultural intimacy and relatedness is attenuated and loses it creative zest in an increasingly anonymous world of people and power?

For example, both the Europeans and the North Americans in the twenty-first century assume the continued retention of a nationality that undergirds their respective political systems. What with immigration and population expansion, the ever more pervasive and abstract communication and transportation systems that now make "home and street" irrelevant, we must concede that the old sense of national/ethnic homogeneity out of which traditional nations were built is today largely a rhetorical device. The respective flags and military embodiments are more symbols of mercantile and economic integrity, than deeply held centripetal feelings of history and fraternity, not to say religious place and setting.

We have the nineteenth-century exemplar of rapidly expanding nations, in wealth and population, centralized political power absorbing the ancient local loyalties. Still, there then exploded rich esthetic as well as intellectual and scientific progress. For example, France was spuriously united under Louis XIV, realistically after Napoleon. Gradually, an ethnically unified French music, arts, literature, philosophy, science came into being.[7] It was as with Rome that the French as a people, a united culture, not as ancient feudal fiefdoms, produced this explosive ethnic civilization. So, too, this richness of cultural invention characterized greater Europe. The same process of maturation in civilizationnal *élan* was reflected in the United States, in its own self-conscious nationalistic century of esthetic and intellectual creativity, 1850-1950.

There can be no hard and immutable rule which will tell us when a creative ethnicity gets too large or bogged down in tradition, then to decline and wither. But there is a hard bound rule, that the key to maintaining a social environment of creative ethnic and national inputs lies first in the protection and nurturing of the national intelligence profile.

As Aristotle argued, the human search for knowledge, of nature, even human political nature, can be sought for and argued from the standpoint of objectivity, the universal rule of reason. When it comes to making policy decisions we can hope to gain a measure of success by searching only for modest surety.

Think in terms of probable success. How to live wisely as a political entity? Reasoned analysis will help us make better choices.

Ethnicity and Nationality

The Jews are the most obvious example of an ethnicity without a nationality, and this for millennia. At first, part of the Canaanite, Sinai, North Arabian complex of Indo-European/Semitic tribes, they united in the second millennium BCE to form a national state, a monarchy based in the hill country of eastern Canaan.

They were presumably united by the laws received by the prophet Moses from the great wilderness God of the southeast, *Yahweh*. Their second leader, King David, captured the ancient Jebusite (Indo-European) citadel of Jerusalem, c.900 BCE, and declared it the holy capital of the Israelites. The United Monarchy lasted about one hundred years, 950-850 BCE. The tribes then split. The northern group, of the religious tradition of the eastern Semitic god El, established Israel as its state; eventually its capitol was Samaria. The southerners, led by the tribe Judah, closer to the Yahwist traditions, retained Jerusalem.

Israel disappeared c.700 BCE through the arms of Assyria; Judah, in 586 BCE, at the hands of Babylon/Chaldea. The Persians returned the Jews from exile, 539 BCE and these former nations became provinces. A new nation, Judea, was established in the disintegration of the post-Alexandrian Macedonian rule, the Antiochenes, c.165 BCE. This nation survived in vassal form until the revolt of 70 CE when its 2nd Temple was destroyed by the Romans under Vespasian and Titus.

In 1948 CE, a new Jewish state was established as part of the Zionist aspirations to return to the homeland after almost 2,000 years of exile. This goal was facilitated by the worldwide desire to absolve Western Civilization of its millennial culpability for the *Holocaust*, the six million European Jews destroyed.

During those 2,000 years, ethnicity was maintained, not necessarily through the linguistic ties to the ancient Hebrew, but through the moral and scriptural glue provided by a belief system that was gradually transformed into an intra-ethnic breeding system. The evolution of Jewish ethnicity in both the Islamic and Christian worlds was conditioned by the press of discrimination and isolation. When external rule was beneficent, the Jews would tend to intermix with the dominant culture.

Otherwise, under the harsh conditions of persecution and pogrom, where the choice was often conversion or death, the Jews tightened their endogomatic restrictions for marriage only within the faith. The gradual disappearance of Jews in the West in the late twentieth century, where they became an ever smaller "minority" group, and increasingly liberal in the interpretation of the ancient rituals and beliefs, has come about through the concomitant liberalization of religious restrictions and clerical domination by the larger Western community.

The Jews have become socially powerful through the evolution of this centripetal ethnic glue. The dominating force was a dialectical literacy imposed upon them by their own community. Here the most literate and intellectual leader was the *rabbi*, the teacher. It was he who demanded of the people literate acceptance of the ancient guides for lawful living, the Torah and Talmud.

In easier times, the Jews contributed this heightened defensive community intelligence to the universal world of general commerce, literature, philosophy. Some argue that it was this high Jewish intelligence, their "chosenness" to obey the laws of their God, that heightened anti-Semitism. If so, it explains the all-encompassing hatred for this ethnicity that led to its European extermination. Likewise, it can be argued that it is the military, cultural, and economic achievements of the Jews in Israel, in the latter half of the twentieth century that has led to the fanatical obsessions against this democratic land by the vastly numerous Arab states.

The Kurds are another example of an ethnic people without a nationality. They are Indo-Europeans in language, a remnant of the ancient Medes, partners of the Persians in the destruction of the Mesopotamian empires, c.650 BCE. The Kurds are Muslim in religion, now spread among the nations of Turkey, Iraq, Iran (Persia), Syria. A relatively poor minority economically, and submerged within their Semitic- and Turkic-speaking neighbors, they have been enveloped by these surrounding dominant nationalities. They still remember the great Islamic empire achieved by their renowned and liberal Kurdish ancestor, Saladin. Their recent guerilla war for independence, against Turkey, failed. The attempted absorption into Turkey sponsored by the Western powers following the disintegration of the Ottoman Turks in the twentieth century has continued to fuel the Kurds' restiveness.

So, too, the Christian Armenians would have been without nationality had not their ethnicity been recognized by the Soviets, after 1917. They were recognized as a semi-autonomous republic within the Soviet Union, a remnant of a once greater Armenia. The Armenian homeland was divided up during this period, facilitated by the expulsion and controversial "destruction" of Armenian populations during the Turkish and Kurdish genocide of these Christians, in 1915. There is thus a politically independent Armenian nation today, a living repository of an ancient Christian people, now a small remnant, surrounded by an eastern, western, southern sea of Islam.

As with Israel, Armenia, with its rich civilizational tradition, can as both ethnicity and nationality receive from ethnic Armenians throughout the world a cross-fertilization of cultural values that transcends its small geography and national population. It can as a nationality establish itself as a cultivator of a new

Armenian tradition and mentality having both a universal civilizational outlook and the integrity of an historic culture built face-to-face for ethnic life.

In the world of post-twenty-second-century civilization building, it is difficult to accept the reality of wandering, politically disestablished ethnicities existing without some geographical base. It requires political and cultural autonomy of all such groups, such as the remnant Amero-Indians. They must be free to preserve what they value from the ancient ethnic tradition. The ludicrous identification of the Amero-Indians ethnic group with state-sponsored gambling casinos is a great tragedy for this people. It has undercut much of their claim for contributing to the rich mix of cultural meanings required by humankind.

How to achieve a union between ethnic identity and national autonomy is the great question, both for the survival of Israel and all the other small national enclaves throughout the world. There are many other as-yet politically unrecognized peoples, having history, language, religion that they wish to preserve. In obtaining cultural, even political rights of self-determination, it is difficult to believe that they would not attempt to harmonize this self-determination by their participation in the major social and scientific movements of the global community.

Why Nationality?

In our hearts, we wish to see all peoples upon our earth live in peace, prosperity, unity. Why not a big global family in which we protect the rights of all humans to express themselves fully, in which we are tolerant of the idiosyncrasies of our neighbors, whether they be down the street or across an ocean? This is the ideological chant of contemporary "liberalism."

Thus, it is illiberal to force Muslims to give up their four or ten wives and concubines, to censor crotch-grasping Michael Jacksons or vulva-undulating Britney Spears, to prohibit "great" art in public museums that subsidize themselves by presenting exhibitions of paintings of a dung-covered Virgin Mary.

A truly modern global culture, so it is argued, must protect free artistic expression, sexual choice, and, of course, tolerate religious and educational freedom. This, even if the tax-exempt religions advocate jihad and terrorism toward non-believers. It is only fair that state-supported schools be allowed teach creationism, this according to the orthodoxy of cultural relativity, and thus the promoters of the "imbecilization" of humankind.

Counter argument: to live together rationally, to be able to face the great issues that will eventually challenge the survival of the species, we must take an alternate route. On an international level, education involving state support should sharpen the critical abilities of all learners. The young need to become skeptical of the tricks of the demagogues, the ideologies that attempt to short-circuit the cortex to plug into the mammal emotional system. This is the first step in creating an internationalism that can bring an end to war.

Scientific knowledge is open. It does not lend itself easily to surety. Any community setting will contain dissenters. Democracy provides for the protection of dissent. It requires constitutions, laws, and a polity willing to protect an individual's right to posit new ideas. However, today, one lone community dissenter instituting decade-long appeals in the courts can often paralyze the life of a community, prohibit it from putting into place any policy consensus.

All humans should have the right to migrate, where their beliefs might flourish, to have a bit of turf to think apart. The conundrum of community consensus, the right to agree *versus* the need to entertain deviant ideas, values, and practices will become the great balancing challenge for humanity in the centuries to come. Within a world of 1.5 billion humans rather than the ten billion to come by the year 2050, a Roger Williams could again be free to make his way to a New Providence, Rhode Island.

The argument for nationality, the political and legal recognition of the legitimacy of ethnic and esthetic difference, is constructed from the recognition that these human cultural elements touch the deepest strands of human creativity. Here, as epitomized in the philosophy of cultural pluralism, we answer to our brain's need for the *tychistic*, the new, the unexpected explosions of human symbolic meaning.[8] Observe the constant ebb and flow of automobile design over the decades, often with only minimal technological improvements. The flow of stylistic change in civilizational life infuses itself even in areas of gross survival economics, patterns of agricultural land use, the aesthetics of the instruments of the hunt, gun or bow and arrow.

We cannot live without symbolic innovation. The trillions of excess neurons and "interconnects," constantly firing off these energies in search for new meaning, demand it. There has to be an external object, (a thought, a sound, a colored vision) as focus for our search for neuronic meaning. Call it catharsis, the eureka moment, the breeze that recalls the memory of one's beloved. These symbolic energies are ephemeral, but constantly renewed. They constitute the life blood of human sensibility. Without them, all human activity is meaningless.

New symbolic envisionments, whether in cuisine, gardening, or corporate structures, may turn out to be but small rearrangements of the given. Revolutions begin with tiny steps, innovative insights. For us to live as full humans, these novelties of perceptions must be allowed to float freely and interact socially with the insights of our neighbors down the street. They cannot be mandated or controlled from afar by the political or the business/cultural commissars. The present technological globalization of "culture" may not fail from the standpoint of pure economics and trade. It could collapse from ennui.

Universality and Nationality

The civilization of the twenty-second century and beyond will require membranes of cultural and esthetic difference. If we be not separated by the big issues of life or death—for these, we have federal governments or, heaven forbid, the United Nations—the small decisions, over sexual normality, noise levels, art worthy of subsidization, will be subject to community consensus.

Do we really think, for example, that Israel can continue to be a Jewish state with historic and contemporary Jewish values when within its borders a surging Arab demography stands apart? Multiply this dilemma by the hundreds of other conundrums that face a world intent on becoming global and homogenized. Is it likely that Iraq will survive as a nation unless it finds a way for the Shiites, Sunnis, and Kurds to live together in economic and cultural parity. Is it possible for them to commit to universal values in education, science, technology, and democracy, all the time practicing their own religions, at the same time respecting the religions of others? Even the multinationals may go national.

Nationality connotes some rights of rejection, of the outsider, challenging the homogeneity of values of the insider majority. The Greeks called the foreigners *barbaroi*. Caracalla, 212 CE, granted citizenship to all peoples—even the Jews—living within the compass of Roman law and Roman arms (a tax scheme). The Union said "no" to the Confederacy's claims for slavery and secession. The then-contemporary elimination of Russian serfdom echoed a universal sensibility toward humanity. The Ottoman Turks were then also imploring their Arab confreres to shed the slave trade and concubinage. When the latter revolted against the proposal, the Turks withdrew. Not too long after, the Ottoman world disintegrated in chaos.

Lincoln taught the Union that this young United States could not hold together, two associated nations, too loosely united in political outlook. Here might evolve in one sub-continent an extreme diversity of cultures, one slave-ridden and looking backward toward a colonialist agricultural existence, the other without slave labor moving with the industrial/scientific revolution. The southerners saw this Union utopia as a nation of immigrant factory/labor "serfs." History was with Lincoln and the Union.

In any future global human setting, universal behavioral and material standards and values must exist, enforceable upon all nationalities. On the other hand, art is the benign pluralist. Gaze out at the skylines of Hong Kong, Shanghai, and Beijing. The engineering and architecture are modernist, almost universal. But the esthetics are immediately apparent. Chinese flavors or Communist conformity?

Here is the nucleus of a creative regenerated world society of the future, nations, provinces, states, towns. Unless we plan seriously for the right to secede into the intimate cultural dimensions of life, in reality the central elements of what it means to be human, there will be no point in striving for a world society that must live in peace with itself. The globe must sing the hymn of human unity and freedom. With *Homo sapiens sapiens*, the essence of this freedom lies in the esthetic, the ethnic, the national homeland.

Endnotes, Chapter 10

[1] Eliade, M. 1961. *The Sacred and the Profane*, N.Y.: Harper and Row; Freud, S. 1962 (c.1935). *Civilization and its Discontents*, N.Y.: W. W. Norton; Bataille, G. 1962. *Death and Sensuality*, N.Y.: Walker.

[2] Cassirer, E. (1923-1929). *The Philosophy of Symbolic Forms*, 3 vols., trans. R. Manheim, New Haven: Yale Univ. Press; Langer, S. 1967-1982. *Mind: An Essay on Human Feeling*, 3 vols., Baltimore: Johns Hopkins Univ. Press.

[3] Schilpp, P. A., ed. 1951. *Albert Einstein: Philosopher-Scientist*, N.Y.: Tudor.

[4] Marx, K. 1967 (1835-1847). *The Writings of the Young Marx on Philosophy and Society*, trans. ed. by L. D. Easton and K. H. Guddat, N.Y.: Doubleday/Anchor; Nisbet, R. 1953. *The Quest for Community*, N.Y.: Oxford Univ. Press.

[5] Rothstein, Edward. "The Brain? It's a Jungle in There," in *The New York Times*, 3/27/2004.

[6] Pledge, H. T. 1959. *Science since 1500*, N.Y.: Harper and Bros.

[7] Duhem. P. 1954 (1905). *The Aim and Structure of Physical Theory*, tr. P. Weiner, Princeton: Princeton Univ. Press.

[8] Kallen, H. 1924. *Culture and Democracy in the United States*, N.Y.: Boni and Liveright; Itzkoff, S. W. 1969. *Cultural Pluralism and American Education*, Scranton: International Textbook Co.

Chapter 11

Tomorrow

Issues

Morality

A usually rational political commentator, William Safire, opines: "…The looming issue is cloning. Not reproductive cloning; most scientists reject that odious goal, with its danger of monstrosities and designer genes that end human individuality, and there ought to be a law against it."[1] Reproductive cloning is ostensibly evil, so go the directives given today by Mr. Safire and many moral pundits eager to "pass a law against it."

In Canada, a professor can be called before a board and threatened with job loss if he or she utters a thought that even implies the existence of on-average intelligence differences between ethnicities. Supposedly this is hate speech, under moral interdict.

Actions or thoughts that are repugnant exist in a shifting realm of human evaluations and actions. Indeed, hatred and poison in thought and action do exist. And we should be aware of their existence in humans and be clear as to the status of such values. The Arab world sees no moral difficulty in spewing anti-Semitic, anti-Christian epithets over the public airways, in the press, its literature, and its schools. Often, such ideas and communications are prelude to violent actions against the objects of their moral diatribes, *e.g.*, terrorism.

It ought to be clear to the educated that humans are alone in the "moral" world. There are few instincts by which we can define human behaviors. Nature has set us loose in a world where our actions are self-defined as moral or immoral. History is written by the victors, in war and in peace. Forget the moral qualms over the price of conquest, its costs, even "pyrrhic" victories. The moral rules are forever rewritten to absolve the survivors. The Muslim and Christian worlds were artists in their moral legitimization of "holy" crusades. Much earlier, the same attitudes suffuse the Old Testament. Can one doubt that if the Arab fanatics win, destroying the Christian and Jewish infidels in an incineration of terrorism, they will see such a vast genocide as appropriate to the committed sin, and notably, moral.

What it comes down to then, in judging moral behavior, in defining such policies, political, economic, and social, are the outcomes. Who will be able to look back and rationalize behaviors that have accomplished such ends, certainly moral ends?

Here, contemporary debates over important choices with regard to tomorrow's structure of life become relevant. A scant two decades ago, *in vitro* fertilization was viewed as inherently immoral, the risks overwhelming the need. The incipient monstrosities predicated as the certain result of such experimentation cast a cloud over the research. Forget the anguish of infertility among those who searched for family life without going the route of non-biological affinity adoptions.

Could these gurus of moral legitimacy today face the many thousands of beloved children thus created and tell them that they are monstrosities? What about the normal reproductive process, so conducive to producing tragedy without careful medical analysis and possible abortion? It will be the same when the first human clones are created and they survive as healthy human beings. Who would then stand as moral legislator and say *no* to a 45-year-old mother who through accident has lost her only child?

Go back two hundred years to Prussia of the 1780s. A debate raged over the moral and legal legitimacy of inoculating against the pox It was damned as playing with nature. Even Immanuel Kant, the wise philosopher of Koenigsberg, was asked to enter the fray. In retrospect, except for devout Christian Scientists and other religious fanatics, a moral issue no longer exists here, merely medical orthodoxy.

The battle over the issue of human intelligence variability now takes on the complexities of the racial and ethnic character of intelligence differences, a debate first engaged in within Caucasoid communities in Europe and North America a scant half century ago. The so-called moral high ground is taken by the environmental egalitarians who maintain that those who argue from the psychological, sociological, evolutionary, educational standpoint that there are real and significant intellectual and thus behavioral differences not merely within an ethnicity but between ethnicities, are morally tainted.

Even to raise these differences in an intellectual setting—forget the economic and political re-distributionary aspects—is enough to trigger accusations of Hitlerism, KKK membership, and other besmirching associations. Researchers into the genetics of inheritance were sent to the Gulag in Stalin's day. In the democratic West, this violation of the moral code offers lesser penalties for such violations. They are, however, just as effective in stifling debate and secular analysis.

According to the politically-correct, there are no such intellectual differences between groups. Thus the taint lies on those "white males" who controlled the power strings down through the centuries. They are the ones who have created the historical and contemporary institutional structures that have caused African-Americans and Latinos, for example, in the U.S., and Muslims and Africans in Europe to languish in the ghettos of the rejected and the incapacitated. To speak of genetics or evolution becomes not a mere factual error. Such facts cannot even be debated. They are now moral "verities" that lie beyond conceptual examination.

What happens when labor's fruits, taken from the intimidated "white middle classes," creative labor that now greases this morally legitimized transfer of wealth, run out? If this writer's argument is correct, "what you subsidize is what you get," they will produce lower on-average intelligence levels and weaker national social, political, and economic profiles. Who will suffer around the world when the demographic miasma now facing us—the proliferation of the civilizationally helpless—becomes the majority reality? No longer minorities for the smug wealthy to succor. Now, a vast underclass. The former majorities will be holding on desperately. Why can't we understand that these educated middle classes are essential for the basic functioning of modern societies? Yet they are and will be taxed into submission. What then will be the fate of these helpless billions that were created by the so-called morally upright?

Will those who called attention to this oncoming cloud of civilizational incompetence now wear the moral halo? After all, they warned of these "December 7, 1941," "September 11, 2001" disasters-to-come, realities scorned by the once morally powerful? Where are those who were really *for* the poor minorities and their descendants?

Blundering Crisis Management

Over both the U.S. and Western Europe floats an opaque sense of a future suffused with dark clouds of decay. Under the mesmerizing opiate of ideological optimism, the true nature of the growing crisis cannot be addressed. Thus will arise, over the next several decades, a series of governmental policy palliatives to attempt to slow the decline. Naturally these policy decisions will be propagandized to the public as significant progressive reforms. To the contrary, they will deal only with the surface manifestations of the problem. As a result, the public should be prepared to see the long, slow, self-induced strangling of the present institutional structure.

Immigration reform: No question that this is a hot-button issue, c.2005, both in the U.S. and Western Europe, where both legal and illegal immigration will certainly be more stringently controlled. Unfortunately, the demographic balances have already been tilted; far more reproducing poor than reproducing intelligent middle classes, of all races and ethnicities. Underscore the fact that individual racial and ethnic attributions are not critical. It is the educated intelligence of the individual and the population that counts. If history is evidence, the existing welfare systems will continue to fund the fecundity of the poor, especially in Europe, where Muslims are foreordained by religious law and custom to be obedient and reproduce.

Economic survivability: In the United States, the huge trade imbalances, budget deficits, total national debt, low savings rates, crisis of Social Security viability, Medicare and Medicaid liabilities, all part of long-term entitlement solvency, are contemporary specters evolving from halcyon late-twentieth-century expectations. The American industrial and manufacturing base that once provided for a real middle-class lifestyle for generations of American high school graduates is disappearing before our eyes. China is the supposed villain here.

The economic burden of America's military hegemony can be abandoned, making for enormous cost savings. After all, we have oceans between us and the great overseas Islamic disaster. Illegal immigration from south of the border can be squelched and our seaports and airports can be controlled if the will is there.

Even with an economically disciplined military, altering the declining productive wealth outlook alone will not solve the above problems of deficits and expensive social welfare programs. We can talk reform with a balanced budget, but only at the cost of abandoning much of our luxurious governmental handouts. State budgets, as in California, will need many more of the tax-paying rich to maintain even minimum educational and social services. The average American, as the century proceeds decade by decade will not live the luxurious protected life provided either by government or the private sector. American citizens will still have to pay for oil, police protection, medical pandemics, remedial education, and an occasional natural disaster.

In Old Europe, the unemployment rates are high, due to go higher still, despite new labor laws that will encourage workers to move from their couches and Miami condos. The cheap labor nations are right next door, and they are New Europeans (East), hungry to partake of the high-tech, high-education feast. After totalitarian submergence, they will happily accept $5-per-hour jobs, one-quarter to one-third of what the Old European pampered socialist labor force achieved in the good old days.

The decline in births for the long run would not be bad. It harmonizes with Western Europe's own steadily improving—as in the U.S.—production efficiencies. However, the new non-European minorities, as they increase in proportion, will exert heavy social and economic pressures on the European (Eurabian) style of life. It will not be as much fun living in London or Paris in 2050. Europeans have already begun to feel this decline in standards of living, except for those few in the economic stratosphere.

Assuming that terrorism can be brought under control, the slow modification downward in the middle-, working-class style of life in the U.S. can be stabilized. As the official argument goes, "all thing change, don't they?" But this argues for stabilization in the job scene, the West Europeans staying ahead by virtue of their intelligence and efficiency. Surely, with the New Europeans, Russia, China, and India not too far away and rising fast, there could be a severe downslide in the job situation and with it the tax wealth available and necessary to maintain the welfare state.

As with the U.S., across the sea, the prediction for the old West can only be stagnancy in the economic social zone. Current high culture will also come under attack by the below-the-neck mass media undergirded by an increasingly non-European character.

Lastly, we can predict the implosion of creative scientific and technological research and entrepreneuership. No growth, no free cash flow in society, slim possibilities for the chance-takers, the creators of the new, the veritable collapse of optimism within the global techno-economy. In order to survive, the Chinese, Indians, and other low-cost producers around the world now and in the foreseeable future need paying customers for their products. The prognosis there would be grim also.

War, Terror, and Hatred

If only we could face the truth about ourselves and our world. The core truth that has spun history forward amid the tensions and bloodshed that have marked civilization's regression and progress is the uniqueness of human intelligence and its historic and current variability in quality and quantity. The fact that we cannot confront this reality in our own time defines the crises of the twentieth and twenty-first centuries. Never in human history has intelligence variability leaped so overwhelmingly to the fore as the trigger for hatred, terror, war.

Why? People don't want other people to get "ahead" of them. Getting ahead means being able to accumulate the values of wealth as they are defined at any one time. That is why Napoleon came back to France from Italy with the loot of the Renaissance in his wagon trains, *e.g.*, the Louvre today. That is why Imperial Germany, having made such a great late-nineteenth-century surge to power, would not tolerate the encapsulations that the allied nations attempted to effect after Sarajevo, 1914. The subsequent defeat of Germany, the reparations, the humiliating economic chaos that followed, bred irrational politics and an insane nationalism, which exploded into the *Holocaust*, World War II. The Germans did not want to be second to the Jews, the French, or anyone, given the historic power of their culture, intellect, eighteenth- and nineteenth-century political expansion.

No self-respecting family wants its children to fail either in school or on the streets of economic and social competition. A child is born. First question asked, is the child intelligent? To say that "black" people are less intelligent than "whites" is the greatest derogation. Such thoughts cannot be countenanced today. Yet, the pride of every great civilization lies in its recognition of the power that intelligence and enterprise bring. In the U.S., the majority that once produced this wealth will soon be a minority, and the power will recede.

The ancient Hellenes were proud urbanites, but relatively weak materially, especially as compared to the Persians and the massive extension of their empire. The Persians understood that their superiority lay not in the culture that they brought to the Babylonians, but in the power and arrogance of military competence that then buttressed an ancient and tired civilization.

The Athenians and the Spartans with their innovative citizen armies sheathed in the iron phalanx, the large trireme battleships manned by citizen marines revealed a fatal gap in Persian pretensions to power. Subsequently, the Greeks were able to show the world that they were more than intelligent, tactically successful killers. They created the most innovative civilizational life quality the world has experienced. The rest of the world, including the once-dominant Persians, would henceforth be disdained as *barbaroi*.

People don't have to articulate their intellectual superiority or sense of inferiority in terms of I.Q. It shows up in their life behaviors, abilities, creative skills, often in the wealth-producing skills absent in others. The history of humankind is truly the history of nations, ethnicities, races, families, individuals either attempting to exploit their various abilities, intelligence, talent, bodily strength, else attempting to level the playing field so as to neutralize or extirpate those advantages in their rivals.

Rarely in closely-knit ethnicities—the Athenians in their remarkable decades, or within the cities of northern Italy during the Renaissance, even the U.S. when it was beckoning, and under-populated—are these competitive juice ameliorated. Mutual poverty and defensiveness often help, bringing out, as in the Jewish ghettoes of Europe or in America and Israel, a sense of belonging, where the suffering of the wealthier is not much less than that of the most afflicted.

Today, the hatred of high intelligence is most clearly exemplified in the Arab world and Islam in general. Without the lubricant of oil revenues and the organized knowledge of Western oil conglomerates to assist them in pumping the oil from the earth, the Arab world would not be able to sustain its suicidal demographic orgy. As the people expand in numbers, the oil revenues will dissipate in proportional sustenance while the West, now including the Northeast Asiatic ethnicities moved into the modern technological era, maintaining relatively free democratic politics and intellectual openness, the social competency of the Arabs and Muslims has withered. Even their most educated know this. That is why they became the terrorists of 9/11.

This hatred of the West, Israel, and the U.S.—its emblematic representatives—explains exactly what is happening *vis à vis* terrorism and the womb–like return to clerical obeisance. It has nothing to do with religion *per se*, for, at one time, Islam was in the forefront of philosophy, poetry, science, and mercantile capitalism. It has much more to do with the Arabs' historical retreat into the desert of African slavery, polygamy, concubinage, and the gradual lowering of the intelligence and educational capacities in the modern Arab world.

Of course, there are minority exceptions within this great geographical, national swath. These higher ability groups are differentiated both by social class and ethnicity. But, in general, the lowering of intelligence levels has pushed down the capabilities of many to participate in the intellectual surge of the modern world. The South Koreans, the Japanese, and the many Chinese ethnicities are now making their mark, and this without the oil that has benefited the ruling Islamic thugs.

Arabs and Muslims, in general, despise those in the West, eventually the Northeast Asiatics, too, simply because they, as a distinct religio-ethnic group cannot jump over the intelligence or educational bar. Thus they have reverted in their search for a meaning center to religious fanaticism. They rationalize their present military, economic, historical incompetence, playing on a once-powerful sense of jihad and supremacy. Further, this intellectual deficit and their consequent fall into social irrationality explain the long susceptibility to succumbing under the thumb of tyranny.

No educational, political renaissance exists that will recreate these tragic multi-millions into partners toward building a scientific civilization for the future. True, Islam has raised no regulatory edict against raising the intelligence levels of the masses. The Iranian mullahs have worked hard to propagate the morality of birth control and population limitation. Agreed, such a generalized Islamic program would take centuries. But progress would be seen at all timeline points in this effort. Were there to be a sudden shift in energy use to atomic or hydrogen fuel cell power for our international needs, with much less reliance on oil and gas, the Arab and Muslim worlds could quickly rethink their future as they fall into a *crisis extremis*. Today, except for allowing nature's oil and gas to flow, they produce nothing with their hands and minds that the world wants.

If the world's leadership wants peace, the fraternity of the human species different by race, ethnicity, and history, it must embark on another highway into tomorrow. The necessary first condition: create an equality of ability, cognitive intelligence both within nations, for internal stability, and between nations. In short, they must even the playing field. The sufficient conditions for intranational harmony and international amity will always be complex, never to be attained automatically or easily. Witness the homogeneously intelligent Europeans, for millennia at each other throats, genocide succeeding genocide. Are we wiser today? Potentially, yes, certainly far more capable of achieving a dynamically peaceful harmony of purpose than the ideological pathway to international disaster today being imposed upon us. Remember, there are groups, the leadership/exploitative classes (national and international politicos) that are benefiting from this catastrophe in the making. They will save their hides and their wealth while the masses they presume to succor, suffer the consequences.

Our Technological Revolution

Modes of Production: We must respect the insight of Karl Marx who understood that, to a great extent the sociopolitical structures possible for all societies throughout history depended on the regnant forms of economic production. However, he was not correct in predicting the emergence of only one pattern of sociopolitical life from one basic pattern of economic life. Certainly, the basic forms of wealth production did not change radically from the Sumerian Uruk period to the Sumerian Ur III dynasties, a period of about 500 years, 3000-2500 BCE. Yet, the semi-democratic forms of the former were gradually replaced by the highly urbanized conflicts of a much wealthier society now ruled by domineering kings. (See Appendix.)

What Marx elucidated for us, to his everlasting credit, was the shaping power over society, in general, by the modalities of economic life. To be sure, under ideological or religious intimidations, economic innovations could be dammed up. We witnessed this recently in the communist world. But because there was freedom to experiment and innovate outside these walls, where progress sped forward, the historical economic inappropriateness of the communist/socialist system eventually brought down the walls.

It is probably true that the force of technology will radically reshape our current international political and social system sometime in the twenty-second century. The present order will by then have failed. The intellectual and educational standards required by the new scientific and technological forms of production have and will make many billions of hands redundant. The need to support these many billions, who will not be able to contribute educationally to the wealth and prosperity of the international system, will undermine the viability of the entirety.

What Marx did not fully understand were the reasons behind the power exerted by the material conditions of social life over the form of other social institutions. This needs to be explained.

Tools and Power: Technology, and the empirical sciences that have uncovered its possibilities, are the keys to the dynamic events of today and the realities of the twenty-second century tomorrow. It seems obvious, but also it needs to be explained. Mastering the physical world in order to create surpluses in the basics of human survival has always opened the door to civilizational fruition. Aristotle explained this phenomenon succinctly. Paraphrased: 'We satisfy bodily needs in order to free the mind to engage in intellectual and esthetic fulfillments.' In the evolutionary sense, our minds have run away from our bodies. Without instincts, our bodily needs are at the mercy of our mental awareness. It is high intelligence that re-interprets bodily needs as they relate to our deeper civilizational and mental urgings.

The Appendix chronicles the Sumerian rediscovery, 4000-3000 BCE (after the Cro-Magnons, c.40,000-12,000 BCE), of the intellectual and cultural joys made possible by organizing the human and physical world so that it can yield the bounty of the mind. Their intellectual discipline and pragmatism showed us how *techne,* and then literacy, can make possible the mentally rich life of civilizational discovery.

The Greeks amplified on this discovery. Their technological breakthroughs were not as millennial as those of the Sumerians almost 3,000 years earlier. But the Greeks, too, saw the organization of society as a technological feat, preliminary to mastering the physical world—manufacturing, trading, growing grains and grapes, generating military hardware and tactics, engineering and architecture. In the Uruk civilization, the Sumerians intuited the value of democratic life in the community. It was the key to getting things done efficiently and peacefully. The Greeks were later and more sophisticated in writing about their ephemeral joust with the democratic life. Yet this discovery contained in it everlasting cultural consequences.

The Sumerians and the Greeks confronted intellectual barriers to their expected indefinite advance for their respective technological innovations. They then shifted their energies to exploit the wider civilizational implications of these past productive achievements. Eventually, each of these nation/cultures had to cede political and military leadership to other groups that were equally invigorated by the idea of technology, power, expansion. The long transition from the Sumerians to Akkadians, Babylonians, Assyrians, Chaldeans, and then their successors, Persians, Greeks, and Romans, could be defined by the technological, military, and economic innovation of each successor group, and their ramifications for power and domination.

These groups, the Mesopotamian and Indo-European complexes, were composed of the descendants of the Eur-Asian Cro-Magnons, *i.e., Homo sapiens sapiens*, the now highest levels of long-developing brain power in the evolutionary universe of dominant *Homo*.

In all these cases, indigenous national innovation and technological advance eventually sagged. Perhaps the cause was the deeper emotional desire to exploit other currents of their civilization's mental symbolism. To live with the material achievements that ensured the good life was thus enough. Then, the real fun had to begin.

Ongoing Technological Dynamic: The revolution that we are experiencing in these first decades of the twenty-first century is akin to the revolution that the Uruk civilization of Sumeria first exploded, sometime after 4500 BCE. These efforts led to the conscious realization of the civilizational power of political/social organization; urbanization; literacy. This power resulted in the full release of all the manifold potentialities of the human mind for high civilizational forms of symbolic expression, the cognitive ordering of all the basic psychological needs of humans, here including the most basic life-sustaining requirements.

The phrase that economists use today is "increasing productivity," simply, using fewer resources and labor hours and hands to fulfill the required productive output. To run our 2005 society efficiently, we need much less raw energy for the same outputs than we needed a generation ago, when the Arab oil embargo on the U.S. almost brought us to our knees. That is why sky-rocketing oil prices did not destroy the U.S. economy in 2004. Why has the family farm disappeared? A few machines can do the work of thousands of the farmers of the 1900s. The labor that we need today increasingly requires more education and cognition.

A simple prediction: the requirements of high cognitive production will eventually bring the international culture into balance. If we follow the potent thinking in Karl Marx' model, the forces unleashed by technological productive efficiencies will, over the forthcoming centuries, cause us to find humanitarian means to bring to universal reality the classless vision achieved peacefully in Western Europe and in the North America in the late twentieth century.

As more and more humans are displaced from the evolving technological job market, the twenty-second-century leadership will realize that only two solutions will be long-lasting: 1. Bring the demographic levels on this planet into balance with human civilizational needs, environmental, ecological, social. 2. Raise the intellectual levels of all humans so that they can participate in this pluralistic national/ethnic civilizational potential.

The Battle of the Two Brains

The lower brain, the limbic system and the allo-cortex, the emotional brain, is a steady contender for dominance over the iso-(new) cortex, the planning, predicting, and organizing part of our mental make-up. A great civilization should hold these two elements in a dynamic balance. By definition, ideology makes a play for our presumed intellectual acquiescence of such an interpretation of reality. It will not command attention unless linked to the lower brain's emotional energies. Thus did communism's vision for creating a classless society magnetize the intellectual elites. This emotional glue allowed the communist totalitarian systems to remain in place for many decades. It was the failure of the ideology, the supposedly cognitive, planning dimensions of this cancerous experiment on human history that gradually led to the people's emotional withdrawal and that marked its final collapse. As Marx predicted, the system could not be reconciled with the evolving modes of modern economic productivity, creative technological innovation by free minds.

In our own time, the emotions that seem to opt for human homogeneity of intelligence and productivity, the hoped-for realization of an equality of social and cultural outcomes once the redistribution of wealth from the haves to the have nots is completed, keeps the system temporarily glued together. These deep mammalian emotions still override the skeptics and allow the exploitative international and national ruling classes to maintain their stranglehold on our economic future, in the face of overwhelming evidence for impending international socio-economic decay.

The reality is that, when highly educated people, whether in Germany, c.1934, the Soviet Union, c.1929, the West, anytime post-1950, fail to speak honestly, abnegating their responsibility, the search for truth goes underground. Facts then emerge, tainted by the stained minds of the emotionally and intellectually irrational fringe. Such a situation attended the coming of Adolf Hitler. It is beyond any thinker's capability to truly understand the barriers that one warp of human history erects against rationality. Why can't supposedly educated humans stay the course of tough empirical factuality?

The opportunity for a new generation of the intelligent, a small self-conscious minority of true intellectual revolutionaries to make its case before history, will surely arrive. People will fight politically for the social embodiments of a modern life that nature's high intelligence has made possible.

Without the self-interest of the decadent, with eyes undazzled by mythic emotional ideologies, they will try to recreate something that for long we haven't seen, a new and modern civilization of the intelligent, the rational, and the creative. From our present perspective, we probably would not recognize it as such. But it will be theirs to create, and they will know and cherish it.

Endnotes, Chapter 11

[1] *The New York Times*, 12/15/2004.

Appendix

Western Civilization Begins at Sumer

Prologue
We will search for originating meanings and momentums, as scholars have uncovered them at the dawning mists of history. Out of the unknown north came the first humans who had the opportunity and internal impetus to create what we would call a *civilization*.

Sumer arose at the then-extreme southern end of the Tigris/Euphrates Rivers c.4500 BCE. Its civilizational discoveries would not have been possible without the biological intelligence that was created for this special taxon of humans, *Homo sapiens sapiens*, perhaps hundreds of thousands of years earlier.

As with all animal adaptations created by evolutionary forces impacting on its genetics, time was needed for the creature in question to make full adaptive use of what nature had created. So, too, with the extremely high intelligence of these distant ancestors of the Sumerians. External conditions of climate and ecological opportunity gradually presented themselves. And then, the slow learning about what was inside of this brain and nervous system that could make the civilizational breakthrough possible.

Indeed, we still know little about this inner nature of ours, a nature that flings itself outward, most often with an unknowing and disastrous exuberance. Then comes nature's inevitable disciplinary leash. Unquestionably, this explosive investigation of nature's mysteries, and the systematic attempt to master and control them, was first fully demonstrated by the Sumerians.

Making of the Great Brain
The making and use of tools by the most ancient hominids reflects the basic physical vulnerability of this line of primate mammals. They took the unspecialized route of defense—"stay out of the way"—as a means of survival. Upright, omnivorous scroungers, they had higher than average intelligence, which was derived from a larger brain. But the reward, of mammal domination, was not

automatic. Several million years ago, it was merely one of the possible adaptive options for positive natural selection available to the already highly intelligent primates.

But considering the dynamics of environmental and ecological change, a larger brain had worked for survival, resulting in almost a billion years of vertebrate perdurance. The tools that humans created were extensions of this extrusive intelligence. Tools went beyond the body in time and space as means for obtaining the next meal. This evidences the dawning of the objectivization of experience beyond instinctual automaticity. It argues for a consideration of possibility and predictability. The premeditated fabrication of potentially useful external materials to make a difference in earning this living was critical for breaking with the instinctual past.

There was more to tool-making than its admittedly crucial practical usefulness for a physically unspecialized animal. Tools also give us hints about broader cultural behaviors, even about esthetics. The great revolution in cultural behavior coincides with the morphological revolution in brain size and structure represented in the Cro-Magnons of Europe and West Asia, first encountered at the time level of c.45,000 B.P. (before the present). The material results of this biological revolution are then clearly in evidence.

No doubt this revolution in morphology took place much earlier than indicated in the discovered bones and material artifacts. We needed large enough numbers that could signify flourishing communities. Genetic evidence in contemporary northern populations argues for a very small population of founders, which subsequently spreading their genetic imprint throughout the world.

The surprising creation of such a large brain enclosed in an eggshell-thin skull, a *paedomorph*, retaining its infantile characteristics into sexual maturity, constitutes a revolution in morphology. As a consequence, a revolution, in behavior, cognitive behavior. Genocidal climatic conditions could have allowed for the destruction of many more primitive humans. A sidelined freak of large brain and mind could have leaped through the void. Such an external challenge, since there were no other fauna blocking the way, certainly sped up the selective process, *orthoselection*, or selection of one attribute, the thinking brain, in a progressive line upward.

Nature, having negatively selected less adaptive human groups, would have thus allowed a few smart outliers of thin bone and big brain to survive to procreate for another day. Except for the powerful selective force of language that was rooted in the morphology of tongue, larynx, and brain, modern humans are unspecialized primates. Free of rigid adaptations, they had to rely on their intelligence, with language, to get them out of whatever vale of annihilation faced them.

Civilizational Threshold

The Cro-Magnons, *Homo sapiens sapiens*, bleached white to help them metabolize Vitamin D from the weak northern sun, were different from other northern Caucasoids. They lacked the heavy bone and, presumably, thick hair, large air-warming nose, short and stubby Eskimo-like adaptations of the Neanderthals. These Neanderthal characteristics were shaped to ward off the glacial winds. The Cro-Magnons physically seemed to have originated on the periphery of the northern adaptive zone. The Caucasus region would be one guess as to their origins.[1]

With these humans, our intelligence and our nature were seemingly completed. The cultural and proto-civilizational evidence argues for this climactic evolutionary moment. We need not repeat the concretia of their cultural achievements, the highly finished tools fabricated for a variety of functions; the painting, sculpture, the sacral settings in which this artistic obsession took place, special caves, most often in interior darkness where only oil lamps provided them the required light.

Even in burial, their connecting of thought and wonder about the afterlife unites them with the literate civilizations. They thought no less than the most civilized humans in modern urban settings, about human destiny, birth, death, and immortality. In Russia, in a site dated to c.28,000 years ago, a male and younger sons were found, dressed in leather, ivory- and bone-decorated clothing, as part of a burial ritual, clearly regarded, with love, wonder, and awe. Other careful burials of young quasi-adolescent women interred with their offspring tell us of the hardships of life, the danger for young child-bearing mothers, and the regard of their families and communities.[2]

The Cro-Magnon, or Upper Paleolithic cultures of Europe and West Asia, extended from 45,000 to 12,000 years ago. During that time occurred the gradual evolution of their technology, the art, the manner in which they revered the animals they hunted or with which they were associated. Above all there is an economic stability, a sense that the food and shelter, the clothing, the life of the small hunting/gathering communities were in balance with the larger thrust of this new human mind to find external symbolic expression, beyond the hunting, scraping, tool kit. Art was never detached from the practical, the spear, the dagger, the projectile.

Until the very end of this period, the Magdalenian, the climate was glacial, with benign, cool summers, and early spring-like winters that hovered around the freezing level.[3] This allowed for a wide variety of large mammal life to flourish, clearly a magnet for these peoples as they entered Europe from the east.

Their lives, epitomized in their cultural effusions, express our own dawning nature as *Homo sapiens sapiens*. Held in an economic context, by this moderate late-Pleistocene glacial ecology, they clearly lived good, stable, disciplined lives.

Across the valley, the Neanderthals, crowded at the edge, gradually ceded the better hunting/gathering ranges, no doubt continuously harried, if not ejected by these aggressive, brainy newcomers. Eventually the Neanderthals succumbed, disappeared, (c.27,000 B.P.), not able to reproduce themselves. No doubt they left many hybrid young among the Cro-Magnon dominators.[4]

The Cro-Magnons clearly lived within a context of small numbers within a geographical community, trading with other Cro-Magnon bands. We find amber caches hundreds of miles from their point of gathering along the northern seas. These humans expressed their wonder of the world around them in chronometry, making incisions on their stone and flint tools to record the rhythms of nature— the phases of the moon, the menarche of the mature female, the geographic settings of the sun at the seasonal climaxes, the comings and goings of migrating animals, the budding of the flowers. We recognize the animal protein sexual energies in the signs of vulvas that decorated their voluptuous mobiliary stone Venuses. So, too, with the decorative sculpturing around the caves.[5]

They were not yet seasoned of mind, not threatened in their way of life. However, we do recognize this high intelligence in the quality of thought that went into their material culture, recently discovered after so many thousands of years. Eventually, this cool paradise had to end. The economic basis of their proto-civilization was altered, a change of climate, more continental in nature, wetter, sharper in contrasts. Now came the conclusion of the era of forage for the great mammals, sloths, mammoths, giant elk, saber tooth tigers.

The Cro-Magnons do not seem to have been responsible for this wipe-out. Evidence for herding of deer, domestication of the horse, the dog, all argue that the Cro-Magnons were inherently "green" in their outlook on nature, conserving and protecting what provided for their living and stimulated their mental/artistic desires.[6]

The semi-sedentary life for which this surplus provided disappeared with the advancing forests of the Mesolithic and Neolithic cultural periods, after c.12,000 BCE. The Cro-Magnons now had to follow the herds and migrations of animals.

In contrast to the Upper Paleolithic, some 25,000 years in length, the transition into the Holocene climatic period (after 12,000 BP), the Mesolithic/Neolithic cultural traditions were quite dynamic in certain geographies, relatively late in others. Although we see instances of highly developed technology—microliths, painted stones, geometrical architectural engravings in some cave homes/temples during the Mesolithic—it is probable that at least in the north, life became much tougher. It was difficult to support the luxuriant high-art products of the previous benign ecological environment. So, too, for the sojourners south. The old hunters of the north were forced into a more nomadic way of life, with wandering groups trying to make their living in the desertified contexts of the modern climatic period.[7] From 12,000-8000 BCE, entirely new economic challenges had set in. The old, rich tundra-like hunting grounds became overgrown with vegetation, the herds vanished into the forests, some extinct. We see this transition in the cultural detritus from these periods, the Mesolithic, thence the Neolithic. The latter is so named because of the appearance of clay pottery and the more intense hunting, gathering, herding lifestyle of the south. This gradual change in climate and ecology put pressure on humans heretofore living off the lush highland and lowland (Sahara) savannahs. They were being forced to move toward the ever fewer sources of water.

Mesopotamian Magnet

It is clear that the movement south of the Cro-Magnons was not the first intrusion of modern types of humans along the Mediterranean littoral and the adjoining river valleys, Danube, Nile, Tigris/Euphrates, Indus. Nevertheless, it is clear from the fossil evidence, burial grounds, technology that the first permanent or semi-permanent communities as found in Palestine, Jericho, in Anatolia, and along the Nile and Tigris/Euphrates reveal a taller, Cro-Magnon-like people displacing the then-dominant Natuftians, people probably hybridized with older human taxons.[8]

Sickles made with flint blades cemented into bone or wood handles are now to be found. Baskets woven from natural grasses, presumably used to carry the harvested wild grains and naturally occurring vegetables are also part of the Neolithic economy. Mortars, pestles, grinding slabs suggest knowledge of husking the grains, as well as evidence for roasting, presumably so that they would not sprout. Storage pits evidently used for the seasonal harvests argue for awareness of the economic realities of living in a new economic environment.[9]

Petr Charvat sees this general cultural adaptation for life in the south as evidence of these wanderers taking hold in this universal mid-Eastern context, especially Mesopotamia. He calls this period, 9000-5000 BCE, the age of inspiration. Here, humans who had been so well integrated and adapted to the autumnal northern glacial climate, with its meat protein basis, now had to find a balance between agriculture, hunting, and domestication.

"Deep reaching knowledge of animal life, leading to deliberate and rational hunting practices and subsequently to domestication, preoccupation with plant life, resulting in the protection of and care for the most promising cultigens and, finally in transformation of plant genetic structures to produce new species without wild ancestors—all these results would glorify any of the modern breeding stations and laboratories. These naked 'savages' endowed with a spirit of intellectual adventure worthy of any modern discoverer, handled nature with much more responsibility and understanding than modern industrial civilization....Theirs was the age of freedom: never did the contemporary communities allow any of their material creations to chain them to a particular site, landscape or specialized activity."[10]

Toward the end of this period, c.6500 BCE, the first irrigation channels were being built, in Jericho, and along the lower Danube. M. Gimbutis has noted the building of multi-room houses and meeting rooms, as well as fortifications, along the lower Danube.[11] Great monuments, megaliths, as in Stonehenge, England, 1800 BCE, also are revealed, and along the Tigris/Euphrates valleys, though not as dramatically preserved. The Mesopotamian climate and the ravages of changing human empires precluded our finding more than hints of their existence.

"Such projects, Choga-Mami, Tell es Sarwan—Samarra culture, did nevertheless represent a lesson well learnt. The fame of such superhuman feats undoubtedly circulated far and wide. People must have talked them over around the campfires of their large winter congregation sites in the lowlands, where the multitudes gathered to hunt game in the steppes, catch a winter crop, exchange experiences, and perform the necessary rites before the whole community.

"In the following summers, when these large groups (dispersed? and) went to the higher lying grounds that protected them from the heat and offered fresh pastures to their animals, well watered valley bottoms to their peasant minded members and hitherto untapped wild-life resources for every one, many of these experiences were undoubtedly tested and found useful. Thus the memory of them was not lost and generations of free-born and proud men and women challenged the forces of nature equipped with the experiences of their predecessors. This incessant traffic in the plains managed nevertheless to create a certain 'mental environment' common to all lowland communities among which ideas, experiences and manners of artistic expression (e.g. the seals) circulated at large, coalescing into the first cultural 'koine' of this part of the world...."[12]

These peoples, c.6500-5300 BCE, were in al likelihood part of a Semitic-speaking migration, as they subsequently remained in the central and northern sections of the Tigris/Euphrates valley, approximately sixty-five miles north of modern Baghdad. Cultural development continued in an internal dynamic.

The cultural artifacts that we find from this period are a composite of the new and the ancient Upper Paleolithic Cro-Magnon proto-civilization, still part of their living mental heritage: "Stone sickles, blades, scrapers, stone ornaments, pendants, beads sown on clothing (belts), alabaster vessels, pottery of different sizes and shapes, figurines of females and animals. Grave goods, semi-precious stones, carnelian and turquoise—latter probably from Iran, copper pendants."[13]

Wild grains from the fringes of the watercourses of the Zagros and Taurus ranges became a part of their diet, making the transition from a nut-like snack to a main course staple. "These change {are represented by the transition} from wild two row (chromosome) wheat into einkorn wheat, two row barley, four row wild grasses into domesticated emmer wheat. Soon six row wheats appear and barleys without any known wild ancestors."[14]

Some of these new forms of wheat, with stronger stems and larger berries, were undoubtedly introduced from northern latitudes. These early Neolithic and Chalcolithic cultivators, c.7000-5000 BCE were certainly on the move, especially with the introduction of domesticated sheep, goats, oxen. In the northern hills and valleys, they would have noticed different forms of wheat, barley, flax. Then, the experimentation process would have continued in the south in the winter months. In fact, this alertness through migration, trade, or conquest is what is supposed to have underlain the introduction of southwestern Asiatic forms of grain crops into the Nile Valley. The success of such experiments clearly hastened the agricultural development of Egypt also.[15]

Careful analysis by Neolithic peasants, as with all farmers, of the cultivation process made them sensitive to the fact that artificial pollination of certain kinds of plants would yield better results, gradually departing from the wild prototype. "We may envisage protection of plants, sowing them in specially conditioned plots of land, selection of sturdier and especially non-shattering individuals (because of the losses of the shattering varieties releasing their grains easily in the cutting process), and, ultimately, cross-breeding."[16]

Here, close to the village, artificial irrigation was practiced. Village buildings had expanded to up to 10 rooms. Early hunters in the Upper Paleolithic had long before been accompanied by tame dogs. Neolithic hunters continued this practice by picking out the tamest of the wild goats and sheep that they hunted gradually domesticating them, breeding out the wildness. Even *Bos primigenius*, the great wild ox of Roman hunter fame, was gradually transformed into tame cattle, probably by offering domesticated grain crops as lures into corrals and enclosures, c.5500 BCE. Most early domesticated animals "displayed a high degree of variability and low type stability," clearly for maximum adaptiveness to changing external conditions.[17]

While, as Jean Bottero argues, these early domesticators were from the Zagros Mountains and the Piedmonts of Kurdistan, many other groups wandered widely throughout the Fertile Crescent as it gradually drifted climatically into the semi-arid environment that we see described in the Hebrew Bible. "We know that in this new, muddy, fertile territory people seem to have devoted themselves to the growing of grains, besides the husbandry of small animals and cattle. Due to the extreme climate and the lack of rain, it was indispensable to establish a tight network of canals that would connect the two rivers and give the earth an exceptional fertility. This collective enterprise not only enriched the inhabitants enormously but permitted the grouping of workers, first in villages and soon afterwards in larger agglomerations that became the centers of administration and distribution."[18]

"In all spheres of human life we feel the tightened grip on nature. Peasants now round up the range of cultigens yielding nourishment to their communities and settle down to establish not only fields but even such labor intensive cultures as gardens and orchards. Shepherds start keeping more cattle for food, but perhaps also as an energy source for traction and load bearing. Specialists in all sorts of crafts attack the resources of nature, gather new experiences and apply new know how. Sedentarization implies the necessity of transport in this age, regular traffic on the twin rivers of Mesopotamia, most probably using rafts of inflated skins (*kelek* in Arabic), first becomes a probability. The sedentarization of major social centres now traps whole settlement zones, the inhabitants of which can no longer disperse and congregate at will, being bound by various means to their capitals which constitute the central points of the coordinate systems in which their activities now take place....

"This is the end of sometimes ragged and worn but blessed liberty: People now have to learn to work together, live together and even die together, this incarceration paying for the increase in living standards. Material seizing of the environment walked hand in hand with a better mental grip on things of the invisible world. The holding of private property now appears on the horizon of historical vision, both by individuals and by whole human communities, as is indicated by the establishment of the first extramural cemeteries, which probably anchored rights to territorial segments claimed by particular communities or rather, community clusters. Socially engineered exchange of material goods, which probably constituted the cementing agent of political alliances, is now institutionalized for the first time in history, most probably in the form of reciprocity."[19]

Civilizational Revolution: The Sumerians

A change occurred in the structure of cultural progress during this period. It is as yet an historically and archaeologically inchoate transition. Still, it merits discussion. Because, while we recognize elements of this Neolithic/Chalcolithic stage of cultural life throughout the Near East—Nile and Danube Valleys, Anatolia, perhaps as far east as Persia and the Indus River Valley—something different had begun to occur in the Mesopotamian south.

It is part of this process of sedentarization mentioned above. The success of these evolved Neolithic semi-stable communities, the fact that they laid claim to a territory essential to their economic and community survival, argues for an eventual surrendering of that ancient joy and trial, the movement of the band with the seasons to new beckoning horizons, sometimes dangerous, sometimes alluring in potential. But always the rhythm was, anchors away, onto the "high seas" of travel, we are going somewhere new.

The Tigris/Euphrates valley began to rise from its glacial inland sea after c.6500 BCE. The gradual drying up of the southern world saw the soil rise to emerge from the Persian Gulf, from today's Nasariyah, northwest. It was then still a great freshwater marsh with a rich variety of wild animals, birds, shellfish, vertebrate fish and other water attracted creatures.

Surely, peoples were also attracted to this domain, if not as permanent residents. The mysterious names of the geographical localities reflect the same kinds of reference as do Amero-Indian names in many of America's rivers and cities; names of an unknown language. There were throughout the subsequent historical period languages of many wandering tribes that we to this day cannot decipher or relate to known tongues. The Elamites to the East in today's Iran (Susa) were a highly developed people, part of the Mesopotamian complex. Their language is undeciphered and not established in its relationship to others. Later, the Gutians, Kassites, Hurrians enter our historical purview as conquerors, quickly accommodating their own culture and mysterious languages to the dominant Mesopotamian civilization.

It is in this context that we meet up with the Sumerians. They transformed what was a wide ranging and developing cultural trend (agriculture, water management, domestication) among all the Cro-Magnon peoples who had descended into the south. Now the stabilization of secure communities along these water courses allowed for a gradual development into a full-fledged literate civilization, a civilization critically self-conscious of its accomplishments as compared with the then-contemporary level of life among its neighbors.

We know little about the origin of the Sumerians. That they were outsiders is hinted in their retention of names for places, flora, and fauna that were not Sumerian, Akkadian (Semitic), or Elamite (Iranian). There seems to have been a cultural change, c.4500 BCE, evidenced in the type or potteryware that was being used in southern Mesopotamia and in the trade of the region from that time period. From c.4000 BCE, we find true urban settings with temple sites that indicate a more intensely settled cultural scene. Eridu, Uruk, Ur, Lagas, important Sumerian cities in their heyday, from c.3000 BCE, are sites that reveal the existence of more ancient temples upon which these towns were built, going back to the dim horizons, evidence of a people branding the terrain with its cultural symbols.

The Sumerians always referred to themselves as the "blackheaded" people, in contradistinction to the light-haired Semites around them. Sargon himself, the Semitic conqueror of the Sumerians, c.2340 BCE, boasts of his military, but not his cultural suzerainty, over the "blackheaded people." His daughter, Enheduana, sent as high priestess to Sumer at Lagas, writes a hymn to that event:

"Urukug, shrine which causes the seed to come forth, belonging to the holy An, called by a good name, Within you is the river of ordeal which vindicates the just man, House of widespread counsel, store house which eternally possesses silver and lapis lazuli, Etarsirsir, from which decisions and **me's** {arête'=virtues} come forth where the 'man' greets (the goddess), Your princess, the merciful princess of the land, the mother of all lands, The lady, the great healer of the dark-headed {Sumerians-not Semites}, who determines the destiny of her city, The first born daughter of the holy An, mother Bau, has, O house Urukug, placed the house upon your..., has taken her place upon your dais.....The house of Bau in Urukug {Lagas}."[20]

The Sumerian language was no closer to that of its northern Semitic neighbors, the Akkadians, than is French to Chinese.[21] In its seeming agglutinative structure, it resembles that of the family of Finno-Ugarit-Altaic languages of Central Asia. And, indeed, considering the wandering needs and tendencies of humans it is not improbable that this was a tribe that wended its way south instead of east, as many tribes of this language family later did, Kazakhs, Mongolians, Japanese, Koreans.

By 4000 BCE, it is clear that these people were well settled in the rich marshy environment of the southern Tigris/Euphrates valley. Perhaps they looked at its potential with new eyes, as foreigners often do. In contrast to the harsh barrenness of the northern steppes, this land teemed with resources that demanded an invitation for disciplined exploitation. A potential garden of Eden, the Sumerians saw opportunity.

Based in the city of Uruk, a thousand-year evolution can be traced, the transformation of cultural life into a full civilization. A companion city, perhaps even older and holier, Eridu, became victim to one of the turns of the wayward river Euphrates. It was finally abandoned, its achievements buried in the sands as the river moved to another course. A shrine in Eridu, dated to 4500 BCE, home city of Enki/Ea, later "stranded deep in a sandy and rocky desert.." was finally transferred to the nearest city, Ur, to stay within the complex of the god, Nanna, patron god of Ur. "No one lived there {Eridu} after the early dynastic period, c.2600 BCE."[22] This god, Enki, as we will later discuss, became the the-

thematic Sumerian god of myth, as with Apollo of the later Greeks, his activities emulating the youthful spirit of this innovating people.

Uruk: Civilization's City
Technology:

"Most of the significant developments that were involved in that transformation seem to have taken place in the Uruk period which follows the Ubaid. {5000-4000 BCE} monumental architecture, public art, specialization and standardization of industrial production, the invention of writing and greatly expanded trading horizons....The continuity with the Ubaid period is epitomized in the famous sequence of temples at Eridu, enlarged time and again through the centuries, the latest surviving remnants of the temple's platform are in fact from the Uruk period....excavations from the Anu ziggurat at Uruk itself has shown that the Uruk period temple on its platform was also built over the site of an Ubaid period temple....It is fair to conclude that the major cities of the Uruk period are in part at least an indigenous development."[23]

"Technologically, it was a time of rapid and important changes. In metallurgy we see the use of sophisticated casting processes for the first time. In pottery we see the use of the fast wheel; perhaps most significantly of all we see the introduction of the first pictographic writing on clay tablets. This was accompanied by the introduction of the cylinder seal. The Uruk period was arguably the most innovative and important in the history of Mesopotamia and its influence was felt as far as the Mediterranean and the Anatolian plateau."[24]

"...extensive irrigation systems, and of techniques of alloying and casting not previously found on the plain itself....Some may have been brought in by immigrants from the Iranian plateau, for instance, but they all appear within the span of a few hundred years and transform life. No comparable innovations can be attributed to the succeeding Early Dynastic, Agade or Ur III periods {3000-2000 BCE}; they seem to have built on the new techniques and refined them, but fundamentally the technological tool-kit remained unaltered. So too did the range of raw materials available to the craftsmen."[25]

Uruk period craftsmen and craftswomen embarked upon a course of systematic experiments, some of which succeeded while others failed. Attempts at building in concrete in the Uruk VI period, temples foundations partially made of concrete/cement, 3500-3400 BCE, were abandoned in favor of more traditional material, clay. Of a number of experiments with alloys, the smiths of the period invented the viable formula of tin bronze at the close of the period, 3200-3000 BCE, but in one site only. On the other hand, the invention of the fast wheel for pottery making, c.3800 BCE, explains the plain undecorated mass production pottery of the period.

So, too, the discovery of iron, which enriched human culture for millennia. Advances in metallurgy, mostly of imported materials, trade with Aratta in the mountains of northern Iran, or again with Anatolia is exemplified in smelting copper into wire, sheets, the lost wax casting techniques; single and bivalve moulds. Lead, for the making of bowls, used as a single or compound/alloy, was mostly for repair. As in later Greek and Roman civilizations, much of these advances in metallurgical and other technology were primarily directed to the temple for cultic paraphernalia. Stonework advanced mostly for seals—administration—or works of art.

In Iran, the city of Susa, bitumen and woolen textiles were exported in exchange for Uruk metal tools. Uruk-type beveled bowls are to be found in Pakistan (Makran Province). Raw materials for chipped stones from Iran, obsidian and metals from Anatolia, chert from Canaan are to be found in Uruk sites, alabaster vessels from the Taurus Mountains, pottery from Anatolia.

Uruk-type terracotta cones, used in the decoration of the great temples, painted in different colors show up in Egypt, in the Nile Delta, presumably transported by ship, or overland on sledges or wheeled vehicles. Domestication of the donkey as a beast of burden took place during this time. The names Dilmun, Meluhha, Magan appear in the later written record signifying distant but long-standing trading partners, Indus River Valley, Persian Gulf oases, Ethiopia in East Africa, and again, more surreptitiously, with the Nile River valley.

Uruk farmers continued the experiments of their predecessor domesticators. They attempted to domesticate antelope and/or gazelles. We have discovered illustrated signs that depict the head of such an animal with an ear of corn at its mouth, implying its feeding with grain.[26]

Cultural Elan:

"With the creation of the Uruk corporate entity, {c.4000 BCE} this essentially prehistoric development—the community as the most important social component, came to its climax....The Uruk corporate entity, short of introducing any major subsistence innovations, did the trick by realistic analysis, rational administration, common consensus and intellectual attraction. It simply committed no mistakes and there was hardly any escape from the tyranny of its all pervading success.

"The Uruk culture managers assessed the economic potential of all their component communities, determined the type of enterprise most suitable to every single one of them and arranged for the distribution of results, maintaining a steady flow of goods throughout the entire community and buffering the impact of unexpected events. Tasks requiring specialized knowledge were carried out by the centres and the products released into the redistribution network.

Some of them involved seeking alternative solutions by testing several hypotheses, the erroneous ones of which were subsequently abandoned" (metalwork).[27]

"The founding fathers of the Uruk culture must have 'run their homes precisely on schedule.' The ideal of the Uruk culture leadership must have been a society in which no one actually starved, as the best individuals racked their brains to procure for everyone what he or she needed and to release the potential of the natural resources in accordance with a preconceived vision of the external world in which non-economic aspects were not absent."[28]

"The Uruk culture settlement network included large scaled settlement agglomerations which may be termed pristine urban centres and military bases, presumably with deterrent functions. All this went on in a predominantly egalitarian atmosphere without traces of social stratification other than the ability of the centre to mobilize manpower and with evidence for holding assemblies {Lugal="big man"} essentially for the decision of common matters…"[29]

The sociopolitical terminology of leadership is interesting. *Ensi* was the term for head of state during the Early Dynastic period, c.2900-2600 BCE. This term meant, in the early Uruk period, c.4000-3500 BCE, "tenant farmer of the god," later, c.3500-3000 BCE, "the lord who established the foundation of the temple." *Lugal* also meant "great man." First, in the Uruk period, it denoted a leader of the community. Then in the Dynastic period (city states in competition with each other), after 3000 BCE, *lugal* became the king who lived in the "lugal" or great house, the palace.[30]

Uruk, 4000-3000 BCE: "In all spheres of society the principle of universality and equality comes to the fore and struggles with the particular and concrete manifestations of the visible world in order to make way for human advance. In the spiritual sphere, the torrents, twists, and turns of the mythopoeic thinking in symbols embedded in reality are surmounted, if not straightened out, by application of universal principles and rules. The world perceived as a unity in diversity is accordingly organized into a social whole. The natural variability of communities, in most cases linked principally by the factor of co-residence and accompanied by industrial sites and service holdings {is} interspersed by groupings that see themselves as manifestations of divine will, communities divided among elites and commoners is constantly leveled. The material standard of living is equalized by means of redistribution, external threats are eliminated by garrisons posted to ward off any attack.

"Everyone is close to everyone else, people meet in assemblies to discuss and decide matters of common interest with at least some of the resolution put down in writing. All receive the same treatment both in life and in death. The world is an organized place where the economy thrives because all the discoveries and inventions of previous ages are now put into practice and systematically exploited. Unity of purpose drives the best brains of the epoch to experiments both economic, some of which fail and social and spiritual, some of which succeed. The flow of goods throughout the community is directed and scheduled....The world is weighed, measured, disposed of in organized form, from cake baking to manipulations of time and space."[31]

Literacy
"From the fourth millennium {3000 BCE} on, what we can call an urban high civilization flourished. It was complex and original, and it was the first in world history. Numerous elements were gathered in this civilization, {from 4000 BCE}: social and political organization; the creation of institutions of obligations, and of laws; the production of all goods of use and exchange, procured over-abundantly by a planned effort, and their circulation in the interior of the country as well as abroad; the appearance of superior and monumental art forms, the basis of the scientific spirit {divination and neocromancy, the functions and status of the gods} characterized first of all by a constant urge to rank, to classify, and to clarify the universe.

"And finally, around the year 3000 BCE, came the last great innovation, doubtless the most decisive discovery of an importance that can barely be measured: the establishment of a system of writing. It was at first {4000-3500 BCE} a simple mnemonic device, but in a few centuries it enabled the recording of all that is expressed by the spoken language, and in the way it is expressed by it. This ability of the script allowed people to objectivize knowledge, to organize it in an entirely different way, and to propagate it. Hence knowledge became rapidly more extensive and more profound."[32]

We have tokens from Mesopotamia, Iran, Jericho, that date from shortly after 4000 BCE. These are made of clay in the shape of spheres, cones, bi-cones, tetrahedrons, sometimes with incised marks, indications of personal or corporate exchange. People are negotiating and recognizing these marked agreements over time and space. From the mid-fourth millennium, c.3500 BCE, in Uruk and elsewhere in Sumeria, these tokens contain pictographic symbols, human heads, trees, animals.

Soon, hollow clay balls were devised, *bullae*, again to be found widely throughout Mesopotamia, north Syria and Iran (Elam/Susa). These had incised symbols on the outside to coincide with the clay-enclosed tokens. Such often thumb-sized cylinder seals would be rolled over clay to identify the owner, soon to be followed by pictographic symbols, often denoting the meaning content on small clay tablets. Soon, conventions about meaning had to be established among these pictographs, and more abstract symbols added to clarify rebus and homophonic elements unclear from the pictographs. The requirements of this urban, economic, political revolution necessitated the establishment of clear, accepted legal public agreements, economic, business exchange, long-distance trade between cities, governmental and temple laws.[33]

"The fact that the Uruk tablets, c.3000 BCE, were located in the enclosure of the great temple of that city, and that the pieces clearly constitute accounts of the movements of goods, listing numbers first in detail and then totaled, make us think that this script was established mainly in order to memorize the numerous and complicated economic operations centered in that temple. The temple was the exclusive or principal owner or redistributors of the products of the labor of the land....In other words, Mesopotamian writing did apparently grow from the needs and necessities of the economy and the administration, and therefore any kind of religious, or purely intellectual preoccupation seems to have been excluded from its origins."[34]

"The script, created deliberately by Uruk's sages, put at their disposal both an ordered series for things of the visible and invisible worlds which they could manipulate to their hearts' content and an efficient device for the tracing of movements of material goods throughout the complex circuits of the Uruk corporate entity. Thus they rose to the status of masters of the visible world, guardians and managers of its fertility and creators of a cosmic order. Nevertheless, they bowed low before their gods who represented the highest values of Uruk culture/society, reserving for themselves {the gods-temples} all the most precious goods and justifying the mobilization of a considerable amount of manpower for all-community projects.

"The gods had to determine and to decide first of all the *destinies* of all things, in order to produce and govern the world and the people from day to day. Their orders had to be *written down* in order to give them substantiality, publicity, and force. Utilizing as pictograms and ideograms the *things* to come, which they created as needed, they impressed in them the 'individual words' of their decrees....Whoever understood the code used by the gods, {cuneiform writing}... could decipher the signs and read in them the irrevocable will of their authors." Priests, scribes, and kings could thus associate themselves with a higher order of powers and the future events. The search for meaning in the external world of mostly unique events, beneficial or dangerous, as well as the powers of humans organized to secure their lives, took on a mythological, religious cast. This required of every city its higher commitment to the will of the gods and the temples, as symbols of both dependency as well as the resurgent intelligence of the community under its gods."[35]

Transition:

Charvet claims that the Uruk period was unique in its treatment of life and death. "The citizens who came to the shrines where they sometimes left their personal articles as tokens of faith even tolerated an absolute break in the treatment of their dead who departed to the nether world in a manner radically different from those of the preceding periods. No veneration of the dead was now possible with the new policy of mass graves or the incineration of the dead. Thus we find few graves, the disappearance of cemeteries, as compared with earlier periods."[36]

This claim raises an interesting conundrum. For, in the succeeding Dynastic period we find much evidence of cemeteries close to towns, often within living compounds, at the least, of the extended family. There are, of course, the royal burial tombs in Ur, discovered by the British researcher C. Leonard Wooley. They were discovered, along with a great urban cemetery of c.2600 BCE, hinting of a radical reversion in cultural practice as represented in the transition between the Uruk and Dynastic periods, c.3000 BCE.

A supposition about this transition can be made from the Epic of Gilgamesh, a great Homeric tale of adventure, misadventure that is now believed to have been written c.2700 BCE, but refers to events, such as the great flood, presumed to have taken place c.3000-2900 BCE. This flood had such an impact on the psyche and history of Mesopotamia and the Near East that it reappears in a more moral/religious setting nearly 2000 years later in Genesis, of the Hebrew Bible, now featuring Noah and his sons.

It is not at all unlikely that this catastrophic event, and the necessity to rebuild the Sumerian cities, gave rise to a wholly new cultural outlook and destiny for this people.

Sumer's Achievement
Timeline of dominance:

Fifteen hundred years, 4500-3000 BCE, approximates the Sumerian adaptation to life amidst the swamps and fields of the southern river system. A vast accommodation had to be made by a people wandering from the mountains and plains of the north. Thence, the maturing cities of Sumer become increasingly self-conscious of their history and covetous of their achievements. Eventually they became engaged in disputes and conflicts with their neighbors as we enter what is called the "Dynastic Period". Certainly, irrigation rights, and other economic contestations figure highly. But also pride of place should not be discounted, as urban centers such as Ur, Lagas, Nippur, Uruk, Kish, Larsa, Isin, Umma, begin to figure in the documents. Writing, computing, surveying, all are perfected within the cuneiform system during a five-hundred-year-plus period of

Sumer's international dominance, c.3000-2400 BCE, a dominance that made its civilizational impact well beyond its geographical boundaries.

Whereas in Sumer the development of writing and monumental architecture can be traced back to the fifth millennium BCE, in Egypt it appears suddenly after 3000 BCE, to be taken up as a passion by the ready Egyptians, "why didn't we think of that?" The Sumerian merchants and technicians had clearly visited the Nile kingdoms.

The influence of Sumer over the ancient world lay as much in its conception of civilization as it did from the material achievements. It reached a peak in Ur, as exemplified in the above mentioned discovery by C. L. Wooley, 1920s, of the royal tombs of that city. Here artifacts amidst the sacrificial suicides of a king's entourage, c.2600 BCE, first revealed the extraordinary achieved level of craft and esthetic skills of this people.

Over time the Sumerian cities were a magnet for the gradually infiltrating Semites of the valley and surrounds. They increased in proportion and influence. There were no "outside" Sumerians to repopulate the area. The Sumerians were *sui generis* in Mesopotamia, as compared with the Semites, with no other known related kin. About 2340 BCE, Sargon, from *Agade,* an Akkadian Semite conquered the cities of Sumer to create an empire that extended to the Mediterranean. Culturally and intellectually, he was a Sumerian, even if of a different ethnicity. After one hundred fifty years, his empire was felled by Gutian tribesmen from the north. They seemingly acclimated themselves to this urban culture and ruled for almost one hundred years, thence to be ousted by a new Sumerian dynasty, from Ur (III).

This reinvigorated Sumerian dynasty achieved a peak of systematization, a Sumerian forte, in every area of life, political, educational, economic and cultural. Now united by a dynastic force of great brilliance, Sumer's, language and heritage flourished amidst this ever multiplying Semitic demography. It was a relatively brief century long nova. Its disintegration, c.2100 BCE, after another one hundred years plus, was accompanied by a wholly new force of peoples from outside, the Elamites, once a satellite people to the east, the Amorites a semi-nomadic Semitic people to the west and north. It was from this latter and seemingly barbarous infiltration that a new cultural center based in the new city of Babylon (Hammurabi), arose from the Sumerian base.

The Belief System:

Twenty-five-hundred years separate the Sumerian and the Hellenic renaissance, 3000-500 BCE. Both were civilizations of the city state. Each city had attached to it its own tutelary god, which represented the local ethos and protective hand. While the Greeks were in the process of creating a written literature, now including philosophy, science and drama, which the Sumerians had not yet developed, both had absorbed ancient mythological systems and literary epics (*Iliad*, *Gilgamesh*). These latter explained to their ordinary citizens the meaning of their existence as vulnerable beings upon this earth.

During the Akkadian Semitic dynasty of Sargon (2300 BCE), there was catalogued a series of forty-two hymns, including the Hymn of Enheduana, quoted above, by the daughter of Sargon, high priestess to the Sumerians at Lagas. These were recorded as referring to the Dynastic Period, c.2600 BCE, and represented thirty-five cities, each one with its indigenous temple and gods. From Ur, Eridu, Lagas in the south, to Kazallu, Marad in the northwest, to Sippur in the north, Esnunna and Der in the northeast hill region. Although the non-Sumerian peoples who came to rule over Mesopotamia throughout its independent history (before the Indo-European Persians and then the Greeks) added their own special gods to the pantheon, the original Sumerian deities remained a critically important element in this conjoint cultural heritage.[37]

The myth of Enki (called Ea by the Semites) represented to the Sumerians a poetic exemplification of the inner values and understandings of their own achievements. Enki, one of the great gods (originating god of the city of Eridu, later transferred to Ur), offspring of Nammu, universal primordial mother, is lazy. He invents humans to do the work of the gods.

"The triumph of Enki was not only to have invented mankind, an enormous technical success, but also in finding a function for all the human types, even the imperfect but usable ones…(sterile women, the court officer, the blind, a-sexual humans for the court, etc)…Thus Enki is at the same time civilizer, inventor, keeper of all cultural values, but also the most intelligent, the most clear sighted, the prototypical technician, the only one capable of overcoming all hurdles, and of adapting everything for his purposes, of molding matter for every possible use."[38]

"What Enki/Ea does, what he has to do, is never defined in terms of power, of government, or of political authority, but only in terms of organization, of control, of the promotion of life and, to that goal, of intelligence and technical and practical success—and all this, always, in the supreme interests of the divine society {the stable order of things}.

"In the end he was portrayed as being at the head of an enormous and extremely complicated mechanism, which he guarded and animated. Beginning with his infallible directives and passing through his 'foremen,', the minor deities, which he charged with a section of this gigantic machine, this mechanism reached all the way down to the 'workmen,' the people who made it actually function. These people were first of all the 'technicians.' Enki/Ea is the *only god* who, according to the entire tradition, is the patron of all of them and of all technologies, as if he had established all of them: from agriculture and husbandry to writing and exorcism."[39]

"Enki/Ea used the *apkallu*, the scholars, sages, craftsmen to introduce culture in the history of his country, the great technical advances, the successive elements of high civilization that had made, first Lower Mesopotamia in general, then Babylon the cultural center of the world....At the side of authority, of power, of efficient command, of commanding appearance, there was indeed need for a clear and profound vision, of intelligence, of wisdom, to give a positive sense to these orders—what we call 'the technical function of power,' eminently incarnated by Enki/Ea."[40]

"The entire civilization of the country, their entire life and their way of living was first of all based, since the beginning of time, on communal work, the extensive production and transformation of usable goods. In such a system, in the end, everything is directed by a spiritual activity that researches, invents, promotes, and perfects procedures, not so much to *see* better, but to *do* better.

"All knowledge, all intelligence, was thus polarized by production and action, and was materialized equally well in the 'practical judgment' of the artisans, and what we would call 'craft' as in the sagacity of the tactician and his ability to adapt, and as in the 'good sense' and the astuteness of what was known in the old days as an 'upright man'—both on the collective level and in individual achievement...this type of wisdom was incarnated...in a younger god, Enki/Ea as if to stress his capacities not only in knowledge but also in action, in speed and in versatility, which cannot be detached from the 'technical function' or from the 'functions of government' that formed the double aspect of power."[41]

Myths, poetry, a bardic tradition that is imputed in such ancient stories as Enki/Ea, reflect only one aspect of a culture which, by the late Uruk, had found a place in its ideals for leisure, play, song and dance. Illustrations on a carving from an Early Dynastic, c.2900 BCE, depicts banquet scenes with lyres, flutes, cymbals as musical entertainment. There are also stone plaques that show wrestling matches, plus other entertainments, dice, complex gaming boards and their pieces—before the mid-third millennium in Ur, c.2700 BCE.[42]

"Some material culture items do bear out a non-negligible function of dance (a pin in the form of two nude female dancers....The fact that in the 'Curse of Agade' {Sargonic period, 2300 BCE}, Inanna {goddess} assigns dancing as a historically distinguishing feature for young women. This could indicate the existence of age grades or age groups as early as the Uruk period..." (4000-3000 BCE).[43]

Even love merits the conscious efforts of humans to go beyond mere procreation. Here, we can better understand the sacred sexual/fertility sacraments celebrated on the day of the spring New Year by a high priest or priestess. As with the Greek god Dionysus, whose role in the mysteries, at his temple in Eleusis just northwest of Athens, here was proclaimed a conjunction of sex, wine, and the sacral. Such invocations were not merely salacious events, "Sadie Hawkins Day." Rather, they were the ritually inscribed and disciplinary representations of a powerful human drive.

Twenty-five-hundred years separate Sumer and Athens. So, too, twenty-five-hundred years separate Athens from contemporary twenty-first-century Rome. In our own era, Vatican Rome's celebrations are royal and mysterious, invoking the sacredness of non-explicit sexuality supposedly held in check by priestly celibacy. How much further have we advanced in the human understanding, the symbolic and ritual acting out of this unique human biosocial force?

"A famous episode found in the first two tablets of the *Epic of Gilgames,* c.2700 BCE....In it is explained how Enkidu, the wild man of the steppe, hairy and barbarous, only intimate with animals and living a life like them, *becomes a man* in the full sense of the word:...a civilized man, a city man who eats bread, drinks beer, and grooms and dresses himself. This transformation is the work of a courtesan from Uruk who came to look for him in the steppe and who introduced him to love; hence not simple intercourse with a female, but love with a real human. Thus, human and refined love, *i.e., free love.*

"Once he had discovered it and had acquired a taste for it, Enkidu could only follow his teacher *to the city*, where she taught him to eat, drink, and dress, and where she completed his transformation. Thus free love is presented as being the point of access to a life that is truly cultural and human. It is difficult to better indicate its worth and its importance."[44]

Marriage contracts guarantee economic, social position and value. Children from marriages established by elders inherit the economic and social base of settled urban life. Such marriages are *pro forma*, and, thus, not usually based on love or emotion. Man is also privileged to take on concubines, slaves for work and sex, if his economic base allows for it. Love, however, is the real key to civilized life.

Beyond Barbarism

Fundamental to the obsessive Sumerian efforts to free themselves from the chanciness of the old order, a wandering subsistence existence always threatened by nature and man, was their awareness that the good life for humans is a constructed life, built out of the possibilities of individual intelligence and conjoint human social efforts. The struggle was against disorganization, disorder, and the primitive, accidental flow of events. Here, discovered consciously, expressed in both life actions and the myths and temples that gave intelligibility to their efforts, they would attempt to extricate themselves from the unknown.

The democratic form of cooperative efforts came naturally, as much a part of this new social and economic system as the ancient Cro-Magnon band or tribal unity that undergirded the hunter-gatherer economy on the northern plains many thousands of years earlier. Key to understanding the creativity of the early Uruk period Sumerian achievements, a rich heritage that was mined in subsequent centuries and millennia, was the sense of the possible, the need to push back the mysteries of nature out of which they expected to bring into reality the life vision they hardly understood, but knew they had to find.

The end of the Dynastic Period (2600-2340 BCE) is characterized by dominating elites that tried to use the temple as a repository of secular power. The palace and its *lugal* or *ensi* ("big man") developed independently of the more community-centered tradition invested in the ancient temples. Thus ensued a struggle between individual achievement and the ancient Uruk community classless traditions. Yet, "this age, terminated by the Akkadian (Semitic) conquests of the forties and thirties of the twenty-fourth pre-Christian century {2340 BCE}, saw the emergence of the principle of statehood, the embryonic forms of political democracy, but also the foundations of modern thought, including mathematics, metrology and the first ethical categories, when such notions as freedom or justice but also guilt and sin found their way into human literary culture. One of the most creative periods of Mesopotamian history, this epoch (the Dynastic—signifying kings and competitive Sumerian states, 2900-2340 BCE) enriched human civilization with achievements that affect the lives of humankind up to this very day."[45]

The Sumerian heritage of the free citizen and the secular culture was epitomized in the fact that rarely did Kings try to transform their secular power achievements into theological ordinations, as gods. Narum-Sin of the Semitic Sargonic era, 2290 BCE; Shulgi, c.2060 BCE, a Sumerian of the Ur III, reestablishment; Ishbi-Erra of Isin, c.1950 BCE, possibly an Amorite, are the few that attempted thus to anoint themselves. Considering that Mesopotamia had its share of autocrats and warrior kings over a period of almost 2,500 years before Cyrus, the Persian, he of religious tolerance, conquered Babylon/Chaldea in 539 BCE, this civic restraint was remarkable. These kings, if not gods, however, felt the need to proclaim that they were "called" by the gods to rule.[46]

What strikes as the gift of Sumer, extended throughout each succeeding dynastic empire, was the commitment to preserving, copying, and cataloging the heritage accumulated over the millennia. Thus the sanctified role of the scribe, the scholar, the scientist/medical doctor never waned, in Nineveh (Assyria) as well as Babylon. The last king of Babylonia/Chaldea, Nabonidas, under whose rule the Israelites lamented in Nippur, sent his eldest daughter to be high priestess in one of the restored Sumerian temples in the south (550 BCE).

The Mesopotamians always feared that descent and disintegration could come from the wilderness both within and without the nation.

In the time of the rule of Su Sin, Sumerian king during the Ur III reestablishment (c.2030), after the Aggade dynasties of Sargon and the Gutian hill people, a description of the Amorite nomads of the western desert then beginning to overrun the walls along the Euphrates: "A tent dweller...wind and rain,... who digs up truffles from the hills, but does not know how to kneel, who eats raw meat; who has no house during the days of his life, and is not buried on the day of his death....Since that time the Amorites, a ravaging people, with the instincts of a beast...the sheepfolds like wolves, a people which does not know grain...."[47] A few generations later (c.1900 BCE), the widely disseminated myth of the marriage of Martu made its rounds in the ancient cities. Martu is the god of the Amorites (city of Mari, along the northwestern Euphrates River region). Martu arrives among the southern city dwellers. He engages in a series of wrestling matches with the king's heroes. Martu wins. The king offers him gold and silver as a reward for his achievements. No, he wants the king's daughter in marriage. Her friends warn her away, "He is a tent dweller, eats raw food, has no house...." She goes ahead and marries Martu.[48]

These Amorites, whose West Semitic dialect (also Hebrew) could not be understood by the Tigris/Euphrates, East Semites, became the Babylonians of Hammurabi, he who introduced new concordats of laws, created a rich and glorious city, to continue and amplify on this powerful civilizational tradition.

Bottero sees the living Uruk tradition modifying and limiting the excesses in class and inter-city warfare until c.2600 BCE of Sumerian dynastic experience.[49] By the time of the Amorite takeover of the ancient civilization, c.1900, BCE, Sumerian was no longer spoken, even in the ancient cities of the Uruk period, Ur, Lagas, Uruk, Kish, Nippur. It was, however, the language of the scribes, taught in the academies, and was the secondary official language of the cuneiform tablets.

"....Sumerian remained, until the very end, the scholarly and liturgical language, as Latin was to us in the Middle Ages. That is undoubtedly the best proof of the intellectual preponderance of the Sumerians in the Sumero-Akkadian cultural complex."[50]

In giving a postscript to the achievements of the Sumerians, Postgate sees the inner character of Sumerian advance as constituted of literacy, urbanization, and bureaucracy. This civilizational pattern was subsequently disseminated to the rest of Mesopotamia and the ancient world.[51]

Chronology—Sumeria/Early Mesopotamia

40,000-12,000 BCE	Upper Paleolithic, Cro-Magnon, modern *Homo sapiens sapiens* Eur-Asian peoples
12,000-5000 BCE	Mesolithic-Neolithic, small lowland communities, ceramics, mixed agriculture—proto-Semites
5000-4500 BCE	Possible arrival of Sumerians in Mesopotamia
4500-4000 BCE	Formation of first towns Eridu, Uruk
4000-3000 BCE	Domination of Uruk culture, writing
3000-2350 BCE	Dynastic period, various Sumerian cities
2350-c.2200 BCE	Sargon, Semitic Dynasty of Akkad
2200-2100 BCE	Gutians, unknown people from north
2100-2000 BCE	Sumerians at Ur dominate, flourishing culture
2000-1800 BCE	Breakdown, Isin/Larsa, Semitic Amorites, also, Elamites, unknown language; Sumerian spoken language in decline
1800-1600 BCE	Semitic Babylonians, Hammurabi, d. 1750 BCE
1600-1150 BCE	Population movements, Kassites rule, unknown language. West Semitic Aramaeans migrate into the river valleys.

Bibliography, Appendix

Barker, J. W. 1966. *Justinian and the Later Roman Empire,* Madison: Univ. of Wisconsin Press.
Bottero, J. 1992. *Mesopotamia,* Chicago: Univ. of Chicago Press.
Bowra, C. M. 1971. *Periclean Athens,* N.Y.: The Dial Press.
Charvat, P. 2002. *Mesopotamia before History,* N.Y.: Routledge.
Chiera, E. 1938. *They Wrote on Clay,* Chicago: Univ. of Chicago Press.
Cottrell, L. 1965. *The Quest for Sumer,* N.Y.: Putnam.
Crawford, H. 1991. *Sumer and the Sumerians,* Cambridge England: Cambridge Univ. Press.
Diamond, J. 1997. Guns, Germs, and Steel, p. 111.
Durant, W. 1950. *The Age Of Faith,* N.Y.: Simon and Schuster.
Frankfort, H. 1956. *The Birth of Civilization in the Near East,* Garden City, N.Y.: Doubleday Anchor.
Gimbutas, M. A. 1982. *Goddesses and Gods of Old Europe, 6500-3500 BC,* London: Thames and Hudson.
Gimbutas, M. A. 1989. *The Language of the Goddess,* N.Y.: Harper and Row.
Grant, M. 1960. *The World of Rome,* N.Y.: Mentor.
Gurney, O. R. 1964. *The Hittites,* Baltimore: Penguin.
Haldar, A. 1971. *Who Were the Amorites?* Leiden: Brill.
Herodotus, 1954 (c. 430 BCE). *The Histories,* trans. Aubrey de Selincourt, Baltimore: Penguin.
Jones, T. B. 1969. *The Sumerian Problem,* N.Y.: John Wiley and Sons.
Kramer, S. N. 1959. *History Begins at Sumer,* Garden City, N.Y.: Doubleday Anchor.
Kramer, S. N. 1963. *The Sumerians, Their History.* Chicago: Univ. of Chicago Press.
Laessoe, J. 1963. *People of Ancient Assyria,* trans. by F. S. Leigh-Browne, London: Routledge and Kegan Paul.
Lyber, A. H. 1913. *The Government of the Ottoman Empire in the Time of Suleiman The Magnificent,* Cambridge: Harvard Univ. Press.
Mallowan, M. E. L. 1965. *Early Mesopotamia and Iran,* N.Y.: McGraw-Hill.
Morrison, M. A., and Owen, D. I., eds. 1981. *Nuzzi And The Hurrians,* Winona Lake, Ind.: Eisenbrauns.
Oded, B. 1979. *Mass Deportations and Deportees in the Neo-Assyrian Empire,* Wiesbaden: Reichert Verlag.
Popovic, A. 1999. *The Revolt of African Slaves in Iraq, in the 9th Century,* Princeton, N.J.: Markus Wiener.
Postgate, J. N. 1992. *Early Mesopotamia,* London: Routledge.
Saggs, H. W. F. 2000. *Babylonians,* Berkeley: Univ. of California Press.
Smith, P. 1995. "People of the Holy Land from Pre-history to the Recent Past," p. 65; Bar Yosef, O. 1995. "Earliest Food Producers, Pre-Pottery Neolithic (8000-5500 BCE)," in Levy, T., ed., *The Archaeology of Society in the Holy Land,* London: Leicester Univ. Press.
Thomson, M. L. 1987. *The Sumerian Language,* Copenhagen: Akademisk Forlag.
Thucydides 1954 (c.410 BCE). *The Peloponnesian War,* trans. by Rex Warner. Baltimore: Penguin.
Toynbee, A. 1953. *Greek Civilization and Character,* N.Y.: Mentor.
Toynbee, A., ed. 1952. *Greek Historical Thought,* N.Y.: Mentor.
Wooley, C. L. 1930. *The Sumerians,* Oxford: Clarendon Press.
Yoshiwara, R. 1991. *Sumerian and Japanese, A Comparative Language Study.* Japan: Chiba.

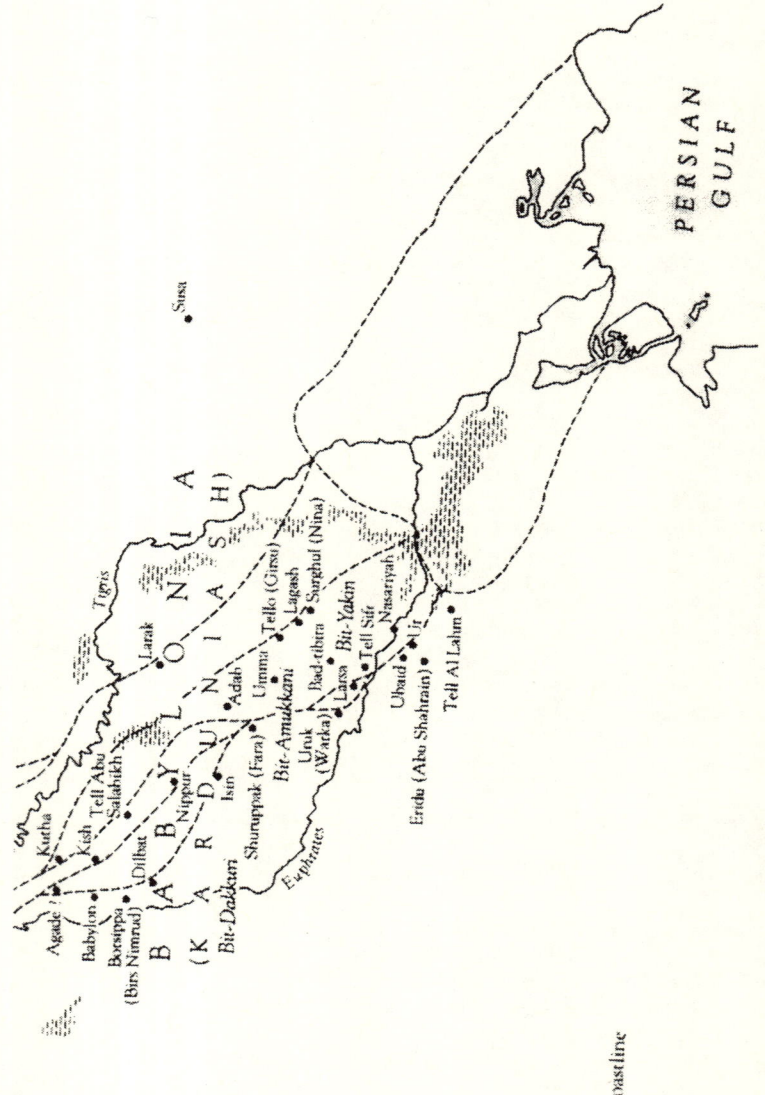

Appendix: Western Civilization Begins at Sumer

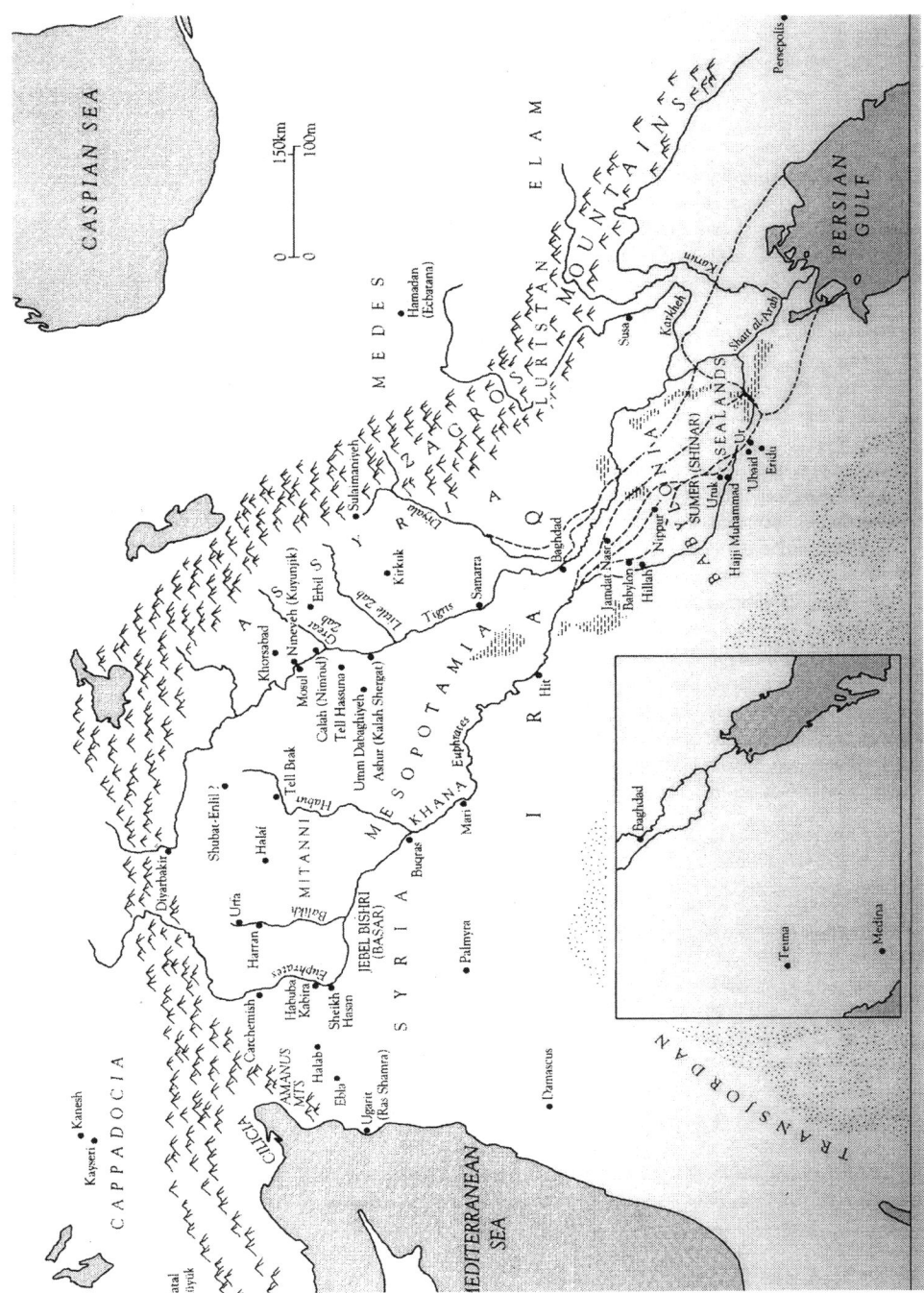

Endnotes, Appendix

[1] Bar-Yosef, O. 1993. "The Role of Western Asia in Modern Human Origins," in Aitken, *et al.*, eds. *The Origin of Modern Humans and the Impact of Chronometric Dating.* Princeton, N.J.: Princeton Univ. Press, pp. 132-147.

[2] Tattersall, I. 1995. *The Last Neanderthal,* N.Y.: Macmillan, Illus. 129, pp. 186-187.

[3] Guthrie, R. D. 1984. "Mosaics, Allelochemics, and Nutrients," in R. S. Martin and R. G. Klein, eds., *Quaternary Extinctions: A Prehistoric Revolution,* Tucson, AZ: Univ. of Arizona Press, pp. 259-298.

[4] Trinkaus, E., and Zilhao. 2000. *Proceedings of the National Academy of Sciences,* Washington, D.C.; Wilford, J. N. 1999. "Discovery Suggests Man Is a Bit Neanderthal," *The New York Times,* April 25.

[5] Conrad, N. 2003. "Thirty Thousand Year Old Carved Figurines," *Nature,* December 18; Clottes J., and Courtin, J. 1996. *The Cave Beneath the Sea,* N.Y.: Abrams.

[6] Leakey, R. 1981. *The Making of Mankind,* N.Y.: Dutton, pp. 193-196; Clottes, J. 2003. *Chauvet Cave: The Art of Earliest Times,* Salt Lake City: Univ. of Utah Press.

[7] Schenk, G. 1961. *The History of Man,* Philadelphia: Chilton, pp. 158-164.

[8] Smith, P. 1995, in T. Levy, ed. 1995. People of the Holy Land: From Pre-History to the Recent Past," p. 65; Bar-Yosef, O. 1995. "Earliest Food Producers, Pre-Pottery Neolithic (8000-5500 BCE)," in Levy, T. *The Archaeology of Society in the Holy Land,* London: Leicester Univ. Press.

[9] *Ibid.*

[10] Charvat, P. 2002. *Mesopotamia before History,* N.Y.: Routledge, pp. 235-237.

[11] Gimbutas, 1989. p. xix.

[12] Charvat, *op. cit.,* pp. 235-237.

[13] Charvat, *op. cit.,* pp. 22-27.

[14] Charvat, *op. cit.,* p. 26.

[15] Personal communication from Dr. Thomas Boyle, Professor of Botany, Univ. of Massachusetts, Amherst.

[16] Charvat, *op. cit.,* p. 26.

[17] Charvat, *op. cit.,* p. 27.

[18] Bottero, J. 1992. *Mesopotamia:* Chicago: Univ. of Chicago Press, p. 47.

[19] Charvat, *op. cit.,* pp. 25-27.

[20] Postgate, J. N. 1992. *Early Mesopotamia,* London: Routledge, p. 26.

[21] Bottero, *op. cit.,* p.48.

[22] Postgate, *op. cit.,* p. 299.

[23] Postgate, *op. cit.,* p. 24.

[24] Postgate, *op. cit.,* p. 170.

[25] Crawford, H. 1991. *Sumer and the Sumerians,* Cambridge England: Cambridge Univ. Press, pp. 118-119.

[26] Charvat, *op. cit.,* pp. 120-131.

[27] Charvat, *op. cit.,* pp. 158-159.

[28] Charvat, *op. cit.,* p. 131.

[29] Charvat, *op. cit.,* pp. 235-237.

[30] Mallowan, M. E. L. 1965. *Early Mesopotamia and Iran,* N.Y.: McGraw-Hill, p. 88.

[31] Charvat, *op. cit.,* pp. 158-159.

[32] Bottero, *op. cit.,* pp. 47-48.

[33] Saggs, H. W. F. 2000. *Babylonians* Berkeley. Univ. of California Press, pp. 46-51.
[34] Bottero, *op. cit.*, p. 70.
[35] Bottero, *op. cit.*, p. 101.
[36] Charvet, *op. cit.*, pp. 150-152, 237.
[37] Postgate, *op. cit.*, p. 26.
[38] Bottero, *op. cit.*, p. 240; also see Postgate, *op. cit.*, p. 299.
[39] Bottero, *op. cit.*, p. 246.
[40] Bottero, *op. cit.*, pp. 248-249.
[41] Bottero, *op. cit.*, p. 250.
[42] Crawford, *op. cit.*, pp. 118-119; Saggs, *op. cit.*, Illus. 38, p. 64.
[43] Charvat, *op. cit.*, pp. 158-159.
[44] Bottero, *op. cit.*, p. 193.
[45] Charvat, *op. cit.*, p. 239.
[46] Saggs, *op. cit.*, p. 136.
[47] Postgate, *op. cit.*, p. 84.
[48] Saggs, *op. cit.*, pp. 92-93.
[49] Bottero, *op. cit.*, p. 238.
[50] Bottero, *op. cit.*, pp. 47-48.
[51] Postgate, *op. cit.*, p. 302

Index

Rebuilding Western Civilization
Chapters 1-11

A

Affirmative action, 25-26.
Africa, "out of," human evolution theory, 75-76.
AIDS, 12, 46.
Akhenaton, Pharaoh, 172.
Arabs, see Muslims.
Aristotle, 163-165, 167, 174, 189.
Armenians, 176-178.
Art, 117-118, 124-125, a-political, 168; criteria of, 145-146; elitism in, 156-157; European, 171; exhausted forms, 154-155; folk, 157; meaning of, 146-147; and musical form, 150-153; and sensation, 147-150; and technology, 151-152.
Anti-Semitism, 19.
Asia, and art, 149; Northeast achievement, 18, 26, 28, 38, 40, 46, 55-56, 66, 138, 149, 187; ethnic origins, 77-78.
Assyrians, 158.
Australids, origins, 78.
Averroes, 143.

B

Bach, J. S. 151.
Baroque style, 169.
Bauer, P., 19.
Benbow, C., 73.
Benedict, R., 14.
Beauvais Cathedral, 151.
Binet, A., 60.
Borges, J. V., 41.
Bouchard, T., 65, 67-68.

Brain, growth, 86-87, 167; structure, 170, 178, 190-191.
Brown v Bd. of Education, 62.
Bruno, G., 134.
Buckley, W., 127.

C

Cage, J., 155.
California, bubble, 52-53.
Calvinism, see Protestantism.
Capitalism, 117.
Caracalla, 179.
Cassirer, E., 136, 164-165.
Catholic Church, 30, 40, 103, 129-130, 133, 137; music, 168.
Chavez, H., 106.
Chicago, University of, 102.
China, architecture, 179; challenge, 46-47, 49-50; 54, 138; conservatism, 56; literacy, 77; population, 40,93.
Civilization, 11-12, and arts, 157-159; challenge of, 50-51; egalitarian, 123, 126-128; and high intelligence, 13-14, 21, 78-79, 87-88, 91-92, 98; origin, 21; Western decline, 12-13, 23-26, 183-185.
Cloning, 92, 95-96, 181-182.
Columbia University, 102, 158.
Communism, 118, 120.
Computer Systems Policy Project, 54.
Coon, C., 76.
Copernicus, N., 134.
Corporation, see Economics.
Cremona, 173.

Index

Crisis, management, 183-185.
Cro-Magnon (*Homo sapiens sapiens*), 21, 76-78, 86, 88, 90, 117, 131-132, 141, 146, 189.
Culture, relativism, 14-15, 90; change, 167-171.
Cuvier, G., "catatrophism," 75.

D

Daalder, I., 43.
Darwin, 31, 60.
Democracy, 30-31; 41-43; civilizational problem, 100-102; and industrial America, 102-104; and intellectual decline, 104-107; middle-class conditions, 107-110.
Democratic Party, 53.
Demography, see Population.
Deng Xiaoping, 47.
Denmark, artificial fertilization, 97.
Dewey, J., 102-104, 113, 136.
Dimasio, A., 71-72.

E

Economics, American debt, 51-52; optimism, 43-45, 46-47; of democratic polity, 110-111; corporate corruption, 120; corporate executive pay, 53, 122-123; end of great corporation, 124-126; productivity, 114-116, 124, 188-190; Third World poverty, 12, 27, 41-42, 46, 48-49; U.S. taxation; 53, 55; wage competition, 46-47.
Edelman, G., 170.
Education, 16, 54-55; Catholic Church and, 103; progressive, 102-104; U.S. decline, 106.
Egalitarianism, see Ideology.
Egypt, ancient religion, 131-132, 172-173.
Enlightenment, 30-31.
Ethnicity, and intelligence, 17-18, 64-65; and nationality, 175-177; power of, 171-175.
Eugenics, and dysgenics, 19-20.
Euripides, 120.
Europe, Western decline, 184-185.
Evolution, human, 14, 21, 86-88, 167; and art, 146-147; of intelligence and religion, 140-141; intelligence variability, 74-78.

Eysenck, H., 65.

F

Fiorina, C., 54.
French art, 168, 174.
Friedman, T., 45.
Future, utopian, 15.

G

Galilei, G., 134.
Galton, F., 19, 60-61, 65-66.
Gardner, H., 70-71.
Genesis, 131, 137.
Genocide, 19-20, 28, 34; and intelligence, 63, 104.
Germany, unemployment, 115.
Gershwin, G., 149, 155.
Geschwind, N., 73.
Globalization, 13, 23, 45.
Goleman, D., 71.
Goldstein, K., 71.
Goldstein, S., 73.
Greeks, ancient, see Hellenes.
Guarneri, J., del Jesu, 147.

H

Halstead, W., 71.
Hegel, G. W. F., 32-33.
Hellenes and art, 149, 154, 156-157, 171-172; civilization, 108-109, 118, 120, 189; education, 158; militarism, 186; modern decline, 105; religion, 132-133, 142-143; *theoria*, 162-164.
Herrnstein, R., 69.
Hitler, A., 19, 21, 28, 191.
Holocaust, 11, 19, 29, 104, 175, 185.
Human nature, 85*ff.*
Hume, D., 98.
Huntington, S. P., 50-51.
Hussein, S., 15.

I

Ideology, 16-20, egalitarian, 34-36; 38-39 and irrationality, 26-29.
Immigration, illegal, 16, reform, 183-184.
India, 44-47, 112-113.
Intelligence, and arts, 157-159; and brain, 190-191; choosing, 96-97; and competition, 185-188; and democracy, 107-110; evolution of, 74-75; factors of,

70-73; male/female, 63-64, 73-74; and religion, 138-139; and social inequality, 36-37, 47-49, 61-62; 69-70; taboo, 24-25, 59-60, 68-69; variable, 16-18, 20, 64-65, 74 *ff.*, 181-182.
I.Q., development of, 60-61; and ethnicity, 17, 28, 64-65; "g" factor, 65*ff*; and genetics, 20, 27, 65-68, 96; minorities, 61-62; national power, 26, 104-107, 167, 169, 186-188; and race, 64-65; regression, 119; testing, 60-65.
Internationalism, 39, 161-163.
Iraq, 179.
Islam, religion, 133, 137-138.
Israel, 28-29, 179.

J

Jakobson, R., 71.
James, W., 102.
Japan, 18, 42-43, 93-95; origins of, 77-78.
Jefferson, T., 107, 119-120.
Jensen, A., 65-66.
Jews, Anti-Semitism, 28; Ashkenazi intelligence, 64-65, 95, Biblical tradition, 147, 175; as nationality, 175-176, 179.
Johns Hopkins University.

K

Kant, I., 19, 135-136, 141, 164, 182.
Kerry, J., 53.
Klinkenborg, V., 85-86.
Korea, South, 45, 56-57; origins of, 77-78.
Kurds, 176.

L

Langer, S., 164-165.
Language, 169-170.
Leibniz, G. W., 21.
Li Kuan Yu, 13.
Lindsay, J., 43.
Lincoln, A., 179.
London, Shakespeare's, 156.
Luria, A. R., 71.
Lynn, R., 65.

M

Machaut, G., 152.
Maimonides, 143.
Mao, Tse-tung, 93, 138.

Marx, K., 24-25, 31-33, 38-39, 111-113, 126-128, 129, 188, 190-191.
Mead, M., 14, 90.
Mesopotamia, 189.
Mexico, 49-50.
Midgette, A., 27.
Mohamad, Mahathir bin, 28.
Money, J., 73.
Morality, economic, 122-123; and social policy, 36-37, 181-183; welfare, 120-122.
Morris, Gouverneur, 30-31.
Murray, C., 69.
Music, and gender, 27; form, 150, 150-153, 168.
Muslims, decline, 18, 56-57, 137-139, 186-188, women, 15, 177, slavery, 30.

N

NAACP, 103.
NAFTA, 49-50.
Nationality, 161*ff.*; and ethnicity, 175-177, why?, 177-180.
Nazis, 21.
NEA, 103.
Newman, Cardinal, J. H., 143.
New Deal, The, 102.
New York Times, *The*, 27, 45, 71, 145.
Newton, I., 21.

O

O'Brien, T., 123.
Old Testament, 131.
Optimism, bureaucratic, 40-41, 43-45.

P

Page, E. B., 64.
Palestrina, G., 152.
Peirce, C., 102.
Piano, 152.
Pindar, 171-172.
Pius XI, Pope, 137.
Plato, 37, 109.
Plomin, R., 65, 67-68.
Political correctness, 181-183.
Population, China, 40, 56; and civilization, 24, 45, 91; demographic optimism, 40-41; expansion, 88-89; genetic change, 104-107; middle-class future, 46, 88-

Index

91, 115-116, 183-184; U.S., 16; urban, 32; world, 11, 24, 41, 92-94; 124.
Print, 151.
Productivity, see Economics.
Protagoras, 142-143.
Protestantism, 134-136, 142.
Pythian games, 154.

R

Race, hybrids, 17; and intelligence, 64-65; irrelevance of, 20; origin of, 76-78.
Rameses II, Pharaoh, 173.
Reformation, 30.
Religion, and Enlightenment, 129-130, 136; and intelligence, 137-139; meaning of, 130-134, 140-143; and science, 134-137, 141-142.
Renaissance, 30, 134, 172.
Reproduction, asexual, 92, 95-96; techniques, 89-91.
Rome, ancient, decline, 49, 50, 57; culture, 173-174; universalism, 162.
Rousseau, J. J., 31, 98.

S

Safire, W., 181.
Samuelson, R., 18, 53.
Schillinger, J., 150.
Schönberg, A., 150, 155.
Science, 141, 164-166, 178; and religion, 134-137, 143.
Silicon Valley, 52.
Servetus, M., 134.
Slavery, 30-31, 179.
Smith, A., 111.
Social policy, class and revolution, 33-34; and classlessness, 126-128; and intellectual inequality, 36-37; responsibility, 120-122.
Socialism, 31-32.
Socrates, 108, 142-143.
South Korea, 45, 57.
Spearman, C., 65.
Spears, B., 177.
Spengler, 11.
Stalinism, 156-157.
Stanley, J., 73.
State, withering of the, 111-113.
Stenhouse, D., 71-73.

Stern, W., 60.
Sternberg, R., 71.
Stradivari, A., 147.
Sumer, 172, religion, 132; Uruk civilization, 117, 151, 188-189.

T

Technology, dynamism, 18, 188-190.
Terman, L., 61, 64, 67, 70, 72.
Terrorism, 185-188.
Theology, and ideology, 29.
Third World, 42.
Thomas, St., of Aquinas, 143.
Thucydides, 108.
Time Magazine, 16.
Trotsky, L., 103.
Turkey, and Islam, 105, 176, 179.

U

United Nations, 15, 42-43.
United States, Bill of Rights, 122, 129; democratic tradition, 47; demographic change, 105-108; dominance, 174; hegemonic decline, 49-54, 184; portent, 49-56; prospect, 54-56.
Universalism, see Internationalism.

V

Varèse, E., 145.
Violin, 147, 152.

W

War, and intelligence, 185-188.
Washington Post, The, 43.
Weber, M., 134-135.
Weiss, V., 67-68, 70.
Will, G., 53.
William, of Occam, 143.
Women, Muslim, 15, 177.
World Bank, 116.